Praise for *Choosing Excellence*

"John Merrow is at it again. Investigative journalism of the first rank, *Choosing Excellence* is precisely what American education needs when it needs it. Hard-hitting and tough-minded, it offers a spirited critique without being mean-spirited. Merrow looks at modern schools without blinking, but his commentary remains humane and generous. Readers from both sides of the aisle will find *Choosing Excellence* a must read."
— Denis P. Doyle, chief academic officer of SchoolNet.com and coauthor of *Winning the Brain Race* and *Raising the Standard*

"*Choosing Excellence* is vintage Merrow: thoughtful, engaging, and delightfully opinionated. With passion and common sense, he provides a tonic for parents fed up with the testing mania and looking for better ways to evaluate schools."
— Jerome T. Murphy, dean and Harold Howe II Professor of Education, Harvard Graduate School of Education

"*Choosing Excellence* is especially powerful because Merrow supports his clear vision of excellent schools with a focus on specific strategies. His in-depth discussion of a wide range of issues affecting the social and academic climate of schools will be very helpful to teachers, parents, and all whose work impacts the development of children."
— James P. Comer, Maurice Falk Professor of Child Psychiatry, Yale Child Study Center, and associate dean of the Yale School of Medicine

A 'how-to-think-about-schools guide' that is sophisticated, thoughtful, and down-to-earth. Everything you need to know with a sensitivity and carefulness that few how-tos manage.
— Deborah Meier, vice chair of the Coalition of Essential Schools and author of *Will Standards Save Public Education?*

"This is a must read for all those who care about schools and children. This is also a book for caring parents who need guidance on the right questions to ask of teachers and administrators."
— Thomas H. Kean, president of Drew University and former governor of New Jersey

"John Merrow has been observing schools for 25 years, and this book provides an engaging accumulation of his good sense and wisdom. The 'Questions to Ask' at each chapter's end are as good a guide to excellence as you'll find."
— Mike Rose, professor at the UCLA Graduate School of Education and author of *Possible Lives: The Promise of Public Education in America*

"His premise of looking, listening, and asking questions is a refreshing way to examine schools. Merrow is obsessed with getting us to ask the right questions rather than impressing us with how much he has to tell us."
— *The School Administrator*

"Avoiding bromides as well as tirades, John Merrow provides a candid, vivid, sensible, and useful guide to excellent schools."
— Howard Gardner, John H. and Elisabeth A. Hobbs Professor in Cognition and Education at the Harvard Graduate School of Education

"There are only a handful of premier thinkers in this nation concerning matters educational, and John Merrow is certainly among them. . . . Getting to the chase of what makes a school excellent and what holds schools back from creating excellent learning environments, this book is an absolute must-read for anyone interested in the current status and the potential of education in America."
— Edward Zigler, Sterling Professor of Psychology, Yale University

"A lucid, sensible, and sensitive account of where American 'school reform' is heading."
— Ted Sizer, professor emeritus at Brown University, chairman and founder of the Coalition of Essential Schools, and author of *Horace's Compromise.*

"John Merrow has given the parents and citizens of the U.S. a wonderful gift. He has written a preview of what to look for and the questions to ask if our children are to have excellent schools."
— Arthur Levine, president of Teachers College, Columbia University

"*Choosing Excellence* provides great information for parents to begin to ask the right questions and make informed choices."
— Sharon Darling, president of the National Center for Family Literacy

"An unusual combination of researched opinion on education, and practical tips for parents and others. John Merrow writes with balance but passion, and no fear of giving his own opinions. And well informed opinions they are indeed, based on years of visiting and observing public education systems."
— Augusta Souza Kappner, president of The Bank Street College of Education

"Always spirited, and sometimes edgy, his points are fueled by stirring and sometimes heartbreaking stories. . . . Add to that expert testimony from educa-

Continued on last page of book

CHOOSING EXCELLENCE

"GOOD ENOUGH" SCHOOLS ARE NOT GOOD ENOUGH

JOHN MERROW

THE SCARECROW PRESS, INC.
A Scarecrow Education Book
Lanham, Maryland, and London
2001

SCARECROW PRESS, INC.
A Scarecrow Education Book

Published in the United States of America
by Scarecrow Press, Inc.
4720 Boston Way, Lanham, Maryland 20706
www.scarecroweducation.com

4 Pleydell Gardens, Folkestone
Kent CT20 2DN, England

British Library Cataloguing in Publication Information Available

Library of Congress Cataloging-in-Publication Data

Merrow, John.
  Choosing excellence: "good enough" schools are not good enough / John Merrow.
    p. cm.
  Includes bibliographic references.
  ISBN 1-57886-014-8 (pbk : alk. paper)
    1. Teaching—Standards—United States. 2. Education—United States—Evaluation.
  3. School improvement programs—United States. I. Title: "Good enough" schools are not
  good enough. II. Title.

LB1025.3 .M49 2001
379.1'58'0973—dc21   00-0151572

⊗™ The paper used in this publication meets the minimum requirements of
American National Standard for Information Sciences—Permanence of Paper
for Printed Library Materials, ANSI/NISO Z39.48-1992.
Manufactured in the United States of America.

For my children, Josh, Elise, and Kelsey

CONTENTS

FOREWORD

For nearly thirty years, John Merrow has been a generous and healing presence in the frequently contentious world of public education policy in the United States. One of the most perceptive and capaciously discerning journalists reporting on the status of our schools during these years, Merrow has brought an empathetic ear and an engaging sensitivity to reportage that always goes beyond the dry statistical abstractions.

Now, in this refreshingly clear-sighted work, he gives us an amalgamation of his insights in a book devoid of pedagogic jargon and therefore accessible to ordinary citizens—and, most important in this instance, to the parents of school children.

Common sense and an uncommon shrewdness intermix in the good counsel that he offers here, especially to parents who are trying to make judgments on the merits of a school, a classroom, or a teacher. Cautioning parents not to draw conclusions on the basis of a single visit (a familiar error, not just on the part of parents but on that of all too many journalists as well), he urges us to look beyond the test scores, beyond the isolated moments, and beyond whatever methodologies may be in use on any given day. Instead, he counsels us to base our judgments most of all upon those innate qualities of personality in teachers who are able to infuse a chemistry of energy and optimism into even the most mundane details of the day—an emphasis that cuts against the grain of pedagogic fashion nowadays, but one with which I personally concur.

The recruitment of such gifted and exciting teachers by school systems, he observes, is not so great a problem as some press reports imply. The greater challenge is to keep them in our schools beyond the few initial years in which they are impelled primarily by the ideals of youth. Retention of such teachers, as he accurately notes, will not be possible until their gifts are matched by the rewards accorded by the scale of pay and level of respect that they deserve.

Merrow is perceptive too about the adverse consequences of the high-stakes testing emphasis that has been thrust upon our public schools in recent years. Unchecked, he says, this often pathological obsession with the numbers derived from a machine-scored test will choke the life out of exciting schools and drive inspired teachers out of public education altogether. Unfortunately, as he observes, the advocates of high-stakes testing have more faith in a machine than they appear to have in teachers; he urges parents to resists these biases and to insist instead upon the kinds of tests, portfolios, and other measurments of progress that good teachers and enlightened principals have been constructing on their own to counterbalance the effects of narrowly empirical assessments.

In a cautionary note, he also warns us of the growing danger that reliance upon high-stakes testing will encourage schools to view with equanimity—and even sometimes with relief—the loss of students who drop out. Since drop-outs are commonly those who do most poorly on machine-scored tests, their departure from a school raises the average score by which a school is judged.

Merrow's warnings about testing should be accorded wide attention. So too should his insights into charter schools, which, he notes, are seldom given oversight by public agencies until their charter is to be renewed. As a consequence, they are sometimes exploited by charlatans and profit-seeking corporations with no abiding loyalty to children or to education. The bluntness and irreverence of his observations about charter schools and other currently accepted trends will doubtless irritate some propagandists but will be invaluable to parents forced to make important choices for the education of their children in the face of often superficial and deceptive blandishments.

Merrow values independent thinking, so he probably won't be surprised that I do not concur with every judgment voiced within this book. I don't agree that school administrations are routinely bureaucratic or that teacher unions are consistently obstructive to reform. I also see far less substandard teaching in public schools than certain passages within this book seem to imply. But Merrow is writing to empower parents, and his efforts to provide them with the instruments of critical evaluation are, in general, well taken and much needed. In an age when market-driven forms of mechanistic competition, frequently disguised under the cover-term of *parent choice*, have come to be a substitute for civic virtue and collective efforts to improve the opportunities of all our children, Merrow has given us a primer in the art of choosing wisely. For this, above all else, the parents of our nation's children will be grateful.

— Jonathan Kozol, author of *Savage Inequalities* and *Ordinary Resurrections*

ACKNOWLEDGMENTS

A number of friendly critics read and responded to various chapters of this book: George Madaus, Karen Pittman, Samuel Halperin, Lisa Walker, Joel Tolman, Joe Nathan, Josh Merrow, Mary Lee Fitzgerald, Deborah Meier, Ted Sizer, Andy Tuttle, Elise Merrow, and Joan Lonergan.

Others helped, either sharing their benchmarks of excellence or suggesting questions. They include Anne Henderson, Anne C. Lewis, Jay Mathews, Sue S. Bastian, Kate Folmar, Joseph Garcia, Marsha Guerard, Bess Keller, Andy Mollison, Mary Jane Smetanka, Meg Sommerfeld, David Keim, Kathleen Wilson, Linda Kramer, Eleanor Chute, Linda Lenz, Linda Lambeck, Robin Farmer, Karin Chenoweth, Marcia Koenig, Keith Ervin, Jondi Gumz, Breea Willingham, Aisha Sultan, Lori Crouch, and Kelsey Merrow.

Portions of chapters 4, 5, 10, and 11 appeared earlier in *Education Week*, *Principal*, and the *New York Times*.

Associate producer Tania Brief provided thoughtful, often brilliant editorial assistance, as did Tom Koerner, my editor at Scarecrow Press.

Samuel Halperin, Karen Hein, William McAnulty, Joshua Kaufman, John Tulenko, Alexis Kessler, and Sheila Pagan encouraged me to write this book. Any errors, of course, are my responsibility.

PREFACE

This book grew out of a whimsical exercise, a list I drew up on the occasion of my 25th anniversary as an education reporter. The standards bandwagon was rolling along at the time, and we were hearing the first whispers of concern about high-stakes testing. The general public's eagerness for simple measures of excellence has always been evident, and more and more people seem to be hoping that national standards and high-stakes testing would, at long last, provide a true, clear picture of how our schools were doing.

I've been around long enough to know that we will *never* have one measure that tells us, reliably and with minimal possibility of error, which schools are good and which are not. Standardized, machine-scored, multiple choice tests are only one of dozens of measures that we ought to turn to in a search for truths about schools. Too often, however, test scores are the only measure we look at.

So, I said to myself on that spring day, create your own list of 25 measures of excellence, one for every year you've been reporting. The list that emerged was highly personal, reflecting my experiences, convictions, and biases. I believe that a school ought to be small enough so its leader can know every student by name, and something about each one, and so that's on the list. I think that the speed with which teachers leave the building after school lets out also is an indicator of the institution's "educational health." As you will see, my criteria include the rate of teacher turnover, the art on the walls, measures of academic achievement, and much more. The list was the spark that led to our exploration on PBS of "excellent, good enough, and bad" educational practices and "School Sleuth: The Case of an Excellent School" (which in turn led to this book).

I brought the list to the office one morning and gave it to my colleagues, who persuaded me that we should turn it into a program for our PBS series, *The Merrow Report*. At first we envisioned a straightforward treatment. Then, in a flight of fancy, senior producer John Tulenko suggested that we recruit the stars of *Law & Order* or *NYPD Blue* to play roles as detectives searching for excellence. That proved unworkable, and so by default I became a detective, a "school sleuth."

Working with associate producers Tania Brief, Alexis Kessler, and Lisa McHenry, John and I began crafting a script. John found a location for my "office," and we hired professional actors to play my blonde client and the thug hired by "the status quo" to scare me off. I donned a double-breasted suit and fedora, and over three days and nights we created our fantasy. Then came the monumental task of editing.[1] Finally, 18 months after I wrote my whimsical memo, the deed was done. "School Sleuth" aired on PBS all over America on Thursday, November 2, 2000. Not long afterward, this book emerged, and our arguments and strategies for improving public education were made public.

Writing this book became an exercise in joy, as I began to unearth memories of so many wonderful teachers, educational leaders, parents, and students I have been privileged to spend hours and days with over the past 25 years. Almost every morning for six months I woke up with my brain filled with thoughts and ideas for this book. As if it were yesterday, I began to see in my mind's eye hundreds of wonderful teachers I've been privileged to spend days with, individuals destined to fight against a system that mindlessly places hurdles in their way.

As a first-year teacher in the mid-'60s, I learned that public education is full of people who know exactly how to prevent change but haven't the vaguest notion about doing things differently. As Linda Darling-Hammond of Stanford told me a long time ago, "The education system is full of people who know where the brake is but have never heard of the accelerator."

My life as an education reporter has taken me to strange and wonderful places: from the People's Republic of China in 1977 to juvenile institutions and mental hospitals for youth, from Indian reservations to Alaskan bush schools, from posh suburban schools to dilapidated, overcrowded urban buildings that don't deserve the name of "school." The glue in all of these stories has been the unquenchable spirit of children and youth and the determination of gifted teachers.

As my deadline drew closer, I grew increasingly reluctant to send the manuscript off to the publisher, wanting more time to add and subtract, rewrite and polish.

The organizing principle of this book is straightforward: In America, we have three kinds of public schools: bad ones, excellent ones, and those that are "good enough." It's this last category that fascinates and appalls me. These are the schools that we accept, even though we know that our children deserve better. As my client in "School Sleuth" says, "We settle for less, because we're afraid to make change." But I believe that excellence is possible, because I see firsthand that many schools are making genuine progress. Unfortunately, the current misguided rush to embrace "high-stakes testing" threatens both excellence and the development of genuine rigorous national standards.

Excellent schools are *transparent* in their operation and *intellectual* in their purpose, which makes them *legitimate* in the eyes of their constituencies. I discuss these ideas at some length in the chapters that follow.

In our spoof of the hard-boiled detective genre, my client hires me to "stir things up," and I hope this book will do just that. I also hope that the questions[2] at the end of most chapters will prove useful to parents and interested citizens who are determined to push and pull the system beyond "good enough."

Some readers may wonder why I didn't simply publish the list and be done with it. For the same reason that single measures are inadequate, so is a checklist. Unfortunately, there's no substitute for looking, listening, and asking questions, and there's no reliable shortcut. The trip, however, is worthwhile.

1

INTRODUCTION

Choice in public education is inevitable. In fact, choice is now or soon will be a *reality* for most public school parents. The fact that *all* parents cannot freely choose from among a variety of successful schools is a stain on our record, particularly because income and race very often determine which families have choices, and which do not.

However, many American parents now are able to choose the school their children attend and the kind of schooling they will experience, as the numbers make clear. Thirteen percent of children attend private or parochial school, an increase of two to three percentage points from just a few years ago. In the ten-year period since 1990, private school enrollment grew by 3.61 million students.

Parents are choosing charter schools, Edison or other for-profit schools, or magnet schools within their own system. An increasing number of systems are following Seattle's lead and operating "open systems," meaning that parents may choose any school in the system where there is room.[3] Fifteen percent of Delaware's students took advantage of that option in 2000, according to Governor Thomas R. Carper. New York City's District Four adopted a system of choice in 1982, and several other of the city's 32 districts have followed suit. Boston now has citywide choice, as well as arrangements with neighboring districts that allow students to transfer. Cleveland, Milwaukee, and Florida have been experimenting with vouchers that can be used to pay tuition at private schools.[4] The fastest-growing approach to education today is home schooling, although the overall numbers remain small. Finally, high school students in

Ohio, Minnesota, and a few other states have the option of taking college-level courses at local campuses.

A major factor in the growth of school choice has been the economy. Between 1992 and 2000 many thousands of families who earlier might have felt stuck in place were able to move, and they did. The U.S. Census Bureau reports that one out of every five families moves every year.

Charles Glenn has identified two reasons for the growth of choice and the interest in variety. "The first is that parents themselves are better educated and more demanding as 'consumers' of schooling for their children. In increasing numbers, they are not willing simply to accept whatever is provided by the nearest public school. The second reason is the growing body of evidence, notably in the Rand Corporation's High Schools with Character (1990), that schools with a distinctive character, including faith-based schools, are more effective than schools reflecting a lowest common denominator of values."[5]

When families with school-age children pick up stakes, they tend to settle where they think the schools will be good. I believe that most families are genuinely interested in educational excellence, but I also believe that most of us have trouble defining it, or recognizing it. We're too accustomed to what I call "good enough" schools (more about that later), and we're not accustomed to having options in education. As Caroline Minter Hoxby, a Harvard economist who studies school choice, observed, "Most of us don't know how to go about shopping for a Lear Jet or a huge yacht either. Parents have to learn how to shop wisely, and they will."[6]

Parents know very little about how their child's performance stacks up against others, according to Public Agenda. Only 3 percent know how their child compares with students in other countries, and only 13 percent know how he or she compares with students in other states. Most strikingly, however, is Public Agenda's finding that *not even half of parents know how their children compare with others in the same grade in their own school!*[7] What's more, only one in five parents say they know a lot about teacher qualifications.

So parents today are making choices—but based on what? Probably on SAT or ACT scores, image, rumor, and reputation. That's not a particularly rational approach,[8] but it's the way things seem to work. When *New York Times* columnist Joe Queenan asked whether the presence of celebrities attracted people to a town, a knowledgeable real estate agent told him, "Celebrities don't raise house prices. SAT scores raise house prices."[9]

Dennie Wolf, a professor at the Harvard Graduate School of Education, agrees. "We have to recognize what electrifying information test data is. Districts sell real estate based on test scores. Superintendents move from district to district based on what they did for test scores. But 'doing something for test scores' is not the same thing as doing something for the quality of education."[10] As I explain in Chapter 3, when the avowed goal is "doing something *for* test scores," meaningful learning tends to go by the wayside, and children and teachers lose out.

Choice means competition, another fact of life for a new public system. Done right, choice means variety. Without variety, there's little point to choice, in education or anything else. It would be akin to choosing from among Wendy's, Burger King, and MacDonald's. Where there are educated consumers, choice *should* lead to excellence.

But our long history of ideological warfare over schooling has made it difficult for many to determine what constitutes excellence in education. As education historian Larry Cuban has pointed out, the previous century was noteworthy for widespread and often bitter conflict among parents, taxpayers, academics, and policymakers over what kind of schooling is best for children— as if there were one best way. Unfortunately, as Cuban notes, "Few educators and parents have paused to consider that 'goodness' in schools comes in many colors, sizes and ideologies."[11]

I wrote this book to help concerned parents, parents who know there's more to school than a test score, parents who have choices but are uncertain how to choose. I would be heartened, however, if it also helps educators who believe in excellence in their fight against the tyranny of high-stakes testing.

To be perfectly honest, I would be thrilled if this book were to help slow down— or even derail—our mad (and doomed) rush to find a single measure of school and student quality. The current frenzy over high-stakes testing threatens the health and well-being of thousands of struggling schools because it is drawing attention and resources away from other important aspects of learning, even as it is driving talented teachers away from the classroom and destroying the dreams of children.

A "one test score reveals all" mentality is a menace to quality schooling. And while our excessive concern with standardization does not threaten choice, it does pose a serious threat to *variety*—and without variety, choice is meaningless.

The current era of choice and variety means that public schools will never again look the same, unless the regressive pressure for standardization triumphs. Standardization (which is different than standards) will kill experimentation, variety, and choice. If a public system survives standardization (and I believe it's essential that it survive), the new system will look and act much different from the one we have now.

Parents trying to choose the right school need to know that, as far as this book is concerned, there are three kinds of schools: bad, good enough, and excellent. By "good enough," I mean schools that most people settle for: schools everyone wants to believe are okay—even though, deep down, they know better. As I will explain, not enough people are willing to make change, and so they play it safe and settle for less. They settle for a "good enough" school with high scores on standardized exams, a good ranking in the city, and a new building. But there is more to excellence than that. Are the students truly engaged, that is, are they developing a love for learning? Is the environment emotionally and intellectually safe? The status quo survives because it works for just enough kids and parents, and because it's easier to go along with what's familiar. Change is hard work, and changing schools may be the hardest work of all.

Most educational *practices* can be categorized as either "bad," "good enough," or "excellent." Take the issue of school safety: By definition, bad schools are unsafe. "Good enough" schools are physically safe, but many kids are teased and bullied and students who make mistakes are laughed at. In "good enough" schools adults may look the other way as powerful cliques dominate the daily life of the school.

Excellent schools are *emotionally* and *intellectually* safe. That is, excellent schools do not tolerate teasing, bullying, and harassment; excellent schools welcome honest mistakes and encourage intellectual curiosity.

Excellence is not easy to find in public education, sad to say. Most public schools fall into the "good enough" category, but that should *not* be cause for celebration. "Good enough" schools are self-satisfied and reluctant to submit to a critical examination. In "good enough" schools some students excel, but most simply endure, and too many fall by the wayside.

I believe that excellent schools have a strong sense of purpose, and that is the development of the individual and his or her intellectual life, what Deborah Meier calls serious and thoughtful "habits of mind." They do not exist to help students adjust socially or learn a trade or profession. Purposeful schools aid in "building a self," in Jacques Barzun's phrase. At the end of the day, and when you're lying awake in the middle of the darkest night, the self that you have built[12] is your closest companion, your guide and comfort. The quality of schooling determines, in part, whether your "self" is more Shakespeare than *Survivor*, more Mozart than *Millionaire*.

Excellent schools are "transparent," in the sense that Ted Sizer and Grant Wiggins have used the word. That is, the machinery of the school is open for inspection and discussion, everything from rules to curriculum to assessment.

That doesn't mean things are up for grabs, only that those in the school have faith in their approach and are willing to display it openly.

Excellent teachers put a sense of purpose first. They teach to the purpose, so students understand why they're studying a particular subject in the first place. That's different from what happens in "good enough" schools, which stress external rewards. In those schools, the goal is to learn skills or absorb some pieces of the curriculum, so that you can pass a test, or get into college, or avoid making your parents and teachers angry.

I suspect that most professional educators will not recognize their institutions, or their pedagogical practices, as "good enough" or if they do, they'll declare victory and move on. But I mean the term to have an edge, a clear sense of disapproval, because our young people, and their teachers, deserve opportunities to excel. "Good enough" is not a compliment, because "good enough" schools are *not* good enough!

Central to this book and its view of public schools are several beliefs:

1. We owe it to all our children to strive for schools that are exceptional, not merely adequate.
2. Excellence is achievable in our schools.
3. Where we do not achieve excellence, the reasons often have as much to do with self-satisfaction and failure of imagination as with inadequate personnel or insufficient resources.

This book is not about our nation's bad schools, although I feel strongly that we daily contradict our bedrock principles when we allow perhaps 25 percent of our children to go to overcrowded, dilapidated schools staffed too often by poorly trained and/or demoralized teachers. Many of these schools are in urban areas, where fewer than three of every four students graduate on time. In New York City, only 60 percent of high school students ever earn their diplomas. Elsewhere, less than half graduate.[13]

Jonathan Kozol[14] and others have written eloquently about the manifest unfairness of inadequate schools, and two of my children have spent the past three years teaching in some of those schools in our home city, New York. I share their anger, and their hope that we will create more variety and more choices for those children. Toward the end of *Ordinary Resurrections*, Kozol's warm and compelling tale of the children of the South Bronx, he writes, "We owe it to these children not to let the doors be closed before they're even old enough to know how many there are, how many other doors there are beyond the one or two that they can see."[15]

Outrage alone will not improve bad schools; nor will a book that offers some insights into what constitutes excellence. Improving bad schools will require a public commitment of resources, strong leadership, imagination, courage, and honest recognition of the economic costs and social immorality of consigning children to the ashheap. And the recognition that there are no easy answers.

Each chapter in this book explores some aspect of schooling: safety, academics, values, technology, and so forth. At its core, however, this book is about teaching, the noblest profession. My intention is not to shine a spotlight on excellent *schools* as such (I'll leave that to others), but on excellent *practices*. I do this because I believe it's easier for others to copy excellent strategies and behaviors, a little at a time.

Most chapters conclude with a list of questions about practices, behaviors, and strategies that, if asked and answered honestly, will help visitors come to a reasoned judgment about the school and its policies and practices. I'm hoping to help you collect evidence, which is why I've resisted creating a checklist. After all, evidence is *suggestive*, not necessarily conclusive, and I certainly do not want readers to think that, if they can check off 75 percent or 90 percent of the items on the list, then the school is by definition "excellent." I hope you will ask lots of questions of lots of people—including, perhaps, yourself.

Finally, although I am trying to set the bar high for public schools, I write as a loving critic and a strong supporter of public education. I believe that it is important that our children see parents and teachers as *allies*, part of the same team that cares deeply about them and their intellectual and personal growth. As Deborah Meier, one of my heroes, has observed, "The sense that some kids have that their parents don't trust teachers and that their teachers don't trust parents is intellectually and emotionally and morally destructive to children. But it happens to a lot of kids." I hope this book will in some small way help repair that breach.

QUESTIONS TO ASK WHEN CHOOSING A SCHOOL

- What is the school's vision? What makes the school distinctive? Why do families want their children to go here?
- What are the school's academic standards? Are copies readily available for parents?
- Does the school insist that teachers have studied the subjects they are teaching? (Certification alone is not necessarily enough.)

- How does the school make sure that all students learn to the standards?
- How does the school know if the students are getting there? Are grades tied to the academic standards? Besides grades, what are the measures of achievement?
- How does the school help students who fall behind? What provisions are made for those whose first language is not English?
- Who is involved in making sure every student makes it?
- How is the school's curriculum developed? How many courses were developed by national organizations or by the state? Do teachers develop their own courses?
- How are parents involved in the school?
- What decisions do parents have a voice in? Do they help select the principal?
- How does the school encourage them to be advocates for their children?
- How are parents involved in improving student achievement?
- Does the school share overall student performance data with families?
- Is there a school report card or something similar? Ask for a copy. Look to see if data are broken down by grade level, gender, race, or ethnicity. What do they tell you?
- What percentage of students in the school are proficient (at least at grade level) in the core subjects of language arts, social studies, math, science? How does this compare to the highest achieving school in the district?
- What is pupil-teacher ratio? How many students are in the typical class? (Do these two figures match up?)
- Is the school absolutely committed to making sure that students are good readers and writers?
- Do the adults in the school know when kids are struggling? Do they have fallback strategies when instructional approaches fail? Do students get extra learning time when they need it?

QUESTIONS TO ASK IF YOUR CHILD IS IN MIDDLE OR HIGH SCHOOL

- Does the school expect all of its students to continue their education after high school? What is it doing to make sure that happens? Does it have benchmarks, like completing Algebra I in eighth grade, to make this goal real?

- How does the school work with students and parents to set goals for the student's future?
- Does the school place students into tracks? If so, on what basis? What are the tracks, and what is the rationale for having them?
- Is there movement between tracks? How often do students get the opportunity to move up?
- What learning programs does the school offer? Which one would my child be in? Is it a higher level program? How many programs are at a higher level than that one?
- What choices does he/she have? What role do parents play in selecting the program?
- When my child completes that program, what options will he or she have for the next stage (high school, college, technical school, etc.)?
- Will the courses he or she is taking qualify him or her for a good, four-year college? If he or she is in a career program, will he or she learn the same academic skills as students in the AP or honors programs?
- What courses and activities does the school require for graduation?
- How does the school help students get information about post-secondary options and then help them choose?
- Does the school have an advisory system? How does it work? If there's no formal system, who in the school will know my child well enough to advise him or her?
- Who can I talk to about how my child is doing? How many other students is that person expected to know well?

2

LOOK, LISTEN, AND ASK

Are there simple, accurate ways to determine whether a school is "right" for your child? How can you measure the quality of your child's school, short of doing an in-depth study over weeks or months? Even after 25 years of reporting about education, I won't try to tell you that "I know a good school when I see one." On the other hand, I have come to rely on my eyes and ears and my curiosity; thus the title of this chapter, "Look, Listen, and Ask." Here are a number of yardsticks, presented with the caveat that there really is *no* quick and easy way to know that a school or a particular teacher is excellent. And even solutions that are simple (hiring teachers who've majored in the field they're going to be teaching, for example) are probably neither quick nor easy.

To begin at the beginning, the primary purpose of school is intellectual; learning should be paramount. If most students are not acquiring vast amounts of knowledge, the school cannot qualify as "good enough," let alone "excellent." Very little academic learning or intellectual growth occurs in bad schools.

And test scores matter, to get another potential controversy out of the way early. Later on I will argue that we test too much and often for the wrong reasons. How students perform on well-made tests is a decent indicator of learning. However, low marks on *standardized, machine-scored, multiple-choice tests* do not necessarily point to a bad school. For example, schools in high poverty areas, where many parents are unemployed, where crime and drug use are rampant, and where children have less than optimal learning environments at home have to fight an uphill battle to succeed.

Success is possible, of course. Samuel Casey Carter describes 21 high-performing, high-poverty schools in his book, *No Excuses*, and Jonathan Kozol paints a careful picture of an effective inner-city school in his book, *Ordinary Resurrections*. What connects these effective schools, besides high performance, are strong leadership, a commitment to learning, "contracts" with parents, and (surprise?) vigorous programs in art and music. These are not "drill and practice" schools, but energetic and positive places to be. The three that I have visited certainly match what's been written about them.[16]

A caveat: don't assume that high scores on standardized, machine-scored multiple-choice tests are prima facie proof of excellence. Excellence is not so easy to attain.

E. D. Hirsch Jr., the author of *The Schools We Need*,[17] believes there are two ways of distinguishing between "good enough" schools and excellent ones. "One is the objective results that the school is able to accomplish: How well do the children read? How well do they compute? How big are their vocabularies? A second measure is subjective: Are students turned on to learning? Are they enthusiastic? Do they like school? Is teacher morale high?"

Does one measure carry more weight? Professor Hirsch believes that the objective information matters more, but I am inclined to disagree, simply because hard numbers very often lose their precision and firmness when scrutinized closely. I'd give equal weight to numbers and subjective impressions formed on the strength of several visits and careful questioning. That is, a lot of looking, listening, and asking!

INDICATORS OF EXCELLENCE

Want one simple test? Spend a few afternoons observing the faculty parking lot or the building exit most teachers use at the end of the day. My experience suggests that, if most teachers can't wait to get away from the school, then you should have reservations about having your child go there. (A caveat: In some large schools, teachers are told to leave as soon as possible, because of fears for their safety.)

Simple test #2: Ask if you may observe classes in your child's elementary school for a few hours. If getting permission requires going through the central office bureaucracy or filling out forms, you may be in a troubled school. But I would also be upset if the principal simply said, "go ahead" without first asking permission of the teacher because that smacks of authoritarianism. Individual teachers should be allowed to control *when* a parent may visit, but not *whether*.

Another reliable indicator has to do with school's leader: is the principal a "sitter" or a "mover"? I recall spending two days in a large Los Angeles high school from 7:30 till 3, wandering around, visiting classes, and interviewing teachers, students, security guards, and cafeteria workers. In my two days there, I never saw the principal anywhere but behind his desk, and that's enough to start the warning bells ringing in my head, because in most well run schools, the principal is visible.

When I spent several hours in a Washington, D.C., junior high school, I kept bumping into the principal; he was walking the halls, talking with students and teachers, even picking up stray pieces of paper. "Is keeping the halls clean part of your job?" I asked. "It's everybody's job, beginning with mine, because when kids see me cleaning up, they will begin to care too—at least some of them will." Now, walking around isn't everything, and I'll be the first to object if the principal's presence has the effect of keeping classrooms unnaturally tranquil, but I will say this: show me a sitting principal, and I'll show you a detached leader and, odds are, an uninteresting school.

E. D. Hirsch, who created the Core Knowledge program, agrees. "A good principal is always out and about. How can you know what's going on if you're sitting in your office? You need to make everyone think you know what's going on."

Excellent principals are not just walking around. They're dropping in on classes, talking with students, "feeling" their school. As one leader told me, "The halls and classes are where the action is."

Open doors can be a sign of excellence, because it suggests that the real work of both the students and the teachers is open to scrutiny. But many teachers close their doors at 8:15 and keep them closed. Are they reluctant to have others know what's going on, or could there be a benign explanation? Ted Sizer is generous in his appraisal. "Most teachers have to close the doors because of the background whine of the school. It's very hard to have open doors in a very large school where everyone is basically a stranger."

What did he mean, "Where everyone is basically a stranger," I asked Sizer? "Say you have 1,500 kids in the school and several hundred faculty. There are probably 50 new kids every month, and 50 that leave. Nine classes a day of 47 minutes[18] each means lots of hustle and bustle. So it's a building full of strangers, and you end up protecting yourself. You're always thinking, 'I don't know who these people are. Who are they?'"

SMALLER *IS* BETTER

The size of the school is important. When I did a report on home schooling in Texas, I went to see the elementary school that one particular child had attended until his parents withdrew him. It was a cheerful, friendly, well-equipped place, with lots of children's art on the wall. It had the feel of a terrific school, and I wondered why any parents would object to having their kids there. After my quick tour, I asked the principal about the boy, who had been there the previous two years. She thought a minute, then said, "I don't remember him. He must have been in the middle. I only get to know the outstanding ones and the ones who cause trouble. You know how it is." I nodded agreeably, and we moved on.

"You know how it is," she had said—but why is it that way? What's going on when an energetic, seemingly competent principal only knows the kids at the top and the bottom? The answer is size, of course. That elementary school has nearly 850 students, grades 1–6, too big for her to know every child by name—not to mention a little something about each.

In my opinion, that makes it too big. The elementary school years are too important for any child to fall through the cracks. As a parent, I'd want to know that my child is a real person to the head of the operation. High school students regularly complain about being just a number. I shudder to think that second- and third-graders may feel that way too.

So here's my rule of thumb: elementary schools should be small enough so that the principal can and does know every child. I've heard the argument in support of bigger schools: they save money—one building instead of two, one principal's salary instead of two, and so on. Okay, to a point, but when any child falls through the cracks, somebody's saving money at the expense of children, maybe my children, maybe yours.

History has favored big schools. Throughout the 20th century, the size of schools increased tremendously, especially in cities. Nationwide since World War II, the number of total schools declined 70 percent, while the average school enrollment increased by 400 percent. Today, one in four secondary schools has more than 1,000 students. New York City has nine high schools with more than 4,000 students, and one with 5,300 students.

What do today's experts say about school size? Is there a best size, supported by serious research. John Goodlad, perhaps the dean of American education researchers,[19] created a "satisfaction index" to measure school quality. The evaluation process involved everyone with a stake in schools—students, teachers, parents, and other adults. Not one single large school ended up being ranked in the top quartile, an astonishing finding given how many large schools there are in the U.S. "We discovered that all of the large schools were in the bottom quartile," Goodlad told me on National Public Radio.

I asked Professor Goodlad if his research suggested ideal sizes for elementary, middle, and high schools. "Yes," he said emphatically, "We concluded that you top out in an elementary school at about 400 students, in a middle school at about 600, and in a senior high school at about 800."[20]

Rachel Tompkins is president of the Rural School and Community Trust, an organization that has studied small schools extensively. She notes that "small" may mean 200 students in Montana and 400 in Georgia, but the benefits are clear and measurable. "There are more opportunities for adult/student interaction. Kids are known by many adults. They get more individualized attention. They have more chances to participate in more activities."[21]

But small size is not a "magic bullet," Tompkins warns. "You still need quality teaching and effective leadership."

Deborah Meier, nationally known for the quality of the small public schools she has started in New York City, has a rule of thumb: an elementary school should be small enough so all its teachers can have a serious conversation together at the same time. "It's very hard for 100 grown-ups to have a serious conversation. In fact, I don't even know what it means for 100 grown-ups to get together and have a conversation. I would say that the faculty shouldn't be larger than a good class, so everyone can join in the conversation. Twenty faculty members is about the upper limit, which means a school probably should have no more than 300 or 400 kids."

Ted Sizer focuses on high schools. "We argue about what's best, and I settle on 350 to 400. Other reasonable people say that a school needs about 600 students to get a certain richness of experience and variety. Whatever the right number is, it sure isn't 1000. It sure isn't even 750."[22]

Don't be misled by the size of the *building*, because one building may contain several schools. I've been in large, old-fashioned schools with as many as seven or eight small, freestanding intellectual communities. The building is just a holding company. That's easy to say, but it does require a new perspective, because we are accustomed to equating one school with one building. But you may work in an office building. Is your company the only one in that building, or are there other companies, other businesses, under that roof?

One of the first reports I did as education correspondent for the *MacNeil/Lehrer NewsHour* was about the school choice plan adopted by District Four in New York City, one of the city's lowest performing districts. In 1982 its key leaders[23] decided that their large (and largely ineffective) junior high schools would be broken up into small schools. They invited teachers and principals to propose "theme" junior high schools and gave the most appealing proposals the green light. Then they told parents that they, with their sixth-graders, had the right to choose among the variety of schools that sprang up. Schools that few families chose would "go out of business," close temporarily, and reopen under new leadership with a new theme.

The experiment worked, and by 1987, the year I reported on it, District Four's ranking among the city's 32 school districts had shot up, from dead last to the middle of the pack.

It worked for a number of reasons (parental choice, variety, power in the hands of teachers, and effective leadership), but the fact that these were *small* schools was critical to their success. Size doesn't matter if nobody has a clear idea of where they're headed, of course, but other things being equal, smaller is better in education.[24]

Two related measures of excellence are teacher attendance and substitution policy. You have a right to the facts and figures about teacher attendance. You'll want to know how many "medical days" or "sick days" teachers are entitled to in their contract, and then ask how many teachers use their quota each year. If virtually *all* the teachers use *all* the days they're entitled to, that's a warning signal that something may be amiss. If that happens every year, the school has either morale or leadership problems—and most likely both.

Then ask about substitution policy. If the school routinely divvies up the missing teacher's class by sending some kids here, others there, instead of hiring qualified substitute teachers, then someone is putting money ahead of your children's interests.

LOOKING AND LISTENING

Rely on your senses when visiting a school, that is, look and listen. Start by *looking* at class size. Small classes—20 students or fewer—means more attention for your child. And don't take the district's word on class size. Count name tags on classroom doors and look inside the classroom and count heads. Class size reduction is just about everybody's favorite reform. A survey by *U.S. News & World Report* in 1997 showed that 60 percent of parents would be willing to vote for a candidate who advocated raising taxes to reduce class size, and a survey of teachers shows the majority were willing to forgo raises if it meant smaller classes. Research supports the benefits of small classes, particularly in lower grades and especially if the class has no more than 15 or 17 students.[25]

Inside classrooms, look for clues about academic quality in the arrangement of the desks. Alfie Kohn is a hard-liner on seating arrangements. "The last thing you want to see is rows of desks behind each other with each kid stranded on his or her own desk as though on a separate island. What you want to find are kids in small groups, challenging each other in a caring way."

E. D. Hirsch rejects the hard-line approach. "Desks in a row don't bother me. It does bother some people, because it's symbolic of the teacher as the boss and students as subservient, passive recipients of knowledge. But as long as what happens in the room is highly interactive and highly engaging, how the room is arranged doesn't really matter."

Look in the auditorium whenever you're visiting. If you often find students watching videos, you might want to try to make sure your child isn't assigned to that teacher's class. (Unless you want to apply for the popcorn concession!)

Focus your sights on the walls, too. What do you see in bad schools? Nothing but scrubbed cinderblock painted light green. "Good enough" schools cover their walls with interesting projects, but be on the lookout for classrooms where the work on the walls looks pretty much the same. Cookie-cutter work indicates a teacher who does not value original thinking. In excellent schools you will find a wide variety of children's work on the walls, showing creativity and expression—and an academic purpose. As E. D. Hirsch says, "Because the primary mission of a school is academic, the walls should display the art students have produced, and not just finger painting but art that's on subject and really related to learning." In other words, look for evidence of children's thinking in the work that's displayed. Not just teacher-designed bulletin boards but work that expresses the children's own ideas.

You may see young children working *enthusiastically* on tasks that are basically of the cookie-cutter variety, but don't let the enthusiasm fool you. They've probably gotten used to easy work that earns them "smiley faces" or gold stars. All they're doing is following directions, which means, unfortunately, that someone is pouring a weak foundation for serious intellectual growth. When I see that, I suspect that the teacher doesn't believe in his or her kids' abilities.

Just to be sure about the work you're seeing, check the dates on whatever's displayed. I've been in schools with truly gorgeous stuff on the walls, only to find that it's five or ten years old! Less obvious, but also revealing, is when winter's work still hangs in late spring. That suggests that somebody's creative engine has stalled.

Once you've finished *looking*, start *listening*—first for the sounds of silence. As Ted Sizer says, "Silence is, in almost every case, a sign of a weak school." His colleague Deborah Meier agrees, "If you have a classroom where kids never talk, they aren't going to learn how to articulate their ideas very well, and that has consequences later on."

If the teacher's voice dominates in the classroom, that limits and perhaps eclipses opportunities for student to be active participants in making sense of things. And learning is all about kids making sense of ideas.

Listen to the tone of the teacher's voice when he or she is talking to students. Is it respectful? When children talk, can they expect to be listened to, or is there competition to get the teacher's attention? If kids treat each other respectfully, that's a sign that what they're doing seems to them to be important and interesting, even intriguing.

Excellent teachers ask a lot of questions, always probing, digging deeper. They push students, challenge their thinking. But look to see if the teacher tends to always call on the same kids. Excellent teachers try to bring everyone into the conversation.

I asked Ted Sizer what he would look for if a student kept getting the wrong answer. "I would hope the teacher would get interested in the confusion and realize it's not just a computation mistake but an error in thinking things through. That is, the excellent teacher would know enough math to recognize that the kid is solving a different problem, or approaching it differently." That's when the excellent teacher goes into overdrive, Sizer said. "The excellent teacher would be able to figure out how a kid's mind was working mathematically, instead of simply marking the answer wrong." In short, the excellent teacher knows the field (content knowledge) and different ways the subject matter can be expressed in different minds, as well as different approaches to teaching it.

Deborah Meier, who takes the idea of listening seriously, suggests paying careful attention to the teacher's voice, because, she says, teachers have their own genuine human voice and their "teacher voice," which they can turn on and off. I asked her what a teacher voice sounds like? "It's always louder and slower, as though you're talking to 30 people at once, even though you may be talking to only one or two. It's slightly patronizing. '*Now, children* . . .'" She smiled. "I like schools where the voice teachers use with children is not so different from the one they use with their colleagues."

Listen at related school activities as well, such as parent-teacher conferences, back-to-school nights, and even school board meetings. Is the tone respectful and are kids at the center, even when the debate is raging? Chicago is proud of its school councils, elected bodies that have the authority to hire and fire principals and make school policy, but most of the school council meetings I've been to have been marked by negative energy and what struck me as indifference to children and their learning.

A cautionary note about jumping to conclusions: You cannot walk into a classroom and tell immediately whether good teaching is going on. As E. D. Hirsch reminded me, "Learning is cumulative, and both teaching and learning have their disciplined moments and romantic moments." Don't expect the same scene every time in excellent classrooms.

How students react when you walk into a classroom will tell you something important as well. If most kids become distracted by your presence, it suggests they aren't engaged in the material or aren't interested in the class itself. In excellent schools, kids will glance at a visitor and return to the matter at hand. If the teacher suspects that the visitor may be able to contribute, she may invite him to participate. That's also a good sign.

I suggest you ask kids what they're studying. Many will say, "American history" or "social studies" and leave it at that. Press them and they may add something like, "We're reading Chapter Six." You may get a blank stare if you ask, "What important ideas are you thinking about in this class?" because no adults have conveyed that concept to them. In excellent schools, students understand that they have the right and opportunity to explore ideas and principles, or to dig into why things happened. In excellent schools you will see students doing research, creating projects, using the library, conducting experiments, reading independently, and having discussions. Many of them will be eager to talk about what they're doing. They can tell you why it's important and whether they are doing good work.

In excellent classrooms, you will often hear a buzz of activity, and it's the sound of students figuring things out and trying on ideas. That will spill over into the hallways too, so don't get trapped into thinking that hallway noise is automatically bad.

In fact, some yelling can be good, believe it or not. You have to listen to what the teacher is yelling. If the teacher is yelling, "You are just so dumb! You never do anything right. I don't see how you're ever going to make it through middle school. Look at this!" that's not a good teacher. But, as Lisa Delpit told me, "If the teacher says, 'You are too smart to give me work like this! Do you see this? I have worked with you before, and I know you are brilliant. How could you give me this kind of information on this paper?' that's good yelling."

The teacher who demands excellent work, even if she occasionally yells, is exactly who you will find in excellent schools. High expectations are essential, and nothing lowers student performance faster than a teacher who anticipates mediocrity. If teachers do not believe that their children can and will learn, those students are doomed to being "good enough" or worse.

There's also good and bad noise in the hallways. Bad noise is hectoring, harassing, mindless, but good noise conveys engagement. It doesn't have the highs and lows of bad noise but it does have a certain intensity. Even if you can't distinguish the words, you can sense and feel the involvement of the students as you walk up and down the hallways. But, as Ted Sizer notes, "If it's a big school with large classes that meet for only 47 minutes, it's pretty hard to get any kind of sustained serious conversation going, in class or in the hall."

Listening to the conversations that students have on their own will tell you a great deal, Sizer says. "The real test of an excellent school is not what students do or talk about when the teacher assigns them a question, but what they do when you're not looking."

You can tell something's important and exciting if they're talking about the material they're studying or if they bring an argument about ideas out of the classroom. If they're not doing either of those things, then you can assume that nothing is engaging or interesting enough to continue talking about.

Deborah Meier also recommends listening to the ways that teachers talk *to one another*. In excellent schools, the adults engage in serious conversation and seem confident in their own "adultness." In most schools, Meier says, students meet adults who see them as children. "Teachers tell them what to do, lecture at them and explain things to them, but they don't see adults who themselves are curious about the world, who are engaged in trying to make sense of the world."

Meier uses a sports analogy to explain herself. "Kids learn to be soccer players because they see soccer played and because they practice. The same thing goes for tennis. If we want them to become intellectuals, they have to see adults engage in intellectual life, and they have to practice intellectual skills together."

Unfortunately, most schools do not operate on the assumption that teachers need or want to talk to one another, and many union contracts specify that teachers do not have to arrive early or stay late. That is, everyone with power has acted to limit the possibilities for serious conversations about teaching and learning.

As Meier notes, policymakers have assumed that teacher time is the same as student time. "Kids come at 8:30, so teachers should come at 8:25. Kids go home at 3:00, so teachers go home at 3:05. If school starts September 2nd, then teachers should be there September 1st."

"Summer camps don't do things so stupidly," Meier observes acidly. "Camp staff gets together a month before the kids arrive to plan, and counselors get together to talk after the kids have gone to bed."

That suggests another measure of excellence: Does the school believe that it's not enough for teachers simply to be present with the kids and to monitor their homework? Does it try to provide time and incentives for teachers to keep on learning about their own craft and their own particular field? While most school districts don't even debate this issue, it's time they did, because we live in a world in which knowledge is exploding (and a science teacher probably has to learn more science every week!).

It is important to remember that you cannot judge a school or a teacher based on what you see and hear in a single visit, no matter how tempting (or easy) it may be to jump to conclusions. You will need to ask tough questions and persist in seeking answers.

QUESTION #1:
WHO IS TEACHING YOUR CHILDREN?

Expect blank stares and hostile looks when you ask unpopular questions, particularly about the qualifications of the teachers. In excellent schools, the adults teaching the core subjects will have either majored or minored in what they are now teaching. Believe it or not, every year millions of secondary school students are taught subjects like physics, chemistry, and history by teachers who do not even have a college minor in that field. That includes 25 percent of all English and history teachers and 30 percent of all math and science teachers. This occurs even though 36 states have rules requiring teachers to major or minor in the fields they teach. Unfortunately 33 of those 36 state regulations have loopholes big enough to drive a truck through.

So ask, in polite language, "Do the math teachers know math? How many math teachers are math majors or have master's degrees in mathematics?" But subject matter knowledge is not enough, so you might want to watch the math teachers who have an MA in mathematics to see whether they use their mastery in creative ways, or if they just lecture.

I have encountered many teachers working "out-of-field" over the years, but never so many as in Randolph Clay High School in rural Georgia. At that school a junior high coach was teaching high school history, math, and English, while another coach was teaching algebra. The shop teacher also taught math, and another English teacher was teaching history and social studies. The principal's explanation for the fact that more than half of his teachers were teaching out-of-field was that he couldn't attract qualified people to rural Georgia, leaving him no choice. He later told me that he had informed the coaches he was about to hire that they would be expected to teach core subjects if they wanted the job. As one coach told me, "I could have said 'No,' but then I wouldn't have had a job."

I watched a vocabulary lesson in one junior English class. Among the words on the board was "strenuous," which the coach had spelled "strenous." He failed to catch the mistake, even when he broke it into syllables. His students dutifully wrote the word down in their notebooks.

Out-of-field teaching occurs in wealthy suburbs too, lest any reader be thinking that "it can't happen here." Michael Cartwright majored in physics in college and now teaches in an Atlanta suburb. One year his principal assigned him to teach health. He explained how that turned out. "I did a horrible job because I couldn't do the CPR. I mean, legally I could not. It was dangerous. I couldn't do the Heimlich maneuver because I didn't know it, and I didn't know the names of all the drugs. And I simply refused to do sex education."

Because seniority often rules in schools, veteran teachers tend to get their pick of classes. Ask if the senior teachers ever teach lower level classes, or if they take only the honors courses. An excellent principal will push to avoid what amounts to a caste system.

Excellent elementary schools provide a nurturing environment for children by having sensitive teachers and small classes. Another sign of excellence is what is sometimes called "developmental guidance," which requires having a full-time trained counselor on staff. He or she meets regularly with small groups, from kindergarten on, and is a continuing presence in the children's lives as they move through school. In their regular meetings, they discuss such issues as making friends, making good choices, handling rules, etc. in the early grades. Later on topics might include personal safety, good touch/bad touch, and drug and alcohol prevention. The counselor becomes a resource for teachers who feel they need help reaching or dealing with a particular child and for parents as well.

Speaking of parents, lots of schools feel strongly about parent involvement, and so they have parent councils and parent activities. In good enough schools, a small group of parents is very active, but they might be the most privileged families. In most schools, 80 to 90 percent of the parents are not very active in the school. That parent council might meet three or four times a month, but that's not necessarily a good sign—because most adults can't attend that many meetings and therefore may hesitate to become involved.

So the existence of an active parents' group is not, ipso facto, a sign of excellence. It's possible that the group may be excluding or scaring off the majority of parents. As Deborah Meier notes, "You can have a school in which the involved parents are very powerful adults who are protecting their own children's self-interest. The real issue is whether the school has ways to protect the interests, and identify the needs of, all parents, and not just the active ones."

Meier has her own analysis of what matters in parental involvement. "I think an excellent school involves its families, first and foremost, on behalf of their own children. There are lots of ways parents can get to know the teacher and develop a relationship around their child's classroom, not necessarily with the whole school."

The truest test of whether a school is right for your child, particularly for a young child, is his or her attitude toward school. Don't measure it by what he or she *says* because bad-mouthing of teachers and school comes with the territory. Instead, watch what your child does, particularly in the morning. Is he genuinely reluctant to go to school most mornings? Does she clearly feel better about herself on weekends than she does on school days? If you answer "Yes" to either of those questions, then it's time for a meeting with the teacher, to figure out what's wrong.

Parents have no right to expect teachers to love their children or give them straight As, but teachers must respect children as individuals and value their potential. If a teacher is sending your child the message—even inadvertently—"You're no good," then it's time for a change of attitude (or, failing that, of schools). And fast!

QUESTIONS ABOUT STUDENTS

- How do students react to your presence (as a stranger)? Do they greet you easily? Do they ignore you?

- What is the absentee rate for students?
- Why do students leave the school? (In some schools, the population is transient because many students are, in effect, fleeing a sinking ship. The kids will tell you.)
- To what extent are students tracked (for what subjects and at what grades)? Is there any degree of mobility between tracks? When are students categorized, and by what standards?
- Are Advanced Placement classes restricted to students who have proven themselves or open to all who want to try?
- How are students selected for a "gifted and talented" program? Does the program cast a wide net, or is "gifted" narrowly defined by test scores? Are gifted programs and the most challenging courses open to any student who asks for them?
- How many kids are classified as gifted? What support do they get? Some schools still assume that gifted kids should just be given more work, instead of different work. (A gifted child is not likely to get what he or she needs if there is only a handful of them and no additional support is provided.)
- Is there continuity in the gifted program from elementary school to middle school, and from middle to high school? Continuity matters.
- What portion of the student population is actually involved in extra-curricular activities?
- How diverse is the student population?
- What percentage of high school graduates enter four-year colleges?
- What is the average class size?

QUESTIONS TO ASK STUDENTS

- Which courses do you like the best? Why?
- Which is your least favorite course? Why?
- Do you have to work hard in your classes? What do you mean by "hard"?
- What do your classes make you think about? Do conversations in class ever carry over into hallways and the cafeteria?
- Do your teachers really know who you are? Do they really know what you've learned in their class? How do you know?
- What's the longest paper you've written? What was it about? How much research did you have to do to write it?

- How much cheating is there in the school? Who seems to be cheating, and what does the school do about it?
- Do teachers look the other way when there's bullying or harassment?
- Do adults in the school favor one group of students over others? Who are the favorites? Do they get away with more? How?
- Is your teacher fair?
- Is it okay to be smart at this school?
- Is it okay (safe) to say, "I don't understand" and to ask for help?
- Do teachers use incorrect answers as an opportunity to learn how the student who made the mistake was approaching the problem? Or are students who make mistakes cut off and ignored if they don't give the right answer?

QUESTIONS TO ASK (ABOUT) THE PRINCIPAL

- Is the principal a "sitter" or a "mover"?
- Is the principal more of an academic (instructional) leader or merely an administrator who makes sure things run smoothly?
- Does the principal teach at least one class a year? After all, the word was originally an adjective, as in "principal teacher."
- Does the principal have an educational philosophy? Does the staff buy into it?
- Do the students know who the principal is? Does the principal know students on a first-name basis?
- Does the principal foster the best in staff or pit teachers against one another?
- Is there clear communication about school events such as back-to-school nights?
- Does the principal have an "open door" policy to meet with parents and students?
- Does the principal allow parents to visit and observe classrooms? Does the principal spend time observing teachers and talking with students about what they are studying?
- Does the principal encourage volunteerism?
- Is there a clear discipline policy that children and grown-ups can understand? Ask the same question about policies for grading and homework.

QUESTIONS TO ASK ABOUT PARENTAL INVOLVEMENT

- Is there an active parent organization such as a PTA or PTO? Does it meet often? Does it work to support the teachers by, for example, accompanying field trips?
- Does it address real issues in the school, such as (perhaps) cheating, student motivation, or an achievement gap? Or is it largely ceremonial?
- Do parents have a real voice in the school? Is there a council that represents parents and helps decide on school policies? (A council might meet with teachers to discuss standards, plan programs to bring the community into the school, develop community service programs, and so forth.)
- Do parents and school work to create a sense of community by, for example, publishing a directory or holding community events like a flea market–yard sale and class picnics?
- Are there clear ways that new parents can become involved? (A PTA or PTO that holds meetings in an officer's home is a problem because that is intimidating to newcomers.)
- Is there a family center? Is it staffed and does it have useful materials that parents can borrow, such as books, learning kits, toys and games, and educational videos? Can families get referrals to social services there?
- Can parents use the fax machine, the copier, or the computers at the school? Is the library or media center open in the evenings or on weekends? Does the school offer computer classes or math, science, and literacy classes for families?
- Are there child care, transportation, and food when there are family meetings at the school? Are meetings held at times that are convenient for families, such as right after work or early in the morning? How many families come to these meetings?

GENERAL QUESTIONS

- How serious is the school about art and music programs?
- How important is physical activity for all children?
- How does the school honor academic excellence? (Here you might compare that recognition to that given for athletic achievement.)

- What is the school's reputation in the community, and is it deserved? Every school, of course, has a reputation, but sometimes the reputations are better or worse than they deserve.
- Has anyone in the district started (or tried to start) a charter school?
- Can I observe my child's class? Are there any contractual restrictions to arental visits to classrooms? What are they, and how did they get written into the contract?
- Does the school seem orderly or in tight control?
- What safety measures are in place? Are they unobtrusive or glaringly obvious?
- Is the school reasonably neat and clean?
- Are the classroom doors open?
- What's the noise level (remembering the distinction between "good" noise and "bad" noise)?
- Are the walls decorated with student work?
- How long has whatever is on the hallway walls been hanging there?
- Can I sit in on classes before I choose the school?
- Can I see my child's school record?
- Are parents and others welcome to visit classrooms?
- What's the student turnover rate? If it's high, is that because families move in and out of the area for economic or other reasons? A high transient rate reduces the likelihood your child will have longtime friends at that school.

3

TESTING, ASSESSMENT, AND EXCELLENCE

Excellent schools are accountable for their "products," the students who pass through their classrooms, but what exactly do we mean by the term *accountable*? This chapter explores the meaning of accountability, the growth of the standards movement, and an accompanying rise in what is called "high-stakes testing." To be forthright, I believe that high-stakes testing, in its current manifestation, is a serious threat to excellence and national standards. Unchecked, it will choke the life out of many excellent schools and drive gifted teachers out of classrooms. Unchecked, it will lead to debased and unnecessarily low standards.

High-stakes tests have serious consequences for those taking them, and sometimes in the careers of their teachers and administrators. A good example is the high school graduation test that students must pass in order to get a diploma. By the turn of the century, 28 states either already had or planned to have such tests.

A more rational approach is broad-based assessment, which involves *multiple measures* of what a student has learned. Assessment relies on teacher-made tests, teacher evaluations, student demonstrations, etc. all over an extended period of time, instead of one score on a single, largely machine-scored test (even if it includes a writing test). Unfortunately, the supporters of high-stakes testing have more faith in machines than they do in teachers.

The mad rush to embrace high-stakes testing says to me that we are now reaping what years of superficial indifference have sown. That is, for years educators have not held themselves accountable, so now business leaders and politicians are creating systems to hold schools accountable. As I will explain, the move to create standards is out of synch, and we're now testing with a vengeance, before the system has had time to get ready.

All students in U.S. schools are tested, probably too much. In *bad* schools, students spend weeks and months actually prepping for the test, abandoning the curriculum. In "good enough" schools, tests have become the tail wagging the dog, that is, they tend to dominate. What's more, in "good enough" schools, tests are used to rate the school or its students. In excellent schools, tests are aligned with, but secondary to, the curriculum and results are used to *describe* students' strengths and weaknesses. "Describe" is the correct term, not "diagnose," although the latter is more often used. Test results pinpoint weaknesses but do not explain why the student has gotten something wrong. That's the next step, and it requires a skilled human being, not a machine.[26] By those rules, very few of our schools today qualify as excellent.

Standards and their apparently inevitable but unwelcome companion, high-stakes testing, are with us now. In 2000, 49 states had already developed, or were developing, educational *standards*. Iowa chose to let local districts develop their own standards. In addition to the growth in graduation tests, 12 states have tests to determine promotion from grade to grade, and more are jumping on that bandwagon. Every year millions of high school juniors and seniors take the SAT, the descendant of the IQ test, and those scores (or ACT scores) figure significantly in college admission decisions. These tests meet any definition of "high stakes."

Standards-based education reform evolved out of what amounts to a bargain between frustrated citizens on the one hand and educators on the other. In this bargain, the public says, "we'll give you more money if you will provide better results and be accountable," and educators say, "we'll be accountable for achievement if you give us the money." Unfortunately, things haven't gone smoothly. In many cases the tests have gotten ahead of developing standards and reforming, and in other instances the money hasn't materialized.

American business endorses standards as the essential building block of school reform, a necessary step if America is to remain economically competitive. They have captured the linguistic high ground in this struggle, because it's hard to say you're against standards; that's a lot like booing Mom or the American flag. That aside, arguments for educational standards make sense: Americans move around a lot. The Census Bureau reports that at least 20 percent of families move every year. Some urban schools report more dramatic turnover figures: every year half of the students—or more—transfer out and are replaced by other students.

Inconsistent standards make it virtually impossible for parents, teachers, and administrators to know how much students have learned. One elementary principal told me, "Sometimes students transfer in with As in reading, but they can barely read. It works the other way too; a child will come in with a B minus in arithmetic but be terrific by our standards."

As far as educational standards are concerned, the major argument has been over *who* should develop them, although virtually everyone agrees that it should not be the federal government. "Washington would just screw it up," says Wisconsin's republican governor Tommy Thompson. When Roy Romer was governor of Colorado, he told me, "It has to be done locally; that's the American way."[27] Now that Romer is Los Angeles' school superintendent, it's doubtful that he has changed his mind.

BEHIND THE STANDARDS

The push for standards began in force back in 1988, when President George Bush called the nation's governors together for the first-ever National Education Summit, held on the campus of the University of Virginia. Out of that largely theatrical meeting came a set of national education goals, some of which were actually written in the White House basement months later, some of which had been decided upon beforehand.[28]

Goals begot standards, and here the White House has taken a back seat. The prime mover behind standards has been IBM's Louis V. Gerstner Jr., the prominent businessman who has been an education reformer for more than 20 years. Gerstner was the principal organizer behind the National Education Summit meetings in 1996 and 1999, meetings that involved nearly every state governor, America's business leaders, and President Clinton. Gerstner is aware of the growing backlash against high-stakes testing, but he's not backing off. "We can't slow down, because we hurt everybody when we slow down."

I asked him about fears that some children are being put at a disadvantage when new, tougher standards were suddenly imposed. He was visibly annoyed. "The argument that we shouldn't put standards in because some children are going to be hurt because they're not going to pass a test is fallacious. Children are being hurt today because they're *passing* the tests, and the tests are not recognizing that they cannot do what they need to do."

Reformer Ted Sizer is concerned not only about the speed with which the standards movement is moving but also about the driving force behind it, American business. "Business has put a lot of time into this, but in ways that have been simplistic," Sizer says. "But why should we be surprised, because if I were to presume that I could move in and run IBM, I'd get most of it wrong, because I don't know enough." The process, Sizer says, has been arrogant and costly, and the notion that there is one best curriculum to be decided upon by a small group, is dangerous. "Do we want a small group of people deciding what is supposed to go into our children's heads? I don't think so."

Gerstner laughed when I told him about Sizer's concerns. "Forty-nine states are setting standards, and Iowa is doing it in every local community. So we'll have 60 or 70 or 80 institutions in our society creating these standards, and every one of them is different." Gerstner says that in every state parents, educators, business leaders, and others are involved, including experts on standards in other countries.

Voting for standards is a lot easier than actually *creating* them. That task involves two types of standards: content standards and performance standards.[29] Some person or group must decide on content: what, for example, eleventh-graders should master in English. Let's say the group agrees that eleventh-graders must be able to present a complex argument persuasively and must be familiar with drama, poetry, and fiction. Let's go further and say that they also agree that eleventh-graders should read and be able to understand a Shakespearean play. Assuming that they've gotten that far (and that's a big assumption, considering the cultural climate we live in), that's only halfway home. Now it's time to decide what levels of performance are "satisfactory," "outstanding," and "unsatisfactory." How much of that play does the eleventh-grader have to grasp to meet the new standard, and what does a satisfactory essay look like? These questions are neither trivial nor easy to answer.

We now enter the arbitrary process of standard-setting. Just what standards are established depends on who is asked. Each expert will have an idea of what is acceptable, outstanding, and insufficient.[30] Are these ideas to be given arbitrary numerical weights and then averaged? Somehow a number is arrived at, and that number immediately takes on magical qualities—it is what a student must achieve to pass, or to be promoted to the next grade, or to graduate.

The next steps are not trivial or automatic either. The curriculum must be adjusted, and then teachers have to be brought up to speed. Teachers who've grown accustomed to teaching certain materials in set ways may have to, in effect, start over. This may be beneficial for all concerned in the long run, but it will not happen overnight.

Multiply that scenario by the number of grade levels, the number of subjects, and the number of teachers (3,000,000), and you begin to understand the swamp that educators, politicians, business leaders, and others have waded into. And you also may begin to understand why testing has gotten ahead of developing and then implementing standards in many places.

Gerstner is clear about what needs to be done, even as he acknowledges that there will be casualties. "We need to make very significant investments now, to protect the people that will get hurt, because we're imposing a new system of high standards in an environment where there weren't any standards, and some children are going to get caught in the middle. How do we help them? Massive after school and summer training programs. We need to fund those. We need to train teachers to develop ways to bring these students up quickly."[31]

STANDARDS IN ACTION

Students who don't meet the standards are likely to be told to go to summer school, even though serious questions have been asked about the effectiveness of summer programs. Chicago started the trend in the late '90s, but the roster of cities mandating summer school for students who have not met the new standards seems to grow daily: Miami-Dade, Oakland, Long Beach, Greenville (SC), Baton Rouge, Atlanta, Richmond, Dallas, Davenport (IA), Oxnard (CA), Orange City (FL), and New York City.

Dallas has decided that students who attend summer school will be promoted even if they fail the summer course. Atlanta has summer school for third-graders, while in Davenport, Iowa, it's for second-graders. In Chicago, summer school is for third-, sixth-, and eighth-graders.

At one point in the spring of 2000 New York City school officials indicated that as many as 320,000 students might have to attend summer school. In the end, 62,537 were mandated to attend. At summer's end 60 percent[32] failed the reading and mathematics tests, but the board promoted many of them anyway.

This seems to fly in the face of the board's promise to end "social promotion," but the board explained that, because it had used a new, more challenging test that had a higher passing score, some students who had flunked were deserving of promotion, in the considered judgment of their teachers.[33]

Today we are rushing headlong in search of the "Holy Grail" of rising test scores. What seems to be happening is that the high-stakes testing movement has picked up momentum and gotten well ahead of the slower process of developing and implementing standards. Most policymakers are not as sophisticated as Gerstner, and many unfortunate decisions are being made as pressure for "accountability" overwhelms common sense. It's a whole lot easier to give a test than to do the hard work of retraining teachers and preparing students.

The vast majority of the items on these high-stakes tests are multiple-choice questions that are scored by machines, and therein lies the major problem. Where high-stakes tests require a great deal of writing, as the English exams in Massachusetts and Maryland do, their use is easier to defend. Those exams are graded by human beings who, I hope, have been properly trained in evaluating essay writing. This enterprise is far more expensive and time-consuming, and I wonder how long states will remain committed to it. After all, early versions of what we know as the SAT were essay tests graded by real people, and the Educational Testing Service/College Board dropped that practice at the first available opportunity.[34]

MORE CONFUSION

Here's a larger example of confused public policy, this at the state level. Mississippi mandated a statewide test for eighth-graders, to be given in May 2001. The results were to provide a benchmark against which to judge progress on the next results when the test is given a second time in May 2002. Second-year results would have consequences: Adults in poor performing schools and districts could lose their jobs, and of course students would be promoted or retained. This is high-stakes testing at its highest!

Mississippi has signed a $4.4 million contract with McGraw Hill/CTB, partly on the strength of the company's promise to deliver test results in early July, two months after the first test is to be given. That would allow low performing schools to regroup, to change their practices, to retrain teachers, etc. That's a logical and essential step.

But then McGraw Hill/CTB announced that it would not be able to provide test results until mid-November, long after the window for making changes had closed, and only five months before the second round of testing.[35]

Did the state leadership take this into account and postpone the high-stakes decision, which would seem to be a logical step? In a word, no. Mississippi was determined to hold educators accountable, even if it means not giving them a chance to use what they learned from the first round's results to improve their performance. The superintendents and others whose jobs may be in jeopardy are organized to fight back, but the public was hell-bent for "accountability."[36]

The Mississippi case is noteworthy because it's not just the students who are being singled out. As critics have noted, most high-stakes accountability systems punish students only, although adults are clearly part of any educational failure.

Cynics will not be surprised if the Mississippi protest, which is specifically against penalizing adults and schools, is successful. Is it any wonder that the protest against consequences emanating from Mississippi seems louder and stronger than it has been in states where only students pay the price for falling short?

A second, more personal, example of educational folly is from my daughter Elise's teaching experience in a New York City middle school. As the mandated state exams drew near in the spring of 2000, her principal directed her to spend 15 minutes of each class period practicing answering multiple-choice questions, particularly in math. "But, sir," she said, "I teach Italian and English, not math." That did not matter to her school leader. She did what she was told. It did not work, of course, although her students did learn several (unintended) lessons from the experience.

The *first lesson* was that neither Italian nor English really mattered. The *second lesson*, learned after seeing how their teacher had been treated by her boss, was that Ms. Merrow was not in control of her own life and therefore probably not deserving of their respect.

The *third lesson* was that the state test, and only the state test, mattered. That lesson her students learned well—so well that, immediately after the test, about one-third of them simply stopped attending school even though the school year had five weeks remaining. Although most of these kids did not expect to do well on the state exam, they recognized that the test meant everything and, therefore, that nothing else mattered, including coming to school. Stories like these are everywhere, but is anyone listening?

WHAT'S A PASSING SCORE ANYWAY?

When decisions are made on the basis of a single test, teacher judgment is tossed out the window, along with a student's past performance. Students in Chicago were assigned to summer school the same way that New York did. One Chicago parent told me tearfully about her son having to go to summer school. "He's a B student, but he missed the cutoff score by half a point on the test, because he was so nervous," she said.

Setting cutoff scores ("cut scores" in the language of testing) is an inexact science at best. That number which seems so firm and final may in fact be wholly arbitrary and subjective. Why is a 65 passing, and a 64.5 failing? Who made that decision, and on what basis? To George Madaus of Boston College, these situations are "obscene." "We're just kidding ourselves," he told me. "The technology is nowhere near being so precise that accurate decisions can be made on the basis of one or two points, one way or the other."[37]

This is not just test-bashing. As Bob Sexton of Kentucky's Pritchard Committee (responsible for monitoring that state's reforms) says, "Test bashing with no alternative will likely lead to weaker not stronger public schools and give those who are opposed to improvement (such as ideologues or resistant educators) exactly what they want—the status quo."[38]

Having educational standards—as opposed to not having them—makes sense, of course, and most of the public seem to be enthusiastically behind the drive to create meaningful standards and curriculum that is aligned with those standards. But an unofficial "coalition" of frustrated business leaders, misguided politicians, short-sighted citizens, and ideologues is pushing us headlong toward the dangerous practice of making decisions based on single scores on tests that those taking them have not had the opportunity to prepare for.

In too many schools (like my daughter's), students and their teachers are not given a choice: It's pass the high-stakes achievement test or suffer the consequences. I believe that the trend toward high-stakes testing, and the related mind-numbing drill-drill-drill that often accompanies it, is behind the growth in private schools and home schooling.

Defenders of high-stakes tests argue that they are fair because students have multiple *opportunities* to pass them. Often this is true, but it doesn't change matters one iota. Perhaps Elise's students would have hung around long enough to get their scores, tried again if they'd failed, and then left. Is that progress? What we need are multiple measures, not multiple opportunities.

Gerstner does admit to being worried. "Are we creating good standards? Are we really creating the right standards? Do they reflect what somebody really needs to know?" But he believes that most states are "getting it right."

"Getting it right" would mean creating school curricula that are in synch with the newly established standards. Then teachers and students would work together, teaching and learning what will eventually be tested. As Gerstner put it, "Standards are no good unless you've got a curriculum that will allow children to meet those standards." Gerstner painted a rosy picture of school-wide activity. "It's really exciting. There's more flexibility, more input, and great opportunities for teachers to modify, change and introduce new material."

Clearly Gerstner and I have not been talking to the same teachers. Those I've interviewed about standards almost always complain about the curriculum. "We don't have a curriculum any more," one teacher in Philadelphia said. "We have what they call 'frameworks,' which are loose guidelines." She said that she wanted a map, not guidelines.

The Cleveland *Plain Dealer* reported that skilled veteran teachers in that city are concluding that, in the age of proficiency tests, they do not want to teach fourth grade, the year when Ohio students face the state test for the first time. Teacher Marylou Duff told reporter Scott Stephens, "It's all so anxiety-driven, and it didn't used to be that way." Other teachers say that test preparation is dominating classroom time, stifling creativity and imagination, and taking the joy out of teaching.[39]

"I know a heck of a lot of people who sure as heck don't want to be hired to teach the fourth grade and sure as heck want to get out of it," Ashland University professor Dana Rapp told the *Plain Dealer*. But, he adds, "Most feel they can't speak out for fear of retaliation."

THE BACKLASH

IBM's Lou Gerstner does admit to being worried about a backlash against standards. "My biggest concern is that we say that, because some kids are going to get caught in the middle, we should reduce the standards effort for everybody. We shouldn't do that. Instead, let's go work with those kids and help them succeed."[40]

The backlash grew stronger in the summer of 2000, when the two major teacher unions expressed strong reservations about standards and the increase in high-stakes testing. At the annual meeting of the American Federation of

Teachers, AFT president Sandra Feldman told her members, "No test, no matter how good—and all too many of them are not—can possibly capture the sum of education, let alone be a substitute for real education."

The mood was similar at the National Education Association's annual meeting that same summer, where President Bob Chase told the 10,000 delegates in attendance that the enactment of standards had been "perverse" and "absurd." He called for "a massive infusion of common sense—common sense based on real classroom experience."

Feldman and Chase saved their strongest words for high-stakes testing, the "accountability" phase of the standards movement. Chase said that a "testing mania" was taking over the schools, and he compared it to "some education-eating bacteria."

The American Educational Research Association has condemned the use of student performance on a single test (no matter how many times he or she gets to take that test) to make significant decisions about that student's school career. A coalition of 16 of the leading education groups, including both teacher unions, the National School Boards Association, the Council of the Great City Schools, is preparing an equally critical position paper. No doubt these moves will be seen by some as the knee-jerk reactions of the long-pampered "education establishment." I hope not.

BEHIND THE MUDDLE

The idea that student performance on standardized, norm-referenced, machine-scored tests is the primary indicator of school quality, and the principal measure of accountability, has been with us for about 40 years. It shows few signs of going away. We've grown accustomed to international, national, state, and local comparisons based on test scores, and we rarely look into the "why" of a number. Some reformers talk bravely about using other indicators of quality, such as attendance and dropout rates, college attendance, and teacher turnover, but at the end of the day test scores seem to push everything else aside.

American students are tested far more than their counterparts in other industrialized nations.[41] Our elementary and secondary school students took more than 140 million standardized, machine-scored, multiple-choice tests[42] in 1998, and 42 states mandate standardized testing. Eighth-graders are tested most often, with third- and fourth-graders just behind. Poor children face more of these tests than middle-class kids, in part because federal programs mandate testing. Monty Neill, director of an anti-testing group called FairTest, told me about one city's excesses. "At one time the city of Newark was testing the kids monthly. Every kid was tested virtually once a month."[43]

The cruel irony is that *more* testing actually produces more reliable, and therefore more valuable, information. That's because there can be so much variability in individual test results, meaning your child's score may vary by large margins from one day to the next. Stanford University statistician David Rogosa has calculated that if the average fourth-grader were to take the widely used Stanford Nine (sometimes called the SAT 9), twice, he would have a 43 percent chance of having scores that are more than 10 percentile points apart. That is, he could be in the 75th percentile on one day and in the 60th the next. "If you could give the test a lot of times and take the average score, that would be approaching a gold-standard measurement," said Rogosa, who recently published an accuracy guide to the Stanford Nine. "In testing, because it's so expensive, we only get one shot."[44]

According to the same story, the Orange County School District has informed parents that a student who ranks at the 50th percentile in reading actually could belong somewhere from the 40th to the 60th percentile, for example. Orange County spent at least $28 million last year to run the Stanford Nine test.[45]

Richard Rothstein in the *New York Times* compared high-stakes testing to evaluating a baseball player's season with his performance in a randomly chosen week of the season, instead of his total performance.[46] We don't do that in athletics for the most part,[47] so why are we willing to treat our kids that way?

A single number spit out by a machine is powerful and seductive (even if some small portion of that test involves writing, which is graded by humans, not machines). What's more, that number is easy to understand. The fact that it is inevitably *misleading* does not seem to count for very much.

To make the point, let's create some questions for a multiple-choice history test right now:

1. How many wives did Henry the Eighth of England have?
   A. Three
   B. Four
   C. Five
   D. Six

2. In 1066, William the Conqueror
   A. Invaded England on behalf of France
   B. Invaded France on behalf of England
   C. Invaded England and France on behalf of Germany
   D. None of the above

If you are of a certain age, you probably got both questions right, but I also hope that everyone understands how trivial this information is. Knowing either fact reveals *nothing* of a student's comprehension of history. If the history curriculum has been designed to see that students learn facts like these, this amounts to educational malpractice. Teaching this way certainly will not turn our young people into adults with an appreciation for the past and its complexity. It's more likely to kill their curiosity.

But the fundamental problem is that many schools and school districts use standardized test results more for accountability than understanding or diagnosis. I'm not blaming educators for this situation, because they're only following orders.

H. D. Hoover of the University of Iowa defends testing but agrees we've gone overboard. He places the blame squarely on politicians. "They want quick fixes, and they like tests because they're cheap. They mandate external tests because to the public it looks like they're doing something about education when all they're doing is actually a very inexpensive[48] 'quick fix.'"[49]

Hayes Mizell, the thoughtful director of the Program for Student Achievement at the Edna McConnell Clark Foundation, has a different view. He says that educators have come to expect *others outside the schools* to hold them accountable, instead of taking the initiative and holding *themselves* accountable. "They obsess over their students' performance on the state test, rather than over what their students really know and can do." He argues that educators ought to find and present school-based evidence, rather than obsessing over state tests and allowing those standardized, multiple-choice, machine-scored instruments to be the ultimate yardstick. He concludes, "Perhaps it is unrealistic to think that public education can do better, but I worry that if educators are focused more on their accountability to the state or school district than on their accountability to their students, their internal professionalism will wither."[50]

Testing is not evil, of course. A primary purpose of school is academic[51] learning, and we must know whether, and how much, students are learning. Well-made tests are an excellent way to measure learning and diagnose weaknesses. Excellent teachers create good tests, grade them carefully, and get them back to their students in a matter of days. Parents searching for excellence would be wise to ask the better students to describe the kinds of tests they take and the lag time between taking the test and getting it back.

Machine-scored, multiple-choice tests are rarely the best descriptive tool, and, as noted earlier, they're usually not intended as such. George Madaus of the National Board on Educational Testing and Public Policy at Boston College sums up the situation this way. "There are only three ways to test people. I can have you select an answer from a list—that's a multiple-choice. Second, I can ask you to produce an answer in essay form. Third, I can ask you to do something—fix a carburetor, or do a dive off a diving board, whatever—and I can rate you on it."[52]

In our adult lives, most of us take the third kind of test, that is, we're evaluated on performance. Some schools, notably those inspired by the work of Theodore Sizer's Coalition of Essential Schools, require students to demonstrate their mastery, by standing up in front of a group of adults or their own peers to "exhibit" what they have learned.[53]

That's a far better way of evaluating, describing, and diagnosing, but it's also time-consuming and expensive, which means that it's unlikely to ever be more important than machine-scored, multiple-choice tests.

I am not criticizing *standardized* tests, because standardization is the key to fairness. When a test is standardized, it simply means that everyone has to take it under the same conditions. That is, you and I have to answer the same questions, in the same amount of time. As H. D. Hoover of Iowa notes, "It would not be fair to make comparisons if one student has three days to complete the test, and another has only ten minutes. Or if one student has the test questions read to him, while the other does not."[54] Properly used, standardized tests are a source of useful information that helps teachers do a better job.

Tests, whether standardized or teacher-made, must also be both *valid* and *reliable*. Both adjectives are technical terms in testing. Valid[55] tests measure what they are supposed to. For example, actually performing a series of dives would be a valid test of one's diving ability, while writing an essay about how these dives are performed or taking a multiple-choice test about diving would not. A test is reliable if it can be trusted (relied upon) to produce the same score, or nearly so, when it is given to the same group or individual again.

The argument is against multiple-choice tests and their impact on the curriculum. George Madaus supports testing, but he's well aware of the weaknesses of multiple-choice questions. "The adults who write the questions sometimes lose sight of the way kids will read those questions. There's a standardized test question that shows a cactus in a pot, a rose in a pot, and a cabbage, and the question is which needs the least amount of water. To the item-writer 'cactus' was the right answer, but some kids pick the cabbage. And the reason they gave was that the cabbage had been picked and so it didn't need water anymore. That's a perfectly good answer, but the machine had been set to score it as wrong."[56] Students who get the "right" answer have demonstrated, perhaps, that they think like an adult—or like the test-maker. The kid who thinks differently, or whose frame of reference is different, is marked down, and perhaps eliminated from the competition.

As Sizer notes, the real world is not "a series of set, pre-digested answers" but a set of questions. "Take the issue of cloning, an issue so difficult that very few teachers want to talk about it, or know how to talk about it. Cloning raises all sorts of difficult questions. What are the right answers? That can't be put on a multiple choice test."

"At the worst," Sizer adds, "these standardized tests provoke a kind of drilling mentality. It's a game. And so students learn the game. What they learn is to hire people to teach you how to figure the test out. Not the substance, but the test."

And that teaches cynicism. "The lesson learned is 'to get a high score, this is what you have to do.[57] If you want to get ahead in life, jiggle the system.' And that's anti-intellectual and pernicious."

HIGH-STAKES TESTING

High-stakes tests now begin as early as first and second grades.[58] Where high-stakes tests are being imposed by states, it has thrown many teachers and students into a state of anxiety. This is counter-productive, says E. D. Hirsch Jr. "They start prepping for tests, cramming for tests, and teaching for tests, and none of these things are educationally productive. My hope is that's a transitional phase." Hirsch believes in testing but not in studying for the test. "If the tests are good," he says, "the way to prepare for them is to have a good education. High test scores are a by-product of a good education."

I've seen first hand what an obsession with tests and test scores does to real learning. In the early '90s I spent three years at Woodward High School in Cincinnati, watching (and videotaping) as some teachers there attempted to adopt the philosophy and practices of the reform known as "The Coalition of Essential Schools." The ideas are easy to grasp: (1) "Less is more," meaning that students will dig deeply into a small number of topics instead of taking a broad survey approach; (2) for the most part teachers will not lecture but will guide and encourage learning; (3) teachers will work together across disciplines; and (4) students will be evaluated on the basis of their collected work (portfolios) and public demonstration of their knowledge.

For nearly two years the reform effort proceeded like most reforms, two steps forward and a step-and-a-half back, as students grudgingly learned that they couldn't merely regurgitate whatever the teacher said and expect to pass.

In response to growing public dissatisfaction with school outcomes, the state of Ohio had instituted its own exam, a high-stakes test that students had to pass to graduate. The test did not set the bar very high, and students were given at least eight chances to pass, beginning in tenth grade. Nevertheless, as test day drew near, the reform simply stopped in its tracks. No longer were teachers encouraging students to ask questions, to dig, to work together on projects, and to stand in front of their classes demonstrating their knowledge. Instead, classtime was given over to drill. "How many branches of government are there?" "Which branch institutes new laws?" "What is the role of the Executive Branch?" If I'd listened long enough, I'm sure I would have heard some teacher ask, "How many wives did Henry the Eighth have?"

The kids got the message: all this fancy talk about portfolios and demonstrations is just so much gas. Coalition teachers grew dispirited, and those Woodward high faculty members who preferred the old ways grew stronger in their resolve to keep on doing things in the same old ways.[59]

George Madaus of Boston College makes no bones about his position on high-stakes testing. "The use of test information by itself to make promotion or graduation decisions is technically and ethically wrong. We are using fallible technology, which we simply refuse to acknowledge."[60] Others have pointed out that high-stakes testing is particularly suspect in small schools, where the performance of a handful of students may determine funding levels, state rankings, and promotions of adults. California governor Gray Davis has announced plans to award scholarships to high school students based on Stanford Nine scores, and the state's "Academic Performance Index," a tool used to measure school performance, is based only on those scores, at least for now. And some school districts will require students to score at a certain level on the Stanford Nine in order to graduate, beginning in 2003.[61]

The reliance on high-stakes testing creates incentives to exclude some students who might perform poorly. This occurs when schools "suggest" that certain students, often those with disabilities, "stay home" the day the test is given. High-stakes testing encourages school systems to be more tolerant of dropping out, perhaps even to encourage or "push out" some students. The reporting of test results does not include the number of students who do not take them because they dropped out, often, some said, for fear of failing the standardized test. And, as has been widely reported, high-stakes testing encourages cheating by adults whose reputations and careers are at stake.[62]

Years ago, well before the current hysteria, I remember how my daughter's elementary school (in inner city Washington) reacted to her having missed the city's standardized test. She and I had spent a week on an Indian reservation. During that time she had read about the tribes we were visiting, and we had gone to several stores for the purpose of comparing prices there with prices back home. On the way home, she prepared oral reports, as per our arrangement with her teacher. But when she arrived at school, she was taken to a small room and kept there for three hours . . . so that she could take the test. Why, I wanted to know? The principal was candid about it. "We need her score to get the school's rating up."

That would not happen in an excellent school. Nor do excellent schools spend much class time practicing for tests, although teachers may spend some time teaching "test-taking" skills. At most, a couple of class sessions could be devoted to explaining what the tests are like, so students are not intimidated by the format. E. D. Hirsch is very firm about the practice of abandoning the curriculum in order to "teach the test." "Prepping for the tests in the way that's currently done is just an admission that the children haven't been taught the basics they should have been taught long ago."

I asked Hirsch, a strong supporter of the traditional approach to the teaching of reading (the shorthand term is "phonics"), what teachers in an excellent school would do as the state reading test drew near. "They wouldn't do anything," he said emphatically. "As the reading test approached, they would persist in their rich curriculum, which they were already doing, because that's what encourages children to read."

Hirsch noted that a rich curriculum builds curiosity. "If you're teaching about the Nile and Egypt, a child will go to the library and see a book on Egypt and say, 'I know something about that.' And then take out the book and will start reading. Children who read become better readers, and that's also how they acquire a large vocabulary."[63]

Results from Hirsch's Core Knowledge schools, where 50 percent of the curriculum is prescribed, support his assertions. Reading scores have climbed at most of the 950 Core Knowledge schools in 46 states, proving that "a coherent approach to knowledge, with knowledge building upon knowledge, actually makes children better at skills."[64]

Critics have been attacking machine-scored, multiple-choice tests for years, to little avail. In fact, we're testing our kids more than ever, and for higher stakes, largely because of the movement to create educational standards. As noted earlier, 49 states (all but Iowa) have developed and adopted some version of standards already, or are hard at work at it.

However, it's the American way to rush ahead, without much thought about consequences and implications. But implicit in the idea of establishing standards is a promise: achieve them, and you will be rewarded. As the nation rushes to create standards in education, it's worth asking whether the people running our schools honor academic achievement. In my experience, many of them do not.

Even without clear national or state standards, reliable information about school and student performance is readily available. Whatever their shortcomings, standardized tests do allow performance comparisons. Other data, including teacher attendance, student attendance, and parent involvement, allow officials to make reasoned judgments about school quality. In excellent schools, teacher-made tests and evaluations by teachers are the principal means of diagnosing and assessing students, because in excellent schools, teachers know more about their students than an outside test could reveal. As one distinguished researcher told me in a conversation that we agreed would be "not for attribution," "All that most standardized tests really measure is how someone did on the test."

The most trustworthy test of a *school*, the ultimate measuring stick, is the answer to the question, Are parents trying to transfer their children *into* this school?

I say that parents seem to have a better sense of what's appropriate than do politicians, business leaders, and educators, if one can believe the Gallup poll on education done for Phi Delta Kappan. When Gallup asked about the emphasis on standardized testing, the percentage of respondents who felt that the emphasis was "about right" dropped five points, from 48 percent to 43 percent from 1997, the last time the question was asked. The percentage of respondents feeling there is too much emphasis on testing increased from 20 percent to 30 percent.[65] Parents with children in public schools felt even more strongly, a finding that supports the idea that a backlash may indeed be developing.

Another poll question asked what was the best way to measure student achievement. On this, 68 percent of all respondents and 71 percent of public school parents opted for "classroom work and homework," rather than "test scores." Finally, a majority of the respondents (65 percent) said that the primary purpose of tests ought to be to determine the kind of instruction that students need in the future, over "how much students have learned." Sixty-nine percent of public school parents felt this way.

Other surveys reveal the same pattern of doubt. When the American Association of School Administrators questioned registered voters, it found that nearly two-thirds rejected the idea that one standardized test score was an accurate summary of a student's learning. A survey of parents in Virginia showed that only 17 percent agreed that the state test was "an accurate measure of my child's achievement," while 61 percent disagreed.

Parents surveyed by the independent research organization Public Agenda spoke out strongly in favor of higher standards but expressed grave reservations about high-stakes tests. Almost eight out of ten (78 percent) agreed that "it's wrong to use the result of just one test to decide whether a student gets promoted or graduates."[66]

But parents are not making the decisions, as the story you are about to read makes painfully clear.

IGNORING STANDARDS, IGNORING EXCELLENCE

Simply creating comprehensive standards at the national or state level will not guarantee that those in charge will care about meeting them. The story of how bureaucrats decided to close a school[67] in the nation's capital makes the point. The public schools in Washington, D.C., have a reputation for mediocrity, but the system does have a set of educational standards and a slogan, "Children First."

Because Washington's public schools are losing population, the D.C. board has occasionally had to close schools. How leaders make decisions reveals a great deal about their priorities and their commitment to academic standards. Consider this case: In the spring of 1998, the board recognized that a neighborhood with three elementary schools had only enough students to fill two of them. The solution was obvious: close one school and transfer its students and teachers to the other two. But which school?

Richardson Elementary was one of the three schools. Attendance by both students and teachers was high, parents were active, with some even earning their high school equivalency degrees in the school's family center. First-graders and second-graders were reading, no small accomplishment in a city (and a country) with the stated goal of having all children reading *by the end of third grade*! Richardson students tested at or above national norms in reading, language arts, math, and science in nine of fourteen measurements.

By contrast, students at two neighboring elementary schools were below average in every measure, and both schools were on the school district's official list of underachieving schools (a kind of academic probation). At Richardson, third-graders ranked in the 73rd percentile on the Comprehensive Test of Basic Skills (CTBS); students at the other two schools were in the 37th and 21st percentiles. In sixth-grade science, Richardson students scored in the 46th percentile, while the others were in the 26th and 19th percentiles.

The D.C. board voted, 7-1, to close Richardson! School board chairman Bruce MacLaury explained the board's thinking. "Geography. Look at the map," he said, pointing out that Richardson lies between the other two schools. "We're going to assign half of Richardson's students and teachers to each of the other schools. They won't have to walk as far, and we'll end up with two full schools."

He apparently believed that he'd end up with two winning schools, or so he said when I asked him whether anyone worried about "breaking up Richardson's winning team." Nonsense, he said. "These good teachers will be good at their new schools."

Did the D.C. board know about the three schools' academic results, MacLaury was asked? "I was aware that we had better test scores in Richardson than we had in the two potential receiving schools, and the majority made its vote with that information in front of us," he said.

The vote was lopsided, and even the single board member who voted against the decision did not fight hard to keep an excellent school open. "I can say categorically that no trustee stood up and pounded the table and said, 'By God, we're not going to close this school because it's academically excellent,'" MacLaury stated, as if to suggest that the absence of conflict made the decision admirable.

When the board made its decision, it assumed that everyone would go along. Unlike the D.C. board, however, parents, teachers, and the principal did care about quality; more than half of Richardson's teachers found reasons not to accept transfers to the two remaining schools, the principal moved to Pennsylvania, and nearly one-third of Richardson's 330 students enrolled elsewhere. Two hundred parents began a drive to turn the vacant Richardson into a "charter school." They were successful, and Richardson Elementary became Robert Johnson Technology Charter School, which in 1999 became Arts and Technology Academy, a for-profit, K-12 charter school.

Whether the D.C. board learned anything from this is debatable, but at least one Richardson student learned an unfortunate lesson about the value of hard work and academic achievement. On the day Richardson closed, she said, "They punished us for being a good school. That's not fair."

It's unfair and it's hypocritical—as is much of the enthusiasm for educational standards. Until we're prepared to honor academic achievement and reward quality, whatever educational standards we proclaim will only deepen the disillusionment so many citizens now feel as they experience public education.

I'll give the last word on standards to IBM's Lou Gerstner, because the revolution of choice and standards has begun and doesn't seem to be likely to be stopped. "We cannot turn back. Everyday we turn back, 100,000 kids suffer. Every class that passes and graduates without the skills that they need is an extraordinary waste of the most important asset of this country, our young people. And we're short of skills in the country today. These people are left without the resources, the skills to be effective people.

"What would we turn back to? The system that got us here? Nobody wants that."

Gerstner is correct when he says that every day that we do not do something, kids suffer. But are we doing the right "something" if we teach them skills, or will those particular skills not be needed tomorrow? Doesn't it depend on which skills? And who decides? I hope that Gerstner and other supporters of standards would opt for a challenging, broad-based liberal arts education for all students, but it's equally likely that we will return to the "good old days" of a challenging curriculum for some, and skills training for others.

SOME SENSIBLE APPROACHES

The last word on accountability belongs to others. We need a clearer understanding of accountability, and we need more measures of school outcomes that are *not* simply test-based. For example, apart from test scores, shouldn't we also seek to know how many young people finish school and graduate? How many continue their education after high school? How many students are put into special education classes and never leave them? What the attendance rates are for both teachers and students? The list of possible and knowable outcome measures goes on and on, but instead we seem to be willing to settle for that one simple test score.

Walt Haney of Boston College reminds us that accountability refers to more than consequences, but also to conduct, by which he means what actually happens *inside* schools *between* children and teachers.[68] These transactions are tougher to measure; they don't lend themselves to easy numbers, but surely they count.

Emphasizing testing may eventually drive parents away from public schools, particularly from high-quality schools. Monty Neill of FairTest says he's already hearing that from parents in Massachusetts, where his organization is located. "This is not a major factor yet, but it could become one, as parents who think they have quality schools (and often do) recognize the damage that is done when schooling revolves around the search for higher test scores."[69]

I may get in trouble here, because I want to suggest what constitutes excellence in testing and assessment. First of all, an excellent testing policy is *transparent*,[70] that is, it is open for inspection by all who are interested and it is presented in clear English. It is understandable and defensible. It is connected to the curriculum and the goals of the school.

Excellent teachers have such policies. They explain in advance to students just what is expected, how they will be assessed, and why.

Excellent schools do not—repeat, do not—attempt to evaluate, promote, or hold back students on the basis of a single test, particularly a machine-scored, multiple-choice exam. That is, they reject high-stakes testing insofar as it is possible.

Teacher-made tests, constructed by excellent teachers, remain the best means of assessing student progress and weakness. The best teacher I ever had[71] routinely tested his students by having us write short essays. He called them "2-8-2s" because we were given a topic and two minutes to think about it, then exactly eight minutes to write, followed by two minutes to make changes and corrections. He made the rules very clear: A major error (such as a sentence fragment) meant a grade of "zero." We could expect a 2-8-2 at least two or three times a week, but at the end of the semester he would discard our 10 lowest grades. We would get the papers back the next day! Often we wrote on some aspect of the play or poem we were studying, but he was just as likely to give us an obscure quote[72] and instruct us to reflect on it.

These were excellent tests, aligned with his curriculum and the goals of his class. His policy was transparent. Without using any of today's jargon, he made clear to us what his standards (of content and performance) were, he allowed no lag time between the test and its return, and he used the results to diagnose and correct our weaknesses. That is excellence at work, and it is what all schools should strive for.

Holding schools or (especially) students accountable almost solely on the basis of student scores on machine-scored tests establishes a "whips and chains" system. When we do that, we're using tests as a weapon, nothing more.

QUESTIONS WORTH ASKING

- What is the district's policy on high-stakes testing? If no policy, why not?
- How many machine-scored, multiple-choice tests will my child take each year? Are these "high-stakes" tests, and if so what is at stake?
- Who mandates these tests (state, county, the National Assessment of Educational Progress)?
- Do the results have an impact on specific children, or is it the school that is being measured and rated?
- If individual students are not being evaluated, has any consideration been given to testing only a sample of students? After all, political pollsters question only a small sample of voters and predict results with uncanny accuracy. Why not take the same approach with educational testing that measures a school's or a system's health?
- How much time is devoted to test preparation and practice?
- How long does it take for the teachers to get the results, and are they returned in usable form?
- How are the results used? Does the school share the results with students, parents, and the community?
- Are the data carefully analyzed (disaggregated) to make sure that all students are learning? (A few high scores by outstanding students can give a misleading picture about the overall health of the system.)
- Are students doing better over time? That is, do the data indicate that the longer a student goes to school, the more he or she learns (or the opposite)?
- Do teachers use a variety of assessments, including portfolios and exhibitions?
- How significant are machine-scored tests as a part of a student's semester and final grades?

- How much money is the district spending on outside testing? Does this dollar amount include the cost of the time that teachers and administrators spend on the tests and test preparation?
- What are the district, the school, and individual teachers not doing because of these tests?
- How does any particular test influence the curriculum? Has anyone in authority explored the influences of tests on the curriculum? If not, why not?
- Do teachers rely on their own tests for the most part, or do they use instruments created by others?
- Is the student-teacher ratio sufficiently low to allow teachers time to create their own tests, grade them thoroughly, and discuss the results with students?
- Regarding testing, how much can one child's score vary?
- What are the academic standards for each grade? (Some parents will be astounded that some kids were reading and writing in kindergarten.)

4

TECHNOLOGY AND EXCELLENCE

O ur society uses the computer as its central tool for communicating and creating knowledge. "Bad" and "good enough" public schools do not. In excellent schools students and teachers use technology to create knowledge, and
computers can be almost as important as people.[73]

But excellence is hard to find, and most public schools misuse computers,
and some cannot use them at all. Three significant obstacles stand in the way of
the technological revolution schools desperately need: (1) inappropriate teaching methods, (2) stereotyping of students, and (3) obsolete facilities.

I think the new technology represents the greatest threat to organized education ever. At the same time, it represents and offers almost indescribable potential for learning. By "the new technology" I mean massive and instant availability of information in different forms: text, video, pictures, and sound. It's
available digitally through powerful networks, and powerful computers can interact with the content. As LuYen Chou, an educator and developer of interactive technologies, says, "This change is just as dramatic as the invention of the
printing press, and maybe as important as the invention of written language back
in the Fifth Century BC in Greece."[74]

Why do I say that technology is a threat? Because it creates the opportunity
for cheating—widespread dishonesty in an unparalleled way. Most people know
how easy it is now for a student to download something from somewhere else
and say: "This is my work." In fact, 77 percent of high school students say they
now use the Internet to research school assignments.[75] How is a teacher to recognize an individual's work under current conditions: too many students, a

broad curriculum that must be raced through, and, probably, a standardized, multiple-choice test at the end?[76]

The other major threat comes from the values driving technology: that is, if technology is used to make schooling more efficient and cheaper, then we're going to drive people away from learning. If technology is harnessed to try to produce a single[77] measure of learning that is both reliable and valid, we'll end up with even more machine-scored exams, and we'll narrow the curriculum to teach only that which can easily be tested.

As to technology's potential, let me give you an example. Say I'm a history teacher and my class is studying the Civil War. I could say to my class of 20 students: okay, each one of you is responsible for the life of a single soldier in the Civil War. As a student, you would pick—let's just make a name up—Jonathan Logan from the Hartford 108th regiment. Your job would be to become in effect the world's foremost expert on the life and experiences of Jonathan Logan and the 108th in Hartford. As a teacher, my job would be to keep track of you, to orchestrate the tapestry, to make sure you and every other student in the class sees the whole Civil War. As students dig up things on the Web, it's very difficult to cheat because no one else has ever done a life history of Jonathan Logan—there's no one they can copy, because they're doing original work. They are creating knowledge and may discover stuff that Stephen Ambrose or David McCullough don't know. And they're going to keep digging and pushing, because this kind of learning builds up their creative muscles, so to speak.

The technology will allow students to produce multimedia reports. They might find photos, surviving descendants of that family—who knows what else.[78] Perhaps they will discover that Jonathan's brother paid someone else to serve in his stead, information will make them curious about that practice. So they will dig into that part of our history, learning more and more. They are no longer mere students, but fledgling historians.

LuYen Chou believes that the new technology can turn "students" into "scholars." "Scholars don't start with a story. They start with a piece of evidence, or pieces of evidence, from the past or from science or from natural phenomena. And like detectives, they try to create a story that unites those pieces of evidence or data in a compelling way." That, he points out, is the exact opposite of what schools ask students to do. "Textbooks simply tell a story, and then teachers test kids on whether they've learned the story."

The paradigm of school and its accepted practices have to adapt and change if technology is to reach its potential. While the teacher can be responsible for 120 *students*, she cannot work closely with 120 *scholars*. Put another way, technology has already enriched the curriculum and ended the domination of the textbook, but educators haven't caught on to the change, and their time is running out.

A TALE OF WOE

"We have to teach children about computers. After all, computers are the future." The teacher's voice trembled slightly, and for a minute I was afraid she was going to cry. We were sitting in her fifth-grade classroom in an elementary school in the Queens borough of New York City, finishing an interview for a PBS documentary on technology.[79] Her emotion notwithstanding, her comments were misguided in two important ways.

First, she probably did not have to teach her students about computers; in all likelihood they already knew more about modem technology than she did. That "bank deposit" approach to teaching in which the teacher "deposits" knowledge into students may have been appropriate years ago, but it is certainly obsolete today, particularly where technology is concerned.

She was upset because her class's ambitious project, a multimedia yearbook, was stalled in midstream, because the itinerant instructor who had been visiting her school regularly had been laid off. The teacher felt abandoned. "I know there's lots of information, like the folk songs the children recorded at home, in this computer, but I don't know how to get it. And now I'll never learn."

Sadly, it had not occurred to her to ask her students for help, because that's not the way she had been taught to teach. Teachers won't survive, and school will become increasingly irrelevant, if teachers don't change their style of teaching.

That particular teacher is an older woman, long removed from teacher training, but many of those now studying to be teachers are not learning how to use technology in imaginative ways. Law students learn how to access case law over the Internet, engineering students must master the computer as part of their training, and so on, but teacher training lags behind, because schools don't demand or expect new teachers to teach in *new* ways.

And so parents visiting a school ought to ask teachers about technology, their training, and their plans for using it in the classroom.

That veteran teacher's second statement, "Computers are the future," is also incorrect. Computers are *the present*, and that's a fact. The high-tech, information-age parade is well under way. We're living in the digital age now, can you even remember when you had to wait in line at the bank to get some cash? Everywhere we go today—offices, shops, hotels, the supermarket, the dry cleaner—technology is there.

Schools haven't joined the parade. We're told that although most schools are now "wired for the Internet" only 53 percent of teachers say they have access to computers or the Internet, according to the U.S. National Center for Educational Statistics.[80] For years schools have used computers as a management tool, largely ignoring its remarkable capacity for creating knowledge and stimulating learning, and even today only 10 percent of teachers say they use computers or the Internet to find model lesson plans or to gain access to research. Instead, they use computers "around the edges of the class's main work," to reward students who've worked quickly or to drill those who are falling behind. That's not enough to justify spending $6.9 billion.[81]

EDUCATIONAL TECHNOLOGY'S DEPRESSING HISTORY

Technology has been promising to revolutionize education for years, but none of those promises have been kept. Thomas Edison's film projector was introduced in 1896 with the promise that it would make school so attractive that "a big army with swords and guns couldn't keep boys and girls out of it." That didn't happen.

Then came "radio schools of the air" in the 1930s. Enthusiasts predicted this new technology would soon "be as common in the classroom as the blackboard." Wrong again.

In the 1950s it was television's turn to promise a revolution in the way children learn. But that promise was also broken.

New technology—and new promises—kept coming throughout the 1960s: language labs, teaching machines, 8mm filmstrips, large-screen multimedia presentations, and finally the earliest computers. All those promises notwithstanding, not much has changed. Schools still look pretty much the same.

Remember Vice President Gore's clarion call: "We now have a new generation of educational hardware and software that can really make a revolutionary difference in the classroom, and it's time to use it." The technology he was talking about is built around the modern, high-speed computer, and includes modems, CD-ROMs, and the Internet. This technology is fundamentally different from yesterday's slide projector or filmstrip. Those were one-dimensional tools, the schoolhouse equivalent of a hammer.

Earlier educational technologies failed because they were designed to change schools, and schools are among our most change-resistant organizations. Computers and the rest of today's high-speed technology, however, were not designed for schools; they've come along and changed everything else—and so schools don't have much choice in the matter, if they are going to be significant in our lives.

Think of it this way: A hammer can increase your ability to drive nails, but that's it. It's just a tool for your hand. It cannot tell you where to drive in the nails, or which size nails to use, or whether they're going in straight. A hammer can't design a house, or work out a table of mortgage payments you'll have to make to pay for the house. The computer, a tool for your mind, can do all these things, and more.

Of course the computer can be used as a simple tool: to practice math skills, or for word processing. But students using computers can also design cities, compose their own music, or browse through a library in Japan or London. Students not only can learn more, but, using the computer, they also can create their own knowledge (like my imaginary history student learning all about Jonathan Logan). Quite naturally, they take ownership of what they create and become more interested, more motivated learners.

Most students, unfortunately, don't get to do all those exciting things in school, but that's not because schools don't have computers—they have more than four million of them. Public schools have been buying computers for a dozen years or more, using them to drill students and to keep track of grades and attendance. Many of the computers in schools are outdated, incapable of running today's complex computer programs. And even the schools that are now buying more powerful machines don't allow their students to take full advantage of the technology, because the kids know more about it than the adults in the building do. As Linda Roberts, who served as technology adviser to U.S. secretary of education Richard W. Riley, noted: "Kids come to school today very much in tune with computers, video, the electronic games. They know that world."[82]

Or as technology guru Fred D'Ignazio told me, "Today's kids are swimming in a world of technology. They are like fish in the water that is the modern wired world—until they get to school, where they're cast on the desert."

Most teachers—like that fifth-grade teacher in Queens—do not know the world of computers, because from the very beginning schools kept computers in the administrators' offices and in special "laboratories." That unfortunate policy (which seems to be changing in many school districts) kept many teachers away from technology and has kept them technologically illiterate. In 1999 the Department of Education reported that only 10 percent of teachers with access to computers feel "very well prepared" to use computers in their teaching. Another 23 percent say they feel "well prepared." That means that at least two-thirds of teachers need help, fast.

Louis V. Gerstner Jr., the chairman and CEO of IBM, is a man with a stake in computer use in schools. IBM has done research showing that the two groups of people who adapt most easily to technology and the Internet are those under 30 and over 60. "Unfortunately," Gerstner notes, "most teachers are in between, so we've got to help teachers. We owe them an effort to upgrade their skills, to get them comfortable with integrating the technology into what they do in the classroom."

This will not be easy, a computer instructor told me. "In my school, teachers' fears of, and unwillingness to experiment with, technology were the biggest roadblocks. Most of the teachers, who were between 30 and 45, simply refused to come to clinics or let me into their classes. They had learned methods of teaching over the years and weren't interested in changing."

Leadership was also a problem. "The principal steadfastly refused to sit with a computer. He wanted us to have the latest equipment and a technology center, but he wouldn't set an example or push his teachers. So nothing happened."[83]

I've sat in on computer training workshops for teachers and watched them discover the power of technology, with youthful exuberance and palpable joy. Unfortunately, the leader of the workshop told me, they tend to go back to their classrooms and try to lecture kids on what they've learned, instead of allowing kids the same joys of discovery.

Retraining will be a major challenge, it is clear. It's not obvious that the current "professional development" system is up to the task. If many teachers are afraid or if they believe that their current teaching is "good enough," our students are in trouble.

We know that most teachers who have computers aren't using them well. And many teachers don't know as much about computers as their students do. Teaching in a wired classroom shouldn't look exactly like teaching 75 years ago.

Are school administrators up to the challenge? A veteran journalist told me that many of the school districts she reports on do not fill the position of technology director with someone who knows technology; instead, they promote school administrators into those positions.

Add that to your list of questions to ask when checking out schools: What is the background of the system's technology director? Don't be satisfied by assertions about buying the latest equipment, because it's not so much a question of *what* schools are buying, but *how they're using* what they're buying.

While simply adding computers to classrooms may not help students learn more, used imaginatively they are a powerful tool. Anyone who does not know how to use a computer in this world will be at a competitive disadvantage, with a new kind of illiteracy. Parents know this and want their children to have access to computers in schools, and many teachers are convinced that computers can help students learn better.

However, you can't just plop computers into the classroom, wire them to the Internet, and then continue to teach in the same way. Used well, computers have the potential to allow a teacher to tailor instruction to the abilities of each student in the class, to encourage students to explore and connect to people all over, and to connect any student anywhere with up-to-date databases of information.

Technology used properly means teachers will work differently and work harder, but in a much more satisfying way with fewer students. When one of my daughters was teaching in a middle school in Harlem, she was seeing almost 150 kids a day. There was no time to use technology—even if they had it (and they didn't because it's a poor school). Under those circumstances, teachers can't use computers unless they're doing "drill and kill."

And if schools continue to be overcrowded and understaffed, they are just inviting kids to cheat. When a teacher with 150 students in Portland, Maine, assigns a paper and asks them to use the Internet for research, she has no way of knowing if kids do the work themselves or if they turn in papers that they downloaded from someone in Portland, Oregon. (And, if the law of averages holds, 77 percent of her students will turn to the Internet for assistance.) She doesn't have time to know how each kid works or to see the paper develop.

HOW TEACHERS LEARN ABOUT COMPUTERS

Unfortunately, most schools provide little in the way of help for teachers who are unfamiliar with computers. Fewer than half report having a basic computer class available for teachers. This seems to me to be irresponsible behavior on the part of school boards. Most school systems require continuing education (professional development) for teachers who want to climb the salary scale, but too often boards have negotiated contracts that fail to specify what teachers must study, settling instead for vague words about "educational relevance." Here's an opportunity for boards to set genuine standards and help teachers overcome whatever doubts and fears they may have about technology.

However, formal training isn't essential if teachers see themselves as *learners*. Jill Livoti had almost no exposure to computers when she was hired to teach at a middle school in Columbia, S.C. Her wise and excellent principal told her not to be afraid to say, "I need help, I don't know." He said, "Relax and let the kids show you."

Jill is proud to relate what then happened. "When we started on our first computer project, I announced to the children, 'I'm not all that familiar with this, so if you have some ideas please come to me and we will work something out.'"

Her students reacted just as the principal predicted. "They love the fact that I don't know too much about it, because they love to teach me, and it's fun for me because they really are good teachers. Some kids aren't as strong on the computer as others, and it helps when they see that I'm learning too. It's not as intimidating for them."

Ms. Livoti was comfortable with the idea of teacher-as-learner. "I think it's important for children to know that a teacher doesn't know everything," she says. "With technology changing and knowledge expanding, teachers have to understand that there is absolutely nothing wrong with not knowing. What's sinful is not seeking to know, or not caring."

Other capable teachers deliver the same message. Yvonne Andres, a teacher in San Diego, expresses it this way: "We're all in this together, and if we don't start learning side by side, it's going to pass us by. I think it's a very sharing, symbiotic relationship."

And Carla Shutte, an elementary schoolteacher in Arlington, Va., adds: "I don't have to be the one who is the giver of all knowledge, the adult who knows it all. I realize that technology and knowledge are changing daily, and so we're learning side by side."

Giving up control may be the first step. As Ms. Andres says: "What I do, really, is model for them. So when we have a new piece of hardware or software, we attack it together. And they watch me learning. And they learn problem-solving skills and trouble-shooting skills. And sometimes they learn it first, and they teach me. And that's great."

These teachers are modeling excellence. They are unafraid of acknowle͏   g their knowledge gaps, willing to ask for help, and willing to learn. Their behavior undoubtedly contributes to a climate of "Intellectual Safety."

What's more, young people enjoy being challenged, particularly when the work is meaningful. One middle school student compared two of his classes: "It's sort of like going from the future to the Stone Age. We have all these computers in this class, and it's really fun, because you get to explore on the computers and you know what you're doing half the time, the other half you're just exploring. But when the bell rings, we're back in the Stone Age. You just sit there and work in the book for 30 or 40 minutes, and you're just so bored of it that you want to scream and leave."

MAKING LEARNING REAL

Technology can and should make learning exciting. It can break down the walls of the classroom and turn students into travel agents, entrepreneurs, and medical technicians. I choose to mention those three occupations deliberately, because they're featured on the software that I've helped develop with teachers from the Baltimore City Schools and Johns Hopkins University. The software asks the high school student to accept a scenario: he's been hired by a travel agent, she has an opportunity to open a store in the new mall, or he has a new job as a medical information officer for an HMO.

In the role of medical information officers, for example, students (actually) go out into the community and make presentations designed to educate older people about some common medical or health problem, such as breast cancer or sickle cell anemia. They are presumably making the presentation for the fictional Parker HMO, which wants it done for two reasons. First, management thinks that a healthier community—one in which few people smoke—is in the HMO's interest. More immediately, the doctors' time is too expensive to do this for each patient and, besides, the doctors are not very good at explaining.

As biology students, the kids work in teams and dig deeply into the workings of the human body. Because each team has to make an actual presentation to a community group, they must learn all they can about cancer, and in so doing they will cover many of the topics in Maryland's Core Learning Goals for biology. The components of a cell, the process of cell division, and the DNA code figure into the process of lung cancer. But as Arnold Packer (my colleague on the project) has noted, "Instead of seeing these things as external requirements needed to pass a forthcoming exam (and mostly forgotten three weeks later), students are intrinsically motivated because they need this information to make their presentations."[84]

That's not all they're learning. The software has material about careers in the health field. They learn how to make effective presentations[85] to a diverse audience, how to field and answer questions, and how to use technology effectively (for example, using Power Point slides for their presentations).

It's active learning, project-based over six weeks with real and measurable goals. Teachers assess continually, and the software itself allows teams to measure their own progress. In that sense, it's a game with benchmarks that must be met before students can progress to the next level. In this case, however, the levels are measures of knowledge, instead of dragons or monsters that must be blasted into smithereens.

As Arnold Packer points out, "These kids are learning about real careers that generally pay more than the nation's median wage." Packer, who helped write what are called the SCANS[86] skills when he was at the Labor Department, feels strongly that schooling must have real connections to the world outside of the school building. "Students need to master the skills they'll need when they're working: they need to be able to communicate effectively, find and assimilate new information, communicate it effectively, and work in teams." The software helps develop those skills.

It seems to be working. An independent study[87] of the project, running in three Baltimore high schools, revealed that students using the program outscored their peers on state tests in math and English by as much as 40 percentage points. Our students were three times more likely to pass English III, 75 percent more likely to pass Algebra II, more likely to come to school, and less likely to drop out. As one teacher told me, "These kids are here early, and they stay late. I can't get them to go home."

Hundreds of similar projects are up and running, and new frontiers are being explored. The growth of the Internet as a tool may make software-based curriculum obsolete in a matter of years or even months, but that's no excuse for waiting around and using the same old curriculum. If schools don't embrace technology, they will lose their students, beginning with the brightest.[88]

Using technology in these ways makes school more enjoyable (for teachers and students) than the traditional "teach it and test it" approach taken in many classrooms. As Arnold Packer notes, "Solving realistic problems motivates students. They have their own answer to the often-asked question, 'Why do I have to learn this?'"[89]

STEREOTYPING AND TECHNOLOGY

A second obstacle that must be overcome before schools can enter the modern age of technology is the persistent stereotyping of children that has led to very different uses of technology for poor and well-to-do children.

Basically, schools with lots of poor children are likely to use technology to control students. "Free or reduced-price lunch" is a common proxy for poverty, and in schools with 71 percent or more students qualifying for free or reduced-price lunch, drill is the favored application (35 percent). However, in schools with less than 11 percent on free or reduced-price lunch, "research using the Internet" is the most common use of computers (39 percent).[90]

Many schools in poor neighborhoods have computer laboratories equipped with drill-and-practice tutorial programs called integrated-learning systems. Students sit in front of these computers and follow the programmed routine, typing in answers to problems like "12 + 4 – 2 = ?"

Critics call this the "drill and kill" approach, and it would be hard to find a student who would disagree.

But go to many suburban schools and you will see students controlling the technology. They will be up on the Internet, or they'll be creating databases and manipulating spreadsheets and computer aided design (CAD) programs—all of which allow them to create. They are able to express themselves and their thoughts and share that information with one another.

On the books, the per-pupil spending for technology may be equal, but the programs and their impact couldn't be more different. In other words, middle-class students, who probably have access to technology at home, are given the opportunity to use technology in ways that will make them controllers of their lives. Poor children, probably without computers at home, are being denied that power in the one place that could provide it, school. Practices like these serve to divide our society. They also contradict our American myth of public education as the great equalizer, the road to advancement.

An obstacle to using technology in optimum ways is the existing education system's basic structure. If the curriculum is a mile wide and a foot deep and you want your students to burrow into one piece of it, it's hard for you to make that happen, because most curricula are essentially surveys. Teachers are required to cover so many years, or so many battles, or so many literary genres, and so on. But, at least for older students, "less is more," because mastery of one area kindles the desire to know more. On the other hand, racing through history or literature (or almost any subject) at a breakneck pace leaves no time for questions and smothers curiosity.

"Deeper" is also more interesting, especially if there's a skilled teacher helping kids make choices. What's more, it is not written in stone that the school year has to be divided into semesters—which are a bureaucratic artifact for the convenience of adults. A school could, for example, have a three-week-long class in some specific issue that students would dig into intensely.[91] Again, the technology would offer great opportunities for specialized study. The technology is more sensitive to the way we learn than the structure of school is. School, like any bureaucratic organization, is set up for mass convenience, and technology doesn't respect that. Technology doesn't know if I'm white or black, young or old, disabled or able-bodied, so why should it be sensitive to semesters, or semester breaks?

WHO'S IN CHARGE?

It's not hard to define excellence as far as technology is concerned. Excellent programs have up-to-date technology—not necessarily the newest and most powerful computers, but machines that are fast enough and strong enough to run complex programs. Most important, however, is the philosophy. Is technology done to students, or do students control and direct the machines?

Some schools fall into the trap of trying to keep up with ever-changing technology, which can lead to diverting valuable resources away from books, teachers, and facilities. LuYen Chou, who develops curriculum for computers, warns against a computer "arms race." "To be excellent a school has to know how to make the best use of the technology it has. Some schools haven't mastered using the blackboard and the textbook, let alone a high-speed computer with a T1 connection to the Internet. And I've seen schools that have unbelievable access to technology that are really doing nothing more than what they could do with paper and pencil. And that's not excellence either."[92]

On the other hand, it's important to be current. "I can't conceive of using technology that's more than five years old," Chou told me. "Not that it wouldn't serve you well, but it simply wouldn't work with most of what's available today." Everyone, he says, has to learn to be nimble.

In Chou's view, excellence comes in figuring out how to make use of the resources that are available to instill that sense of passion in kids, getting them to be active learners, and getting them to strive to create their own knowledge of the world.

IBM's Gerstner agrees that it's how the technology is used that matters. "We don't want to teach students how to use computers in schools. I mean, they'll probably know it before they get there from their experience in pre-school," he say with a laugh. "What we really want to do is use the computer as a tool to learn math, science, history, and all the other things. It is not an end in itself."

In *excellent* programs, students are producers of knowledge. They use the Internet to explore, to dig deeply, and to become experts. It's an old argument, between breadth and depth, and in Chou's view, depth wins. "It's important, and it's more interesting, to dig ever deeper and deeper into a subject than it is to learn more correct facts about a lot of subjects." In excellent programs, technology is a tool that students use to create new tools. Students are programming, and they are involved in planning how the school will use technology in the future. They may be training teachers, too.

In *bad* programs, drill and kill is the order of the day. Programs that are merely "good enough" probably let some students soar, while restricting access severely.

To Chou and others, technology can be a unifying device to cut across disciplinary boundaries. After all, curricular boundaries (English, social studies, history, and so on) are artificial constructs, but they are also powerful determinants of what happens in schools; that is, math teachers don't have to coordinate their curriculum with other departments. It's much easier to teach according to these disciplines, because all of the commercial teaching materials that schools buy and that teachers use adhere to those disciplines.

Once school is out, however, the arbitrary divisions disappear. As Chou notes, "If you are an architect designing a house, you have to have a mastery of skills that cut across a wide swath of traditional disciplines. Every day you're confronted with situations that require you to integrate your knowledge across a wide range of subjects."

Excellent schools recognize technology's power to cut across disciplinary boundaries, while "good enough" schools often use those boundaries as a crutch for not teaching students to understand that the world does not treat learning as a set of distinct operations that break down into fields. Excellent schools, says Chou, create curriculum that forces students and teachers to think across those lines.

I worry, however, that the movement to save money on education and the obsession with standards will drive kids underground. In "good enough" schools students who want to learn may have to be subversive and do it on their own.

Outsiders often assume that lack of money is a major obstacle to a technological revolution in schools, but that is not correct. In 1999 K-12 schools spent an estimated $6.9 billion on desktop computers, servers, routers, wiring, Internet access, software, and everything else involved in making schools up-to-date technologically. This represents a dramatic increase over the estimated $2.4 billion that schools spent in 1997. As Glenn Kleiman notes, "Education funds are enhancing the bottom lines of Intel, Microsoft, Apple, Cisco, IBM, and other high-tech companies."[93] However, comprehensive planning must not be our educators' strong suit, because all too often someone discovers that the expensive new equipment can't be run without blowing a fuse or burning down the building.

Despite all the hoopla about wiring[94] all of our schools for the Internet, school buildings themselves are a major obstacle. Around 31 percent of our public schools were built before World War II. Another 43 percent went up almost overnight during the baby boom of the '50s and '60s. That is, about half of our public schools are more than 50 years old. These are yesterday's buildings, but they're trying to run today's technology. James Mecklenburger, the president of the Global Village Schools Institute, noted: "You're dealing with buildings that were built in the 1870s and the 1910s and the 1940s when the electrical connections that you needed were likely to be one or two plugs for a classroom, if that. There was no thought of telephone systems or other kinds of electronic connections."

When the two worlds meet, bad things can happen. Clark High School in New Orleans caught fire and burned when the demand for power to run the new computers caused a short circuit. In New Orleans, the average public school is 55 years old, and the basic wiring inside can't satisfy technology's thirst for electricity. In fact, as late as 1997 only 10 of that city's 125 public schools were properly wired for, and equipped with, today's technology.

Kenneth DuCote, the director of facilities for the schools in New Orleans, says that students were being shortchanged. "We have gone in the last 200 years through a tremendous shift in society. We were an agricultural society where the main power base was in land. Then we went to an industrial society where the main power base was in capital and money. Now we're in the information age where knowledge and access to technology determine power, and our schools don't have the electrical power to give our kids the power they'll need to succeed."

DuCote took me to schools with fully equipped computer labs that have remained locked and unused for two years because the wiring was inadequate. Those years represent lost opportunities for young people.[95]

Run-down schools are not hard to run across. A study conducted for the National Education Association in 1999 estimated that it would cost $268 billion to modernize our public schools. The Clinton administration in its final budget proposed to spend $1.3 billion for renovation and modernization of up to 25,000 schools, and an additional $24.8 billion in tax credit bonds to build and modernize up to 6,000 schools.

In the past, schools have resisted technology successfully, but that's no longer possible because most of our children are swimming in the sea of technology that exists outside of school. If schools resist technology or if they refuse to take advantage of its capacities, young people will simply turn off. That means more discipline problems, a higher dropout rate, and greater waste of human potential. In other words, schools must adapt, or they will die a lingering death.

"ADAPT OR DIE"

"Adapt or die" may seem harsh, but it's not the grimmest prospect. Today's technology is truly democratic: The computer doesn't know whether the person sitting at the keyboard is rich or poor, male or female, black, brown, or white— only how competent that individual is. If our schools don't give all young people a fair chance to become competent, then the gulf between the "haves" and the "have nots" will grow wider. That prospect should frighten us all and persuade us to help teachers and schools transform themselves.

Computers represent the future in education, but in most schools television is the present, generally in the form of videotapes played on a VCR. In fact, a sure sign of a bad school is a lot of TV-watching, and most schools have never figured out how to harness the power of television to the creative energies of students.

Television is a fact of children's lives. Young people between the ages of 6 and 11 watch, on the average, between 21 and 28 hours of television a week. Put another way, children are spending the equivalent of two months of the year watching television.

These dry statistics come to life in conversations with young people everywhere. One afternoon in a high school in Peoria, Illinois, I was allowed to take over a sophomore English class. "Let's talk about TV," I suggested. Most of the students told me that TV was "boring and repetitive," but what I remember most was not the shows they said they watched or the number of hours; it was the number of TV sets. Three-quarters of these young people had their own TV sets; every household had at least two, and a few had as many as five. The youngsters reported that at least one set was on "all the time."

I asked whether they watched TV with their parents, and, if so, who picked the program? One young girl's answer: "Nobody really chooses. We just watch whatever's on. Mom or Dad may be in the same room with us, watching the same shows, but they're not really with us, if you know what I mean." That conjures up images of television as a soporific, enervating experience that leaves viewers tired, frustrated, and angry—without knowing why.

However, attacks on television watching are all too common and all too easy. Politicians, educators, and religious leaders call on students to "turn off that TV" and "buckle down and study." These lines always draw applause, but students, more than any other group in our society, have already turned their backs.

Older adolescents watch fewer hours of TV than any other group, but they are not using their "extra" time for homework. They have part-time jobs in fast-food restaurants, gas stations, supermarkets—any place they can find work.

Why young people work is, on one level, pretty easy to understand: they want money. One cynic puts it this way: they need the money to pay for a car, and they need a car to get to work. But money is only part of the appeal of having a job.

Working for pay is an important step toward adulthood. Working means contact with a bigger, ever-changing world, and the workplace offers real challenges—or so it seems to young people accustomed to the insular routines of schooling. Most schools segregate students by age (and sometimes by sex or by academic performance). Schools "pay" in letter grades and are set up for mass production, not for individual attention. When technology is used imaginatively, students experience the thrill of discovery and the joy that comes with accomplishment—the kind of "pay" adults hope to get in their work. And the students probably receive high grades as a by-product, a bonus.

TELEVISION IN SCHOOL

For many youngsters, school is repetitive and unchallenging, which, of course, is what they also say about television.

Not everyone attacks television, however. We've had our share of constructive criticism as well. In the past four decades researchers have produced more than 3,500 reports and commentaries about television and children, often calling for more children's programming, for more public access channels, or for "media literacy" training in schools. My experience as a journalist and a parent tells me that a more helpful step would be to let children be *around, in, and on* television.

I am arguing for rethinking how we use TV in the schools. Children want desperately to "be on TV," as any reporter who has taken a camera crew into a school can attest. When I was a radio reporter covering schooling, children would flock around me, clamoring for attention and demanding to know "what channel" they would be on, even though I was carrying only a small cassette recorder. Post-game interviews with athletes are invariably conducted over, around, and through a crowd, aping, waving, or calling out "Hi, Mom!"[96]

What are children telling us when they mob camera operators, making faces and crying out, "Can I be on TV?" I don't think they're demanding the 15 minutes of celebrity that Andy Warhol predicted we'd all get. I think that their mob-like behavior is, paradoxically, a search for individuality. We seem to have become polar opposites of the aborigines who fear that cameras will steal their essential beings. To children especially, "being on TV" proves that they exist. Schools, on the other hand, often send students the message that they're empty vessels into which teachers will pour knowledge. At best these young people see themselves as minor cogs in the vast machine of schooling. They reject that message either by quitting school or by tolerating it, putting in the "seat time" necessary to graduate.

But saying that children are "seeking individuality" when they jump up and down in front of the camera doesn't help the filmmaker, who, after all, only wants them to stop doing it. At first we tried letting them get it out of their systems by wasting 20 minutes or so of videotape, which is fairly cheap. But that didn't work. Our entire tape supply would have been exhausted long before the children were.

What *does* work is making young people part of the production process itself, sitting down with them and explaining everything, answering every question.

That gives them power (knowledge is power, remember) and a stake in the outcome. Understanding how television is made—actually helping to make it—provides young people with an even greater sense of self.

Because children learn quickly what they want to understand, only rarely do we have to explain something more than once. That's because television is so much a part of their lives, their "friend and neighbor." But it's more than that: television is their common language and the collector of their experiences.

Even children who rarely watch TV know what's on and what's happening to which characters on which series. My own children showed me that. We restricted their TV watching to a couple of hours a week at most, with special emphasis on *Sesame Street* and *Mister Rogers' Neighborhood* when they were small. Despite this restriction, they always seemed to know everything about *Charlie's Angels* or *M*A*S*H* or *Dallas*.

More proof of TV's power with children can be gained by watching them watch the tube. My children always liked commercials best of all. At first the razzle-dazzle (what we call "production values") drew them in. Later, the seductive power of the ads did battle with their desire to understand the how and why of the message construction. We often talked about the ads—not about whether such-and-such a product really had more cleansing power but about whom the ads were aimed at.

I think there's a message for the schools in all of this, a message that excellent schools already understand. Most schools generally use television as a medium of instruction. Draw the shades, lower the lights, and watch videotapes in science or social studies class. Teachers attuned to "media literacy" often acquire scripts of network series and build lessons around them, as a way of teaching writing and other skills. But these uses of TV do not tap children's creative energy and desire to learn in the way that actually *making* television can.

High schools (and a few middle schools) in prosperous districts might have their own production facilities, perhaps even closed-circuit channels; a few cable systems broadcast programs produced entirely by children, for children. Today, however, the advent of low-cost digital cameras and computer-based editing systems means that most schools can afford one or more complete systems.

Excellent schools have this equipment *and* use it creatively. I've been in elementary schools that produce their own news programs, complete with fake commercials. These programs were shown throughout the school, and copies of the master tape were distributed to local TV stations. Today, however, the gates are down, and school productions do not have to rely on traditional broadcasting. The Web is a more convenient outlet, and student programs could be Webcast to (potentially larger) audiences everywhere in the world.

The possibilities are endless. For example, every junior high school social studies class could make a news program about a particular historical period, and a panel of judges could choose the best one. Or a chemistry experiment could be videotaped and tightly edited to teach both the new material and lab technique. Any competent music, art, physical education, or dramatic arts teacher can think of dozens of creative ways to have students use the equipment.

Let me give an example from my own high school teaching in the 1960s. I decided to try to bring Shakespeare's *Macbeth* to life by putting Macbeth and his wife on trial for first-degree murder. Some students took roles of major characters in the play, which required them to know the play well enough to testify accurately. Other students served as attorneys, and the principal was the judge. But this was a large class, and there weren't enough major parts to go around, which meant that some students had the less interesting job of juror.

Introduce a video system, however, and a whole new dimension emerges. Student "newscasters" could deliver regular reports on the trial (careful writing required here); a panel show could provide a forum for interviewing the defendants (more careful study of the play required); technicians would be needed to tape and edit the proceedings (I'd also have them prepare a written plan and a subsequent report); and so on. Some curious students would probably end up analyzing the plot, perhaps comparing it to one of the daytime soaps. Everyone would learn something about the cooperative nature of television production— and a great deal about *Macbeth* and Shakespearean tragedy—as well.

Before we left *Macbeth*, we'd probably try our hands at acting and videotaping some scenes and speeches. I'd have the students watching different actors in TV dramas and ask them to figure out where the camera was, and why. They'd be thinking, and writing, and learning.

In the early 1980s, the Markle Foundation recommended five sensible objectives for realizing the educational potential of television:

Availability. Programs directed at children should be at the hours when children watch television.

Diversity. The range of content, style, and subject matter should be as broad as a child's curiosity and needs.

Selectivity. Programs should use television for purposes it meets better or more efficiently than other forces influencing children.

Focus. Different programs should be made for children of different ages.

Innovation. Programs should try concepts and tasks not yet extensively explored.

I strongly suggest a sixth objective: **access.** Children should be given access to information about how television is made and to the TV-making equipment itself. Access invites inquiry and encourages curiosity and creativity. So as not to scare anyone, I have labeled what I'm talking about "access," but in fact I mean power—giving young people more control over their own learning.

Actually, all I'm doing is recognizing in what ways television is important, even central, to the lives of young people. It's time to recognize that television, the most powerful medium of mass communication ever invented, is also a wonderfully effective way to acknowledge individuality and foster cooperation.

Hands-on involvement with television makes schools places young people want to attend, and interested students make school a more satisfying place for everyone else. Hands-on experience with television makes children better educated, better informed consumers of television, which will lead them to demand better television—and to avoid inferior programming. Some educators call this "media literacy," an insider's term for a level of understanding that is essential today.

To those who worry that TV and other media will replace the textbook, I think there is a real possibility that the text*book* may go out of fashion, but *text* itself will not disappear. Words will always matter. In my experience, students who become avidly media literate remain curious about the world around them. They read to learn.

The new technologies have the potential to drive a stake through the heart of the high-stakes, standardized, machine-scored multiple-choice test, which (if it happens) would put the standards movement back on track. I say this even though the current momentum is very much in the direction of more testing. Those tests come from a tradition, a time when it was conceivable that an educated person could know everything there was to know about a subject. Those days are over, with knowledge doubling exponentially. Today employers in high-tech industries are looking for people with an appetite for learning and an inner core sensibility that allows them to find and process facts faster in sophisticated, more efficient ways. Not someone who knows a lot of facts, but individuals who know how to dig ever deeper and deeper and turn facts into a coherent story. Politicians are trying to standardize schooling and the measurement of its output, but technology is making learning more focused on process and depth. We need new measures of capability and achievement, because, with technology, less is so much more.

QUESTIONS TO ASK ABOUT TECHNOLOGY

- Does the school have a philosophy about technology? What is it? Who developed it?
- Is the computer seen as a tool for specific tasks, or as a vehicle for research and exploration?
- Does the school use Macintoshs or PCs? (Actually, it doesn't really matter; what's important is how computers are used.)
- Does the school use the same computer that my child will be using in college or on his first job? (Again it doesn't make any difference, because the technology is changing so fast.)
- Does the school have the same equipment that you find in the self-service department at Kinko's? This is a good barometer of what's current.
- Are students programming? In how many languages?
- Does the school have a full-time person maintaining technology, or is it left up to teachers?
- Does the school have a full-time person responsible for maintaining computers, or is it left up to the teachers? What is the technology director's own philosophy? Is he or she at the school because of a strong commitment to education? (This may be the only good reason someone would work in education when industry is paying so much more.)
- Ask to see some projects that students have finished (and if they all look pretty much the same, ask "Why?").
- What is the ratio of students to computers?
- If there's a computer lab, how much access do students have?
- Does the school filter Internet content? Why or why not? (One sensible policy is to place computers with Internet access and without filters in public places.)
- Don't forget to ask about bandwidth, the school's capability for receiving and sending information. It doesn't matter if the equipment is totally up to date if bandwidth is limited; that's like driving a Lexus on a one-lane dirt road.

- What do students say about technology and its use? Do they enjoy using computers? Do they go to the lab when they have free time?
- How "computer literate" are teachers? Does the school insist on literacy? Does it provide training for teachers? What kind?
- Does the school provide e-mail or file server accounts? Do students have access to these accounts from home?
- Do all students have home computers? Does the school have a program to ensure that all students have access at home?

5

THE "RUSHED, CRUNCHED, AND ISOLATED" WORLD OF TEACHERS

Not long ago I heard a teacher describe his world as "rushed, crunched, and isolated." I'm tempted to add two other adjectives, "distrusted" and "undervalued." It's disgraceful that this string of adjectives is not positive, because teachers have a profound, long-lasting, and (most often) positive impact on the lives of our children. Leadership in the principal's office may provide the driving energy behind an excellent school, but teachers are its heart and soul. Most teachers work hard, most entered the profession for the right reasons, but their overall level of performance leaves something to be desired. I believe the fault lies not so much with individuals but with working conditions, training, and expectations.

Teachers work under difficult conditions, public perceptions to the contrary notwithstanding. While outsiders look at the hours (9–3) and the extended summer vacation,[97] few of us realize how stressful it is to live with a roomful of young children or adolescents. Parents feel that one, two, or three kids is a lot to handle, but teachers must maintain control and manage the learning of as many as 40 students in a small room. Secondary schoolteachers are often expected to teach (and get to know?) 125 students, sometimes more.[98]

In this chapter I will attempt to answer several questions: Does excellent teaching look and sound different from "good enough" teaching? Are there sure-fire indicators of quality teaching? What are the signs of bad teaching? Of teacher burnout? Unfortunately, exploring these important questions often unearths greater complexities.

You cannot identify an excellent teacher by looking into the classroom, because the classrooms of first-rate teachers vary widely in appearance, sound, and teaching styles. Lisa Delpit, who works with teachers at Georgia State University, says, "You may see a teacher working on projects all over the room, things hanging from clotheslines, and the room looks like it's a mess. Or you may see a teacher in front of the classroom, working with the whole class. Or you may see a classroom in which the teacher is working with small groups, and you can't even tell who the teacher is, because she's so low key in the classroom. And all three could be absolutely excellent."

Excellence takes many forms, and a particular teacher may be excellent for some kids and disastrous for others. There are, however, constants. Excellent teachers know their subject matter and they know how young minds work. Excellent teachers care deeply whether their students are engaged in learning, and about their academic progress. Excellent teachers know about "learning styles," that is, they are aware that not all children learn the same way. Some take in information best by reading it, others by hearing it, and so forth.

Excellent teachers know their children by name. Delpit told me about an exercise she often does with veteran teachers. She asks them to write down the names of all of their current students (or students in one class if they're high school or junior high teachers), and invariably they cannot come up with all the names. "They'll be forced to admit, 'I just can't think of that other kid's name.' And that's an eye opener for them."

Actually, excellent teachers know more than their students' names. When Delpit asks teachers to write down an important interest that each child has outside of school, most cannot. "And then I ask them, 'Which of these children give you the most trouble, or which ones are you most concerned about?' And often it's the ones who they know the least about."

One important caveat here: most school systems mistreat teachers by making them responsible for far too many students for them to get to know. How many is too many? "If a teacher has 65 kids to get to know," Ted Sizer observes, "I would tell him that he has a shot at it. But if the answer is 165, I would tell the teacher that he's in the crowd control business." In other words, don't be quick to judge teachers harshly if they haven't connected with all of their students, because your school district may be putting them in "the crowd control business." Teachers are crunched under the weight of that crowd of kids.

Don't make a judgment about a teacher on the basis on a single visit, because the best teachers vary their methods, presenting new material directly in lecture form, engaging in discussions, breaking the class into groups, and so on. If you happen to be there on the day she's lecturing, you won't have enough evidence to make an accurate judgment.

Whatever their ages, your children can tell you (often indirectly) whether they are in the hands of an excellent teacher. If your child can tell you—and wants to tell you—about a classroom discussion, that's a good sign. If your child tells you that the teacher makes cutting remarks about *other* children, that's not a good sign. If your child tells you that the teacher doesn't seem to care whether they do well or not, that's also a bad sign, because excellent teachers tell the children that they believe that they can and they will be successful. You want a teacher who captures the attention and the imagination of your child.

Excellent teachers genuinely like children and young people. As Deborah Meier says, "I'd rather have my grandchildren in a classroom whose curriculum and pedagogy I'm not so crazy about as long as the teacher likes and respects them. That's better than having them with a teacher whose educational philosophy I agree with completely but who doesn't seem to like my grandkids."

What does excellent teaching look like? A wonderful example can be seen on a video made as part of TIMSS, the Third International Math and Science Study. In this video of a high school math class, the lesson concerns finding the area of an irregularly shaped, four-sided figure. Rather than simply giving the students the formula and leading them through some practice problems, the teacher draws the figure on the chalkboard. Then he tells the class to imagine a bent line dividing the figure roughly in half. "One side is your land," he says, "and the other side is my land. We want to have a straight dividing line," he tells them, "But neither of us wants to lose any land. How can we do it?"

Having engaged the students' interest, he suggests they sit alone and think for a few minutes, then move to sit with a friend to share ideas. After five or ten minutes, he says, they will have a discussion to see if anyone has figured out how to do it. Students huddle together, scribbling on their papers and talking quietly. Then the teacher calls for ideas. The first few are examined and found wanting, but before long a formula emerges. The teacher asks if this would work for figures with other dimensions. Students show him that it does.

What have they accomplished? You might say that they have solved only one problem and are therefore not productive enough. (You *would* say that if the curriculum prescribed solving some large number of problems each day!) But the proper way to describe what they have accomplished is this: they have *discovered* something; they have taken a real problem and found a workable solution, and then they have proved that their solution has general application.

Is this better teaching, and more permanent learning, than if the teacher had lectured on the formula and then led students through a drill-and-practice routine of solving a dozen problems? Of course it is.

Incidentally, the example of excellent teaching was found in a typical Japanese high school. In the video of the typical American high school class studying the same problem, the teacher lectures and then drills, while many students blatantly ignore him. Perhaps we Americans can learn a great deal about teaching by looking elsewhere.[99]

TEACHERS AND STANDARDS

In an earlier chapter about testing and assessment, I argued that people behind high-stakes testing do not trust teachers to set high standards and hold to them. My own experience suggests that teacher-made tests are the truest indicator[100] of student accomplishment. It's also been my experience that most teachers, if they are lucky enough to work under conditions that allow them to get to know their students, can be relied upon to uphold the integrity of the school. I have a favorite story that makes my point.

Five years ago the hero of this story was teaching in a New Hampshire high school, and one of his courses was an elective class for juniors in ethics. He explained very clearly on the first day just what his standards were. Everyone, he said, had to produce work of either A or B caliber. No one would be allowed to get a lower grade. No one will get a C or D or F. His students nodded, yeah, sure, but he persisted. Don't stay in class if you can't accept these rules, he warned again. I will be giving only three grade: A, B, and Incomplete. Why are you doing this, one student asked. Because, he said, this is a class in ethics, and I don't want you to go out into the world thinking that as workers, employers, parents, and spouses, that you can do C or D work then. The school won't let you off the hook with an Incomplete either, he warned.

At mid-semester he gave out a handful of letter grades (just As and Bs as he said) and more than a dozen Incompletes. No one seemed particularly worried, and at the end of the year a dozen students failed to produce A or B work and thus received grades of Incomplete. As he had told them, he would not flunk them.

Fast forward now to senior year, when these dozen students are called in to the guidance office and told that they will *not* be able to graduate because of the Incomplete on their transcript. They rushed to his classroom and demanded an explanation. It's as I told you last year: Only A or B work is acceptable. That was the rule then, and it's the rule now.

Please flunk us, several implored. We've been accepted into college, and we have enough credits to graduate. An F will be fine, please. He refused.

One student took his complaint[101] home to his father, who just happened to be the head of the local school board. Dad came to call upon the teacher and asked him to "be reasonable." Is that the ethical lesson you want your son to learn, the teacher asked quietly? Do you want your son to learn that substandard work is okay and that influence is what really matters? The father left, chagrined.

In the end, the dozen students revisited their earlier essays and papers, rewriting them until they measured up to the standards that their teacher had made crystal clear from day one. They learned a lesson in ethics that, let us hope, they have not forgotten.

High standards, but no high-stakes test; a "transparent" system; a courageous principal; a dedicated teacher, and an intellectual (not merely academic) purpose. This represents excellence.

"TAKE OUT YOUR PENCILS PLEASE"

Gilbert Grovesnor of *National Geographic* once gave me a demonstration of excellent teaching, and all it required was a #2 pencil. He was arguing, as one might expect, for more geography in the elementary school curriculum. He was not calling for a return to what once passed for "geography" in most elementary classrooms—memorizing the 50 state capitals[102] and the world's major rivers. Requiring kids to memorize kills their curiosity, Grovesnor said. They certainly don't come away from that painful experience wanting to know more about the world.

So how should geography be taught, I asked him? He reached into his coat, withdrew a pencil, and handed it to me. With this, he said with a smile. Then he asked me to identify the component parts of the pencil. After looking it over, I told him, wood, paint, metal, pencil lead, and an eraser that I guessed was made of rubber. Okay, he said. Now let's figure out what "pencil lead" is, what the eraser is made of, and where those materials might have come from. The answer, he told me, would involve many countries. The teacher can expand this, he said, by having kids figure out where the pencils are made, how the raw materials got to the factory, and how the finished product is distributed.

A pencil is only a beginning. Grovesnor went on as he warmed to the task. The teacher can ask each student to bring in a common object from home, analyze those with the class, and ask the same questions. If the object is old, figure out how it's made differently today and where the new materials come from. Students will be discovering the world this way, he concluded, not memorizing places on the globe.[103]

Gilbert Grovesnor has the luxury of designing a better way of teaching geography, a "deep" way, because he does not inhabit the crunched and rushed world of public school. In that world, the curriculum is broad by design, so that by its nature it discourages depth. Tests and test preparation wield great influence over the curriculum, and machine-scored tests rarely contain questions that reward those who've dug deeply into a subject. It's enough to know the year when Hannibal crossed the Alps; you get no extra points for knowing about the historical debate about the three possible routes he might have followed during that winter crossing with the elephants.

I recall a painful conversation with a teacher of advanced placement physics at an elite private school. He wished that he could teach the principles of flight by having each student design a plane with the school's CAD (computer-aided design) program. "Once they had finished the design, the computer would show them whether it would fly. If it didn't fly, they would have to figure out why and fix it. If it flew, they would have to explain why. Both ways, they would *discover* all the fundamentals of the physics of flight, instead of my *telling* them."

Why the long face, I asked? "Because I can't do it that way. It might take too long, and I have too much material to cover so they will be ready for the AP test." He was, in short, rushed by the demands of the curriculum and unable to teach in a way he knew would be better.

Students could do this on their own, and some do. But they do it at their own peril. They are rewarded for skimming many surfaces, not for exploring. My sophomore year in college the guy across the hall flunked an American literature course we were both taking because he fell in love with William Faulkner's writing. Instead of reading only *Light in August* and then moving on to Hemingway, Fitzgerald, and the rest, he read everything Faulkner wrote. That meant he couldn't write glibly about "common themes" the way the rest of us did on the final exam, but he learned more and knew more than we did.

In short, breadth is the enemy of depth, just as "good enough" is the enemy of excellence.

THE SENIORITY DILEMMA

Where seniority rules—and it rules almost everywhere in education—new teachers are likely to suffer. They are often assigned to the least desirable schools, given the "worst" classes, the most preparations, and the additional assignments nobody else wants. But here's a radical thought: seniority, at least in its most rigid forms, hurts veteran teachers as well.

It's not difficult to find administrators who dislike the rigidities of seniority. I once asked an assistant principal how his elementary school went about hiring teachers. "You want to know how we fill vacancies? *We* don't fill them. A day or two before school opens, someone shows up with some paperwork and says, 'I'm your new fourth-grade teacher. Where's my classroom?' And we take the paperwork and point to the empty room."

His distaste was palpable. "What other profession doesn't allow the professionals to select their colleagues?" he wanted to know. "How can we create a genuine learning environment when we can't control who teaches here?"

When teachers have seniority, who benefits? That's a question I've been pondering ever since I happened to meet Marlene, a middle-aged veteran of more than 20 years in the classroom.

"This is the worst school I've ever taught in," the woman muttered to herself, just loud enough for me to hear. We were watching several hundred high school students streaming into school on a fall morning. "How long have you taught here?" I asked. "It's my first year," she said, with some bitterness.

Because her union is fiercely protective of teachers' seniority rights, I assumed she had made the decision to teach there, and I asked her why? Her answer stunned me. "It's the closest school to my home, and I wanted a short commute."

We introduced ourselves and talked for a while. I don't know what sort of teacher Marlene is, but it's easy to hypothesize that she's a burnt-out, bored worker counting the hours until she can go home for the day. I can imagine her contempt for the school playing itself out with her students. And given that she is white and virtually all of the students in her high school are African-American, it's hard to conceive of happy endings for this story.

Is she Exhibit A proving the evils of the seniority system, or could there be more to the story? I'm assuming that, 20 or 25 years ago, Marlene was a typical new teacher: idealistic, energetic, and determined to contribute to the growth and learning of her students. What happened to make her view her profession through such a narrow prism? Have the rewards of teaching been so slight that *commuting time*, not her colleagues, the curriculum, or the work environment has become her highest priority?

Unions fought for seniority to protect their members from what they perceived as arbitrary decisions of administrators, and any veteran teacher can tell horror stories of being treated contemptuously or indifferently. Does that still happen? Do administrators still treat trained teachers as if they were "interchangeable parts"? Sadly, in many places they do.

I recall watching a first-year teacher showing high school sophomores how to determine the area of a rectangle. She gave her students the formula and did three sample problems on the board. Each time she gave the answer in meters. No one in the class, including the teacher, knew that the answers had to be in *square* meters.

What she's experiencing in her first year on the job actually supports the need for seniority privileges. She had been hired to teach *physical education*, but on the first day of school her principal assigned her to teach two sections of algebra, a subject she had not studied since high school. A teacher with seniority might have been able to refuse, but not a first-year teacher.

"Teachers as interchangeable parts" seemed to be the operating principle of that principal.[104] Elsewhere in the school an art teacher was teaching basic Math and a basketball coach was teaching English.

That fundamental attitude of anti-professionalism goes beyond individual administrators. It's built into laws and regulations. For example, Georgia (where that young woman was teaching) says it's okay for teachers to spend 40 percent of their time teaching subjects out of their field without being categorized as "out-of-field." Could a podiatrist spend 40 percent of his time performing brain surgery without running afoul of the authorities?

That's a rhetorical question, of course. Defenders of teachers are fond of medical analogies, but they're not necessary to make the point. Perhaps a more persuasive analogy has to do with automobiles. Think about this: A mechanic licensed to repair Porsches would not spend 40 percent of his time repairing Toyotas or Fords, but a phys ed teacher can be to told to teach two physics classes! So cars are more important than children—or other people's children anyway.

The world of teachers is one of small victories . . . and dozens of routine in-dignities: constant interruptions from the main office ("Please send Joey Brown to the office"), hall patrol, cafeteria duty, and the impossibility of taking a bath-room break when nature calls.

Over the years the treatment takes its toll. Many teachers simply leave. Thirty percent of those entering teaching leave within five years, an exit rate that is far higher than in law, medicine, nursing, or the ministry, professions that teaching is often compared to.

What happens to those who stay? While thousands continue to do wonder-ful work, despite it all, many become, in the current lingo, "burnt out." That is, they're on the job, but they've lost sight of why they became teachers in the first place. Perhaps that's what happened to Marlene.

Seniority gives veterans—finally—the opportunity to thumb their noses at these indignities, and that's how I explain Marlene's way of choosing her school.

There are alternatives, ways to allow teachers to be professionals. In Seattle, for example, progressive union leadership pushed through an agreement that al-lows teachers to be part of the hiring process at individual schools while, at the same time, allowing schools to hire without regard to seniority. That meant that teachers were able, for the first time in their professional lives, to participate in choosing their colleagues, in building a professional team at their workplace.

Improving the system, however, cannot *start* with doing away with seniority. Most teachers I've known want to be good at their job, but they're working in systems that don't let that happen. Seniority is a desperate protection, and if I were a teacher I'd fight to hold on to it, until management demonstrated its com-mitment to teaching as a profession.

In the eyes of many observers, the public school system is set up in ways that discourage excellence and drive out capable teachers. As John Goodlad of the University of Washington has noted, "Even some *reformers* do not want well ed-ucated, thoughtful, creative teachers, because they get in the way."[105] He notes that teachers have never had much of a voice in the curriculum or anything else, and what evolved was a paternalistic system with nonteachers making decisions for teachers. Today, however, education is attracting idealistic, bright, able peo-ple, and, Goodlad said with a laugh, "They are good crap detectors. They're alert to the stupidity of much of the simplistic reforms that are being proposed, which they know won't work. Their bosses don't want bright people around who are going to resist when they impose things on them. So the schools lose the best, and who can blame them for leaving?"

"GOOD ENOUGH" TEACHER TRAINING

On a warm spring afternoon in Texas, about 25 education majors, all young white women, are waving plastic toys in the air, giggling and singing "Row, Row, Row Your Boat." They're pretending to be five-year-olds as part of their teacher training.

In rural Georgia, 850 miles to the east, a young man is leading his ninth-grade English class through the day's vocabulary. One of the words is "strenuous," which he has written on the board "strenous." During the lesson he reviews the definition, the spelling, and the syllabification, never catching his mistake. His students dutifully copy his spelling mistake into their workbooks.

And in Oakland, Calif., an eleventh-grade biology class is having its 163rd consecutive class meeting without a certified science teacher . . . a parade of substitute teachers for an entire year. [106]

Taken together, these three anecdotes would seem to support the widely held contention that we are facing a major crisis in teaching, that we need more teachers, and we need better-trained teachers. For at least five years experts have been saying that our schools will have to hire more than 2 million teachers over the next decade.[107] The Clinton administration budgeted $1.38 billion for fiscal year 2001 to recruit, hire, and train teachers, the first spending of a planned $12.4 billion over seven years.

I would make a different argument. I believe these vignettes, and the circumstances behind them, demonstrate that our education system has an unacceptably high tolerance for "good enough" teachers and "good enough" training—although quite often the results have been mediocre, that is, not even good enough. What's more, national, state, and local policies merely reinforce the status quo.

Despite the fact that some regions of the country are having difficulty finding teachers and that serious shortages exist in science, math, and special education, we actually produce more teachers than we need, at least 30,000 a year by some estimates.

Where shortages exist, they are often what should be labeled "self-inflicted wounds." They fall into three categories: schools underpay and mistreat teachers and eventually drive them from the profession; inept school districts cannot find the qualified teachers living under their noses; and substandard training ill prepares young men and women for the realities of classroom life.

Excellent schools do not assign people to teach subjects they have not studied. The clear majority of teachers in an excellent school will have majored in whatever subjects they are teaching (in private schools that number ought to approach 100 percent).

Excellent schools and school districts are committed to the continuing education ("professional development") of teachers and administrators. Here the program should be well designed and continuous. If teachers are free to take whatever courses they choose, many will choose to take whatever's easy and convenient. And that alone should persuade parents with the power to get their kids out to start packing immediately!

EVERYBODY INTO THE POOL?

Consider this metaphor: A swimming pool with a serious leak. You wouldn't expect that pouring more and more water into the pool would in time fix the leak, but that's precisely the approach we are taking toward the so-called teacher shortage. Everyone's noticed that the teaching "pool" is low, and getting lower. Impending retirements, increasing student enrollments, and legislation mandating smaller classes, particularly in the lower grades, are the reasons, we're told.

The response has been to recruit more people into teaching, using a variety of strategies including public-service-announcement campaigns, $100 million in federal money, hiring bonuses, help with mortgages, and recruitment trips to Spain and other distant lands.

Dire warnings are not new, and neither are these strategies. Almost every U.S. president since Harry Truman has warned of teacher shortages, and large-scale recruitment efforts have followed.

Yet the pool keeps losing water because no one is paying attention to the leak. That is, we're misdiagnosing the problem as "recruitment" when it's really "retention." Simply put, we train teachers poorly and then treat them badly—and so they leave in droves.

As it happens, interest in teaching among our nation's university students is growing. A 1998 survey of over 300,000 entering college freshmen revealed that more than 10 percent of them say they want to teach after they graduate. The results were encouraging—interest in teaching has doubled since it hit its low point in 1982.

On the surface, the news is encouraging, but just because 22 Princeton undergraduates want to teach (up from three a few years ago), no one should assume we're out of the woods. We aren't.

"Interest" in teaching is not enough. We need to train them well so that they are just busting to be with kids in classrooms. The country's 1,300 schools and colleges of education *already* graduate enough teachers, but three out of every ten do not go into classrooms. Some never intended to; they were majoring in education because it's an easy way to get a degree or to have a "fallback" option. Others found they couldn't get teaching jobs in their hometowns, and so they found other work; that is, staying home was the goal, not becoming a teacher.

Of the remaining seven who do go into the classroom, two will leave teaching within five years. Half of the new teachers hired to work in urban schools leave within three years, a truly astonishing exit rate. At the very least, this is an inefficient use of human and material resources. To call for greater recruitment efforts in the face of overwhelming evidence that the system cannot *keep* people seems odd, to say the least.

Education's real problems lie within the system that is already in place, and no influx of idealistic men and women will change that. Our 1999 investigation into the teacher shortage for a PBS documentary found a system-wide pattern of mediocrity and incompetence that begins in teacher training institutions and infects the entire system.

We found that school administrators frequently assign teachers to teach subjects regardless of whether they had majored or even minored in those subjects in college. For example, the young man who couldn't spell "strenuous" was a middle school physical education teacher and coach, but he'd been assigned to teach English, history, and math at the local high school. He knew he was in over his head, but he had no choice.

We found certified teachers who simply couldn't penetrate incompetent school bureaucracies. Katherine Scheuermann, armed with a California license to teach science, applied for a teaching position in Oakland in June 1997 and again in June 1998. She finally got a response—nearly two years later—in the form of a letter inviting her to apply for a position in bilingual education. Without much difficulty, we found two other certified teachers who told essentially the same story: the school district's bureaucracy was impenetrable, so they looked elsewhere.

Oakland is not an anomaly, according to those who have studied the issue. City school systems tend to be run by overstuffed bureaucracies. And, as mentioned, cities lose teachers at an alarming rate. For example, Oakland has to replace up to 30 percent of its teachers every year, even though it pays well for a school district. Teachers leave because they burn out. Veteran Nancy Caruso described her teaching conditions. "I had no water, and I was supposed to teach science. I was toting water from a decaying toilet, basically little gallon containers, one at a time, and it was just very frustrating for me. I'm in a decaying building. It's graffiti-ridden, trash everywhere, and it seems like nothing that could get done gets done."

New teachers seem to be treated even worse. Caruso, who left Oakland High School after ten years there, observed wryly, "Administrators give new teachers the hardest, most challenging classes and the most preparations, so they have maybe four different classes to prepare for every day, and then administrators expect that that's going to make them excited about teaching. It's just not conducive to retaining young, enthusiastic people. They get burnt out, and so they go to the suburbs or they leave teaching completely."

HIGHER EDUCATION'S "CASH COW"

But mediocrity and incompetence begin earlier at most of the 1,300 institutions that train teachers. Their parent universities tend to treat education programs as "cash cows" for their overall needs, diverting tuition paid by education majors into law, medicine, engineering, and nursing programs, for example. As Stanford University professor Linda Darling-Hammond notes, "If you are preparing to be a teacher, you can expect about half of the tuition money that you put into the till to come back to support your preparation."

Training teachers on the cheap means large classes on campus, rather than intensive (and more expensive) work in real schools with real children. That's why those would-be teachers at Texas A&M were earnestly pretending to be five-year-olds for 50 minutes at a stretch. "It's as close as we can get to the real thing," one student told us, apparently unaware of the existence of a dozen elementary schools within a few miles of campus.

Training on the cheap means more part-time faculty and lower salaries for those with full-time jobs. It's no secret that schools of education are at the bottom of the university pecking order. On the bottom rung of the education school's own ladder of prestige are those who actually train teachers.

It's likely that unimaginative training has an unintended consequence: It breeds contempt for the very profession these students are getting ready to join. We asked a class of seniors, on the verge of graduating and moving into classrooms, whether they were having doubts about their career choice. Virtually every hand went up.

Universities like Texas A&M, and their schools of education, actually know how to train teachers well, but that requires more time and money. About 30 percent of A&M's education students enrolled in a separate and much more rigorous program, one that required them to spend 40 hours a week in a public school, working with a mentor teacher. Throughout the year, these students take most of their university classes in the public school, often taught by experienced public school teachers.

Where were the university's education professors? Most were back on campus, lecturing, writing, and doing research—and for good reason: they will *not* get tenure for doing a good job of training teachers. Tenure is awarded to those who do research and publish. As A&M education professor Jim Kracht noted, "Working in public schools doesn't give teacher education faculty members much chance to do those things that are necessary for promotion and tenure, because it consumes so much of their time." But working in public school classrooms does keep professors in touch with what is really going on and provides them with experiences that would better equip them to prepare teachers.

I asked Professor Kracht whether the aims of the university were incompatible with the aims of good teacher education. He said with a smile that, although they weren't incompatible, "they probably aren't aligned as well as we would like to have them be."

The dean of A&M's School of Education, Jane Close Conoley, was candid in her appraisal of the two approaches. Of the traditional and less expensive method, she said, "I think it's not as good. There is evidence that people who go through the off-campus program are better teachers, they get better outcomes from their students, and they last longer in the field." But, she adds, "It's also incredibly expensive to maintain."

Darling-Hammond of Stanford does not accept that answer. "If Schools of Education received all the money their students are paying, there would be enough," she says. "Many colleges, however, have basically used the tuition that large numbers of education students pay to fund the medical school, the law school, the business school and the other parts of the university."

AN ALTERNATIVE ANSWER?

How much training is necessary? Are good teachers born and not made? Frank McCourt, the author of *Angela's Ashes* and *'Tis*, is a former teacher with strong views on this subject. When I interviewed him for our National Public Radio series, he spoke his mind. "Can you teach somebody how to be a poet? You cannot. You can help him or her. You can suggest and hint but you can't make a teacher. I think there is an innate quality, a personality." Training would help, McCourt conceded, but only if it's provided by veteran teachers. "You can't sit in a college classroom and learn how to teach, what the chemistry of a class is like, how to open up kids, and how to open yourself up. Ultimately, the only way of finding out is to be in the classroom three or four years in front of the kids. Then you'll find out."

Competition from "alternative certification" programs could force Schools of Education to shape up. These programs, which are designed to attract and train older professionals looking to change careers, generally provide an intensive summer of training and a year of weekend meetings, a far cry from the four- or five-year programs at education school. Some of the nation's 120 alternative-certification programs are suspect, but others seem rigorous. For example, graduates of the state's alternative program in Austin outperform graduates of nearly every traditional School of Education in Texas on the state test for teachers. Alternative programs in Texas graduated some 4,000 teachers in 1998—about a third of all new teachers in the state, and the primary route into teaching for minorities and older professionals. And districts rush to hire graduates of alternative programs.

Darling-Hammond vigorously opposes alternative certification. "A group of kids are being put at risk for somebody who's using them as guinea pigs while they learn to teach," she says. "We wouldn't do that in medicine. We wouldn't say to someone who wanted to be a doctor, 'Hey, while you're figuring out how to do surgery, why don't you just practice in this hospital?'"

Chester Finn, an assistant secretary of education under Ronald Reagan, disagrees with Darling-Hammond. "She has a highly professionalized notion that teachers should enter through a classic route and then spend their whole life in this profession," Finn says. But, he adds, "I think that 200 years of private school history proves her wrong. Parents pay quite a lot of money to have their kids taught by people who have never set foot in a school of education."

I asked Darling-Hammond, a determined reformer, if she felt uncomfortable defending what amounts to a monopoly, the exclusive franchise of Schools of

Education to train teachers? "It's a difficult argument," she admitted. "The Ed School establishment has a lot of low quality activity in many places. Variability is huge. We don't have standards that are being enforced." But, she insisted that the answer was not to ignore the importance of preparation. Don't lower the bar, she pleads, raise standards instead. It's unfortunate that Darling-Hammond is often cast in the role of defender of the traditional approach to training, because she is working overtime to reform from within. Her own teacher preparation program at Stanford stands as a model of excellence; unfortunately, too many of the other institutional programs are mired in mediocrity.

Those who favor alternative certification say that alternative routes into teaching raise standards by definition, because well-qualified people who are not willing to spend class time singing "Row, row, row your boat" *will* commit to teaching *if* they can find a shortcut. That means classrooms end up being staffed with bright liberal arts majors fresh out of Princeton, or retired military men like Jules Cabeen. Cabeen, who acknowledges that he wouldn't be teaching if it weren't for alternative certification, says he's having the time of his life teaching junior high school science. "When I was in the military leading troops I was more of a leader, but here I'm more of a coach, more of a mentor. It really is two different roles, and you have to be able to cross out of that military role and move into that teacher role."

I have been following the adventures of four newly recruited Teaching Fellows in New York City, people hired to staff the city's worst public schools. Under court order to staff those 52 schools with certified teachers and unable to persuade[108] enough veteran teachers to move, the district created, almost overnight, the Teaching Fellows program. Advertised widely in language reminiscent of the Peace Corps ads of the '60s ("Ready to change your life, and someone else's?"), the program attracted 2,500 applicants, including doctors and lawyers and hundreds of young college graduates. From this pool the district accepted 348 and gave them *one month* of training.

To qualify to teach, the Fellows had to be certified, which meant they had to pass the two exams that most new teachers take after four years of college as education majors. Over 90 percent passed, which compares favorably with the 95 percent passing rate for those who've studied to be teachers for their entire college careers! Whether that is a comment on the quality of the Fellows or the simplicity of the exams is unclear.

That the Fellows program attracted so many young college graduates, in an economy where better paying jobs are going begging, speaks volumes about the idealism of youth. It also says a great deal, I think, about the reputation of teacher education. I spoke with dozens of Fellows during their training, and most said, flat out, that they wouldn't want to be teachers if it meant having to go to a school of education.[109]

I confess that I felt the same way when I became a teacher in the 1960s. I had been accepted into the Peace Corps, slated to teach English in East Africa, when just before graduation I injured my back so severely that I couldn't pass the physical. I got a job teaching English in Port Washington, a Long Island suburb of New York City, and began work there as I was recovering from surgery.

I had no training whatsoever, having taken only a History of Education course at Dartmouth, but nobody seemed to care. My department chairman gave me valuable advice and encouragement, as did other veterans. The school was rigidly tracked, 1-5, and rookies weren't allowed anywhere near the Ones or the Twos, the kids who were bound for top colleges. I was given some classes of Threes and one group from the Fourth track. Because the administration didn't seem to care very much about these kids, I was left alone.

I made a lot of mistakes, but I think my youthful energy and enthusiasm made it at least a wash. There were three other new English teachers in the school, and we bonded easily, sharing ideas, victories, and defeats. We all worked long hours, and we pushed our kids to write, re-write, and then re-write once more. I re-member many late nights of grading papers, but I also remember driving to school most mornings eager to get to work.

The teaching Fellows I've met, many of them, remind me of myself 35 years ago, and they remind me of the young people in Teach for America, the alterna-tive program created by Wendy Kopp while still an undergraduate.

Concerned that all children do not have equal access to good schools, Kopp used her senior thesis to propose a national teacher corps of outstanding recent college undergraduates from all academic majors who would commit to spend two years teaching in some of America's toughest public schools. She got the program going right after graduation. Teach for America had some initial stum-bles, usually because TFA assigned corps members one-to-a-school, which led to isolation and unhappiness. Today TFA tries to place three or more teachers in the same or neighboring schools. (I've been in a school that had seven TFA teachers on staff.)

At the turn of the century Wendy Kopp was still the organization's president, and TFA had become an institution. In 2000 over 1,000 Teach for America corps members were in classrooms, and 77 percent of school principals who have supervised them rate them as better than other beginning teachers. TFA reports that 85 percent complete their two-year commitment, and that 54 percent of its "alumni" have continued to work in education.

Alternative certification, TFA, and other programs like Troops for Teachers accounted for only about 3 percent of public schoolteachers in 1998, but they may be having an impact beyond their numbers. I've been in schools that have hired three or more of these nontraditionally trained teachers, and they seem to bring boundless energy to the building, a sense of "can do" optimism. Are they wonderful teachers? I don't know, but I'll opt for positive energy and subject matter knowledge any time.

Harold Levy, chancellor of the New York City public schools, is the man behind the Teaching Fellows program. He believes that the system does not need to be filled with career teachers. "If we can persuade idealistic young people to make short-term commitments to the schools, the system will improve. We need easier paths into teaching, and we don't have to insist that teaching be their lifetime career." Levy notes that today's young people will have six or seven career changes in their lifetimes. "Why shouldn't teaching be one of those careers," he asks?[110]

Lou Gerstner of IBM believes that hiring teachers from places other than Schools of Education actually improves school for *everyone*. "If you could have 5 or 10 percent be people who had worked in the government, had worked in a nonprofit sector, or had worked in a profit sector, they could enrich a school system, and in no way be threatening to the other 90 to 95 percent."

Gerstner dismisses Darling-Hammond's concern about courses in pedagogy. "I happen to think what's most important is a mastery of the subject you're teaching, not that you've had a lot of courses in the mechanics and philosophy of teaching." He noted that almost half of public school math teachers didn't even minor in mathematics in college. "School is all about knowledge, not about procedure," Gerstner says. "Hire a person with a Ph.D. in math who has been working in a private sector company and give him a mentor teacher. No problem."

Alternative certification faces uphill battles in most states. In Texas, for example, alternative preparation programs receive significantly less state funding per student than traditional teacher-training programs, even though alternative certification graduates outperform the graduates of most traditional programs.

Leo Klagholz is the former commissioner of education in New Jersey who developed that state's alternative certification program. He believes that "knowledge of subject matter, and personal traits like intelligence, human sensitivity and caring, communication ability, work ethic, self-discipline, and the ability to relate to children" are more crucial to teacher effectiveness than a degree from a

School of Education. Klagholz issued a warning: "When government uses teacher training as a formal job eligibility screen, it produces the double error of failing to guarantee the competence of those who meet requirements, while also eliminating individuals who have significant capabilities."[111]

The current national policy of recruiting more teachers is a waste of money. It not only lets education schools and public school systems off the hook, but it actually rewards them. After all, those federal training dollars are going to be spent at teacher training institutions. Treating the majority of these institutions as part of the solution is like asking the polluters to clean up the river.

Further, it's destined to fail. As University of Pennsylvania professor Richard Ingersoll notes: "We can recruit all kinds of qualified people and persuade them to go into teaching, but if they get into jobs that aren't well-paid and don't have particularly good working conditions in which they're given little say in the way schools operate, it's not going to really solve the problem because a lot of these people will leave."

Professor Ingersoll is correct. *If* teacher training were rigorous and demanding, *if* the profession were opened up to welcome those entering from other fields, *if* teaching were a well-paid occupation in which expertise was respected, and *if* out-of-field teaching were simply unacceptable, there'd be no teacher shortage. That would fix the leak.

QUESTIONS TO ASK THE TEACHER ABOUT YOUR CHILD

- Is my child's work at or above the standards for his or her age?
- Are most students in the class above or below the standards?
- Does my child understand what he or she needs to do to meet the standards?
- Is my child falling behind in any area? What is being done/can be done to help him or her?
- Does my child have any learning problems? Is he or she getting help? Is it working?
- How can I help my child do better?
- What level class is my child in? How many levels are there? What are they called? What is the difference between them? How likely is it that he or she will move up?
- Is my child learning the same things as students in the higher level classes?
- How will the school help my child meet high standards?

- How will my child catch up to where he or she should be? What can I do to help?
- If my child stays in this program and does well, will he or she be able to get into a higher level program next year?
- What classes should my child be taking now to be qualified to attend a four-year college?

QUESTIONS TO ASK ABOUT TEACHERS

- What is the absentee rate for teachers?
- What professional development is offered to teachers? How is it related to student achievement? Do teachers have choices of courses and programs? Is professional development a series of occasional workshops, or is there continuity?
- Does the principal support staff development? Does he or she participate?
- Do teachers have time to talk with one another about their work? To visit one another's classrooms?
- Do teachers have the opportunity to visit other schools? Are teachers part of on-line conversations about their work with teachers in other parts of the country (or the world)?
- Are there provisions for teachers to observe their colleagues?
- What is the teacher turnover rate? How long do teachers stay at the school?
- Is the staff a good blend of veterans and newcomers?
- What do veteran teachers do to help teachers who are having trouble?
- Are all teachers certified or nearing certification?
- Do they have degrees in the subjects they teach?
- Are they knowledgeable about the research in the field of teaching and in the subjects they are teaching?
- Do they feel supported by the parents at the school? Are they enthusiastic or discouraged?
- Are there only a few teachers that every parent seems to want, or are there good teachers in most classrooms?
- Are there hands-on lessons?
- Is homework meaningful?
- What do teachers want students to get out of homework?
- Is homework ever used as a punishment?
- Do teachers ever design homework that will engage families?

6

SAFETY AND
EXCELLENCE

The argument of this chapter is that, as far as schools are concerned, there are three kinds of safety: physical, emotional, and intellectual. Excellence demands all three, while "good enough" schools are simply physically safe. Unsafe schools are bad by definition.

Because most public schools are *physically* safe places to be, I am not going to devote many pages to the subject of physical safety.[112] Even with the rash of school shootings we've had over the past three years, the odds of being shot to death in school are one in six million. There were nine gun-related homicides on school grounds in 1999, and school enrollment is about 55 million. Less than 1 percent of the 2,500 child homicides and suicides in the last six months of 1997 took place at a school or on the way to and from school.[113] School crime continues to decline, even faster than the nation's overall crime rate. By the numbers, our neighborhoods,[114] homes, and highways are far more dangerous places for young people. It's understandable, however, that school boards are concerned about security; they certainly don't want to have another Columbine on their hands and have to try to explain away a decision not to install metal detectors, surveillance cameras, and so forth, even though many security experts say that metal detectors are less efficient than low-tech approaches. What's more, most metal detectors are unsuitable for large schools, which have a dozen or more entries.

However, schools are thinking security—Philadelphia put metal detectors in all its high schools at a cost of $5 million. Chicago did the same in its middle schools. Other schools are doing random searches, installing security cameras, and adding guards.

Is this an overreaction? Probably, because most school violence doesn't involve guns or knives, but good old-fashioned fists. Still, teachers must be wary, because they know that lethal weapons are easily available.

Many schools and districts have adopted what's called a "zero tolerance" policy, meaning that *one* offense leads to automatic suspension or expulsion. Some policies require calling in the police as well. Under these codes, a gun, a box cutter, a plastic fork from a fast food restaurant, a fistfight, and a hostile shove in the hallway are equally serious offenses. One elementary student was suspended when he waved around a miniature sword, the sort that's used to hold the olive in a martini, around on the playground!

It's easy to laugh at the ridiculousness of the latter, and in the face of public scorn that suspension was withdrawn. But zero tolerance has had deadly, irreversible consequences. It's not far-fetched to say that Rob Pace, an 18-year-old honor student, is dead because of his school's zero tolerance policies.

In April 2000 Rob Pace went on a field trip with his fellow Riverhead High School seniors. At the entrance to the Great Adventure Amusement park in New Jersey, security guards discovered marijuana in his backpack. Arrested at the gate, he was processed and released by the police, but Riverhead High School officials refused to let him accompany the group back to Long Island. "He's gonna have to take a train or he's gonna have to do something," the school's associate principal told the police. Removing Pace from contact with other students was consistent with the district's zero tolerance policy: students caught with drugs must be removed from school activities.

But the policy also states that *parents* are to do the removing, implying—but not stating explicitly—that students shouldn't be left on their own. By the time a school representative reached Rob's parents, Pace, who had already been accepted into college, had set off on his own. As the *New York Times* reported, "Mr. Pace made it to Bethpage on the Long Island Railroad before deciding he could go no further. 'Please tell anyone who ever knew me that I'm sorry for letting them down!' read a note he left on his seat. Then he jumped between train cars to his death."[115]

I fear that our devotion to making schools safe from physical violence—guns—may be making schools emotionally dangerous places for young people. The intense focus on security seems to be having other, smaller unintended consequences. Lately I've been meeting students who've told me that they are afraid to show their own emotions, because they're afraid of being labeled a potential threat.

As a high school senior in Charlottesville, Virginia, told me, "There is pressure not to admit to being on edge or being unhappy because then automatically people are going to assume, 'Oh, that's that kid who's going to fly off the handle at any moment.'"

In September 2000 the FBI issued a report with a list of more than 40 "warning signs" for educators to look for in children and youth. And while Attorney General Janet Reno warned against "unfairly labeling and stigmatizing children," it seems likely that the presence of a list will contribute to the growth of a "checklist" mentality. The FBI's list includes clearly *subjective* behaviors like "hopelessness, despair, hatred, isolation, loneliness, nihilism and an 'end of the world' philosophy." The report also refers to students who are easily angered, who've just broken up with a boyfriend or girlfriend, who have a superior attitude, or who are rigid or opinionated. In short, a laundry list! Despite the FBI's warning that "At this time there is no research that has identified traits and characteristics that can reliably distinguish school shooters from other students," it's easy to imagine school personnel saying "Johnny's been very opinionated lately. Maybe he's feeling nihilistic."

What will they do next? Offer counseling, or put Johnny on a "watch" list? Or maybe suspend him for a few days? Given that the average counselor to student ratio in most schools is 1 to 500,[116] the watch list (and maybe an entry into Johnny's school record) seems a more likely destination.

The FBI's introductory phrase, "At this time," indicates that the authorities remain preoccupied with student behavior and may not be looking into either *school conditions* (i.e., harassment or domination by cliques) or *social conditions* (i.e., gun availability and social acceptance of violence).[117]

Heightened school security itself creates stress. Lisa Delpit, the author of "Other People's Children," is worried about the effects of zero tolerance policies.[118] "People cannot learn under stress, and I find that children are so stressed right now. Because of zero tolerance, children are worried about whether something they bring to school can be used against them. The zero tolerance policy requires that schools call the police if some fight occurs. That's crazy. When we grew up, there were always fights, but teachers took care of things. Now, with zero tolerance, children are seeing other children get taken off by police in handcuffs."

I asked Delpit if children should be able to speak freely about their emotions. Be able to say, "I'm so mad I want to punch somebody." She laughed, "Adults do that all the time, so why can't kids?" Then she turned serious. "The adults in the school should sit down with an angry child and work through the anger, not just let the child go away holding on to it. Adults have to recognize that anger is a normal emotion, not an occasion to call the cops."

LuYen Chou, an educator in New York agrees with Delpit. "We have to be careful that in the name of safety, we aren't quelling an openness to diversity, an openness to expression of different emotions and different feelings. Kids need the safety valve, and if we shut that off, we are asking for trouble."

To Delpit, who teaches at Georgia State University, zero tolerance makes *zero* sense. "It's scary that we have some arbitrary outside rules that require us to respond in a certain way. It means that we're not allowed to use our knowledge of how children function, and it tells the children that we are powerless."

Ruth Zweifler of the Student Advocacy Center of Michigan feels even more strongly about zero tolerance as a school policy. She says that the children most affected are young adolescents (ages 11 to 13), children of color, and handicapped children "whose special needs have been ignored, making it a double crime." In Zweifler's view, parents of children who are expelled must face hostile school boards with little or no information about the law, without adequate representation, and with few avenues to appeal the dire consequences of expulsion. "The zero tolerance hysteria accepts the premise that some children don't deserve an education," she concludes, adding that in her state, Michigan, there's no agency that is obligated to see that expelled students continue their education in some way.[119]

Ted Sizer, the distinguished school reformer, also believes that most schools are overreacting to gun violence. "What you should worry about are the kids who seem to take pleasure in harassing and insulting other kids, the bullies, the ones who see school as a game and are constantly pushing the limits."

Generally it's urban high schools with more than one thousand students that report the most crime. That's what the research says anyway, although there are exceptions. The vice principal of a combined junior/senior high school in rural Indiana told me that, by its demographics, his school should be one of the safest in the nation. "Unfortunately, however, we have the KKK and all its baggage, and that creeps into the school." Did that mean guns, I asked him? "No, but it means bullying, fistfights, and harassment."

How can parents and others determine whether a school is physically safe? It's always good to find out how many students were suspended at your school, and why. Ask school officials, but if they're reluctant, search out student advocacy groups like the Michigan Advocacy Center.

Of course, a lot of trouble goes unreported—unless you know where to look and whom to ask. Talk to students. Ask them about the places in school where they feel unsafe, and check them out for yourself. Bathrooms are a good place to start, because if some kids are being bothered, there's a good chance you'll read about it there. Look for graffiti that singles out kids in a mean or threatening way.

And keep an eye out for stuff that smacks of sexual harassment, because schools now have a legal responsibility to protect students from sexual harassment by their peers. In 1998 a federal court ordered a Wisconsin school district to pay $900,000 to a student for its failure to stop sexual harassment. School systems understand that sort of message.

That includes harassment of gay students. Their problems are often overlooked, and most teachers have not been prepared to cope with them. Ramon Gonzalez is a brilliant young teacher in a New York City middle school, a young man who's studying to be a superintendent while he's teaching math full time. I asked Gonzalez about his awareness of students who might be gay. "Now I'm starting to be aware of the issue. It's hard for me to deal with because I grew up in a very traditional environment, so I'm trying to come to terms with that for myself. I've asked my counselor, 'What do I do?' And they don't know what to do either."

Having lots of adults—and not just security guards—around is one good way to stop violence and harassment. In physically safe schools, the teachers maintain a presence in the halls. They're around talking with students, not as police but as responsible adults. Unfortunately, some collective bargaining agreements place limits on the time teachers can be asked to spend in the halls. To my mind, this is a good example of what should not be negotiated, or need to be. In excellent schools, teachers know most students by name and want to be in contact with them, not just to keep an eye on them but because they genuinely like them.

Excellent schools protect their students from strangers, and you might want to try the "back door test" as a way of determining whether a school is safe. That is, try to get inside using entrances other than the front door. If you can get in that way, that's probably a bad sign. That is, if you can just walk in, so can anyone else.

You should not be able to wander around aimlessly either. If no one stops you at the front door and if the adults you meet in the hallways ignore your presence, that's trouble in the making. In physically safe schools, teachers are coached to speak to strangers and find out what they're doing in the school.

EMOTIONAL SAFETY

The second aspect of school safety is what I call "emotional safety." It's rarer, unfortunately, and harder to spot, but excellence is impossible without it. Recall Ted Sizer's comments about bullies. Most of the bullying in schools is verbal, the so-called "normal" teasing that kids inflict on one another.

As a reporter, I meet students all the time who talk openly about being teased. Jessica is a young white girl in a nearly all-black middle school in New York City. "I'm just sick of some people making fun of me because of the color of my skin, or because of what I wear."

Charles, 17 years old and about 6'2", recalls painful years of being teased unmercifully. "Kids would make fun of my ears, because they're big, and I just hated it."

Carlos, a Maryland high school student, hasn't forgotten how other students react when he tries to read aloud. "They call me stupid, stuff like that, because I get nervous and start stuttering."

John is diagnosed with ADD and on Ritalin. "They'd go, 'Ha-ha-ha, ADD boy, you can't do anything right. You're so stupid.'"

Students told their stories to me, a reporter from outside. What happens if you complain to teachers or to your parents, I often ask? Usually the kids tell me that adults say, "Get tough. That's just normal, so get used to it." Unfortunately, that's the conventional reaction in "good enough" schools.

Perhaps teachers cannot *prevent* teasing, but they can intervene. Deborah Meier, the founder of the world-renowned Central Park East school, believes that most teachers, and most adults, tend to dismiss teasing as normal, something children just have to get used to. But, Meier says, "We turn our backs because we don't know what to do about it."

I recall when one of my children came home complaining about being teased unmercifully about something, and I was concerned enough to visit the head of the school. When I told him what my daughter said was happening, he nodded. "We're aware of it, and we're watching to see how it turns out." His detached attitude and his unwillingness to intervene infuriated me, and I told him so. "Why isn't it your job to intervene," I demanded to know, but he was unfazed. "This is a natural part of growing up, and kids have to get tough." We took our child out of that "good enough" school, because that school leader believed in "going with the flow," instead of taking responsibility.

Deborah Meier, a living example of thoughtful responsibility, has her own definition of safety. "A truly safe school is willing to tackle the tough issues. Teachers are confident enough and powerful enough to say, 'Stop everything! We're not going to move until we have made sure this isn't going to happen again.' "

To Meier, nonviolent teasing and other cruelties are connected to physical violence, and she insists that adults have a duty to become involved, to intervene on behalf of those being harassed.

That apparently did not happen at Columbine High School, the scene of the worst school shooting in our history. There, by most reports, athletes dominated classes and hallways and terrorized those who did not fit in. Some teachers watched and laughed when jocks verbally and physically harassed smaller students (including stuffing one student in a locker and closing it). Among those who were victimized were the two young men responsible for the massacre.

Meier is not the only educator who finds fault with the adults who failed to intervene, and she's not the only thoughtful person who believes that the subsequent shootings might have been prevented if adults had said "Stop!" instead of saying, in effect, "Boys will be boys."

Words sting, and it's why excellent schools pay attention to emotional safety. That means that when children are teased, or frightened, or bothered, they feel confident taking their problems to the teachers, and the teachers won't dismiss them. Lisa Delpit told me about a middle school teacher with his own way of handling excessive teasing. Whenever he sees a child being put down, he makes the "putter downer" stand in front of the class and do "put ups." That means the kid has to say good things about the person until the rest of the class feels that there've been a sufficient number and with enough sincerity to count as a "put up."

Ted Sizer says that in excellent high schools adults don't try to stamp out cliques, because they're part of everyday life. "All you have to do is go into a bar or a faculty room, and see the cliques of adults. There's nothing necessarily wrong with it. Every group of kids and adults will form cliques. The kids who like to play music together. The kids who like to fix cars. The thing is to make sure they're benign."

That can be done, Sizer says, by rewarding healthy, positive cliques with support and encouragement. "An excellent school has cliques of kids who say, 'We don't do that here' when something bad comes up." What Sizer worries about are students who seem to take pleasure in harassing and insulting other kids. "Bullies, and the kids who see school as a game and who are very clever cheaters and who push the limits of the school. Those kids need to be dealt with."

Sizer, who has served as principal of two high schools, believes that kids, not adults, actually run schools. Excellent schools recognize this and capitalize on it, Sizer argues. "We have the illusion that we run high schools, but in fact they outnumber us so much that unless there is an alliance of kids and adults that both groups respect, it's pretty hard to run a truly safe school."

When there is such an alliance, kids know that the school is theirs, and they take pride in it. In such a school, students will approach a teacher to express concern about another student, or will ask a teacher to intervene in support of a student who's being ostracized.

"The truly safe school really starts with this alliance, where, if there's going to be some kind of physical violence or violence to ideas (like cheating), a significant number of kids will feel their reputation will be tarnished if something happens, and they will speak out."

I asked Sizer if he thought that schools, perhaps the most autocratic of our institutions, ought to be democratically run. Should high school kids be part of the leadership? "Absolutely," he replied. "Why shouldn't kids that age be?"

He doesn't argue for formal voting but instead for a collective commitment to the school. That entails conversations with students and families, asking them "What is school for, what's good, and what isn't, and what should be done?"

Do kids actually make the rules, I wanted to know? "I think the kids and adults have to make the rules together. Take the issue of drugs in school. Adults cannot keep drugs out of the school unless a significant percentage of kids say, 'we don't do that here.'"

"You can't have enough cops and dogs. Kids are a lot smarter than dogs. You can have searches and you can only have transparent backpacks and all that, but those are desperate steps after the situation is out of control."

Alfie Kohn, who writes often about schools, agrees, "When kids feel that they have a voice, and when they're learning the skills of democratic decision-making by participating and thinking about matters large and small, school-wide and class-wide, then they tend to authentically develop this feeling of loyalty and commitment to the place and to one another so they wouldn't want to deface the walls."[120]

Arnold Packer, the economist who directs the Institute for Policy Studies at Johns Hopkins, goes one step further. Involving kids makes schools safer in all ways. "People want to be part of the solution, and if you don't give them an opportunity to be part of the solution they're going to be part of the problem."[121]

E. D. Hirsch, the founder of the Core Knowledge program, believes that schools are making progress in teaching and modeling tolerance. With a touch of irony, he says, "Maybe our math scores have gone down and maybe our reading scores have gone down, but in general the atmosphere emphasizing tolerance, acceptance, respect has increased. It's taught explicitly, and whenever some intolerant act occurs, it gets a lot of publicity and a lot of disapproval."

In excellent schools, the adults know the students in the building and approach them with respect. School is seen as a shared enterprise, with students as partners in that enterprise. Not equal partners of course, because roles and obligations are different, but students in excellent schools are not objects to be manipulated or watched.

INTELLECTUAL SAFETY

There's something else about excellent schools—they're not just emotionally safe, they're also intellectually safe. As Ted Sizer notes, "There can't be a climate where the kids laugh at the wrong answer. When that happens, a kid will immediately shut down and refuse to participate. And that's when learning stops."

Sizer warmed to the issue. "For me, the ultimate test of a school is the willingness of any student to display his or her ignorance, because the riskiest thing you can do in a school, whatever your age, is to say, 'I don't know' or 'I don't understand.'"

How common is intellectual safety? "It's not as common as it should be," according to E. D. Hirsch. "That's the kind of safety I'm most interested in, because it's the most closely connected to academic achievement, which is what I think schools should be focused on."

Think about what happens in most classrooms when a student admits to not understanding and asks for clarification. Other students snicker and begin teasing their bewildered classmate. In excellent schools, however, a display of ignorance, coupled with a desire to understand, will be applauded. That sounds like a contradiction, but as Sizer notes, "Unless a kid can say, 'I don't get it, I don't understand,' secure in the knowledge that the adults will try to fill that void, genuinely excellent education is impossible. So in a really excellent school, the kids who are struggling, know that their struggle is respected as legitimate, and so they're willing to expose themselves, to be vulnerable."

Parents should take note that they can (and often do) contribute to a climate of "intellectual danger" by putting intense pressure on their children to "get it right" and earn honor grades. Pressure to achieve those external rewards creates an atmosphere in which kids are afraid to explore, afraid to take intellectual risks, and afraid to say "I don't know."

Frank McCourt, the author of *Angela's Ashes* and *'Tis*, taught English at one of New York City's elite public high schools for 18 years, an experience that brought him into daily contact with parental pressure. In his entire career at Stuyvesant, he told me, only one parent asked "Is my son enjoying school?" McCourt was shocked. "Only one. The rest would say things like 'Oh God, is he doing his work?' and 'I'm worried about his PSATs and his SATs' and 'He hasn't finished his application to Yale and Cornell.'"

McCourt says that forced him to question what he was doing with his own life. He began to doubt the direction public education was taking. "We test and test, because we want to make sure a kid fits, but we don't pursue wisdom in any Socratic way. We ought to want to have the kids think for themselves and not to be afraid to think for themselves, but they're discouraged from doing that because they're told all the time 'the test, the test, the test.'"

Intellectual safety means more than being able to say "I don't know." It means that students feel free to think and question and doubt. It also means being free to take unpopular positions. "Schools must encourage the idea of rational persuasion," E. D. Hirsch says. "A student might have some oddball idea like 'the Holocaust never happened.' That would then be discussible, although I would like to think that reason would prevail. It's the old Jeffersonian principle 'We tolerate any error as long as reason is free to combat it.' I would like to feel that we encourage an atmosphere in which we didn't let a false idea go without at least an attempt at rational persuasion."

An intellectually safe school values ideas and exploration. As LuYen Chou says, "It's an environment where students do not feel restricted in their ability to admit what they don't know. And the teachers feel that they can admit that as well." In that environment, Chou says, there's a communal commitment to knowledge building, instead of classrooms where teachers present a set of facts and ideas that students must learn and regurgitate.

Intellectual safety—freedom to make mistakes and to raise questions—allows real teaching and real learning to happen. As writer Alfie Kohn notes, "In excellent classrooms, the teacher is always listening, always watching, to see what kind of mistakes are being made and what information that provides me about how this kid's mind is working."

I asked Kohn for an example. "Let's say the answer to a math problem is 17 but a kid says 18. A lot of caring teachers in 'good enough' classrooms might try to be supportive and sympathetic and say, 'Ooh, you're close.' But that's silly and counterproductive, because the teacher doesn't know why the kid missed. The kid might not understand the underlying principle and just by luck arrived one digit away from the correct answer."

In Kohn's view, the excellent teacher would push to find out how the student arrived at her answer . . . even when the answer is correct. "The teacher shouldn't just say it when the kid's wrong, because you want to know how the student is looking at this issue. What has he gotten or failed to quite grasp that has led to his answer? When a teacher creates a climate of safety where mistakes are truly welcomed, you have a classroom where teachers understand where kids are falling short and why, and so they're in a much better position to help them."

Kohn believes that the more schools focus on competition and rewards, the less intellectually safe they become. That is, the kids who don't win the gold stars get the message, "I'm a loser." And Kohn believes that competition undermines a school's sense of community. "What competition teaches, above all, is that other people are potential obstacles to my own success. And that is a poisonous message, for winner and loser alike, because now we can't take advantage of the kind of collaboration that leads to genuine excellence for everyone."

Intellectual competition actually is both good and natural, in my view, but if students are simply competing for places on the honor roll, it can work against excellence, as Kohn observes.

Competition for grades reduces student's interest in knowledge for its own sake, because, as Kohn says, "If the point is to get an award, or to get a sticker, or to get an A, now I'm less interested in figuring out the problem. I'm not interested in science now; I'm interested in beating someone else."

In a highly competitive environment, Kohn maintains, students are likely to pick the easiest possible tasks, and that's counter-productive if we want kids to pick the most interesting or most challenging. "They figure, all right, the point here is not to try something a little beyond my competence; the point here is to do what I know I can succeed at, pick the shortest book or the easiest project because the point is not understanding and excellence, the point is getting an A."

Kohn would say that truly excellent schools minimize competition, or at least place community first. That's an oversimplification, in my view. I believe that the marketplace of ideas is competitive; the rewards, however, must be more complex and more thoughtful than simple letter grades or other external rewards.

Excellent schools and excellent teachers try to put that sense of purpose first, and teach to the purpose, so that the students understand why they're learning something in the first place. That's a very different mentality from learning a skill or learning a piece of the curriculum in order to pass a test or receive an external reward like an A or getting into college or not making your parents angry.

Let me end with a simple, commonsense test of school safety, whether it's physical, emotional, or intellectual: "Listen to your children." They will tell you, perhaps not directly but by their behavior, whether they feel safe at school. They may want to stay in bed in the morning often, or they'll have mysterious stomachaches, or they'll have lots of unexplained absences. Those are "illnesses" that a visit to the doctor cannot cure, but a visit to the school might.

QUESTIONS TO ASK

- How do adults in the building react when they see students being teased? Bullied?
- Do adults in the building tend to favor one group of students over others?
- Does the school maintain a rigid "zero tolerance" policy? Who established it?
- Does "zero tolerance" apply to even minor pushing and shoving or playground incidents, or do the adults in the building have some leeway?
- What are the school's disciplinary rules and procedures, and have students played a part in establishing the rules? How often are those rules reviewed? By whom?
- Is the number of discipline referrals low? How many suspensions are there? What other alternatives besides suspension are there to teach children proper behavior?
- How is a playground fight handled? Are attacker and victim treated the same?
- How are disabled students treated when they misbehave? Is there a double standard?

7

HOMEWORK AND HOME LEARNING

I've written that the primary purpose of school is intellectual or academic, but it should be clear that I believe that parents are a child's principal teachers, particularly of values and other intangibles. Ideally, parents and teachers see themselves as allies, ready to work together. There are many opportunities for collaboration and cooperation.

In a thoughtful "back to school" column in August 2000 Orange County *Register* columnist Katie Hickox made a dozen or more useful suggestions for ways in which parents may take the first steps toward an alliance with teachers.[122]

Among her suggestions: Introduce yourself to the child's teacher as soon as possible. Shake hands and indicate that you're ready to work together. Start on a positive note. When our children were in elementary school in Washington, D.C., we tried to write a friendly "thank you" note to the teacher the first time our child came home excited about something. We were genuinely appreciative, but we also figured that she would remember us with a smile, instead of a frown.

Hickox, who is a teacher herself, suggests a number of ways that parents can be helpful, including volunteering: "Visit or volunteer in the classroom during a school day. . . . You can also volunteer to correct papers, read with students, or help with dozens of other tasks teachers need completed."

Take steps to boost teachers' status and prestige, such as providing business cards. One year I had cards printed up for one child's teacher (after first asking her what she wanted on the card). My reasoning was that she was a professional, and professionals carried business cards to hand out. It cost about $25.00, as I recall.

Along that line, Hickox suggests providing supplies. "Find out what supplies the teachers need. In addition to supplies purchased by school districts, many teachers spend their own money to enhance their classrooms. Ask your child's teacher if you can donate something. Some language-arts teachers burn through their supply of pencils by December. A math teacher might love to have that old office stationery for scrap paper."

Of course, Hickox urges parents to be involved, to attend Back-to-School nights and parent conferences, and to find out about key school events so they can be sure to attend. Perhaps her most predictable—but nonetheless extremely valuable—suggestion has to do with keeping your cool when your child complains about "unfair" treatment. She writes, "Talk with the teacher about the problems first. Be sure to hear the teacher's side of the story before you try the principal. Sometimes, communication can be garbled, and the 'unfair' detention your child got can turn out to be a necessary disciplinary action."

That's good advice in this litigious society, but my own experience is that, whenever there's a problem, most parents assume that their child is wrong and the teacher is right. Over the years I have heard dozens and dozens of parents say to teachers words to this effect, "If my kid gets out of line, let me know and I will paddle his butt." So if I were writing Hickox's column, I would ask parents to hold off on the paddling, because teachers can be wrong too.

HOMEWORK

Regarding homework, several questions inevitably arise, especially where young children are concerned:

- How much is too much?
- How little is not enough?
- Should children do homework right after school or wait till after dinner?
- Where's the best place to do homework?
- And, finally, how involved should parents be in homework and in the direct teaching of their children?

The answers vary with the age and grade of the child, but a few common-sense observations seem to hold for most cases.

When?

In the old days, most elementary school children came home after school and found their mothers there. Times have changed, most women work outside the home, and many young children are in after-school programs these days. But that doesn't mean kids now do their homework while they're attending the after-school program. In fact, many very good after-school programs deliberately do not provide time and space for doing homework; instead, they are a break from school and consist of organized play, special help, or group activities like art, ceramics, and computers.

That means that, when you pick up your child at 5:30 or 6:00, he or she probably still has homework to do—the only difference being that now there's less time available to do it. Perhaps a general rule here, something like, "Do half of your homework now and the rest after dinner" makes sense—or "Help me with dinner, and then I'll help you with homework." But if your child comes right home after school then I'm all in favor of a break between arriving home and tackling homework assignments.

Where?

All the books suggest a comfortable, well-lighted, quiet, out-of-the-way place for homework, so let me suggest why that can be a bad idea. No matter how comfortable, etc., the place is, if it's the place that you send your child to do homework, then it's inevitably going to be seen as coercion, even punishment.

Most young children are proud to have homework; it's a sign of being "like the big kids." Capitalize on that and try to make homework a pleasant experience. The single best way to do that is to participate when asked, or when you sense you're wanted. That won't happen if you've sent your child away to the comfortable place, and you're in the garden or the kitchen. One of my children often did her homework in the dining room while I was working at the computer in the same room. When she was overly insistent on my participating, I'd say, "We're both working, and I have to get this done. Please don't interrupt."

As children get older, they will decide that they need to be alone to get homework done, and then they will retreat to that comfortable, place. That's when you'll need some general rules about limiting television and telephone use.

How Much? How Little?

Some school districts have rules and guidelines about hours of homework, in reaction to complaints that school was not rigorous enough. In such cases, guidelines make more sense than hard-and-fast rules and that's true at home too.

I think that, as a general rule, children in the first three or four grades should
not be expected to do more than an hour of homework; the workload can be increased as children grow older. But an arbitrary amount of time can be counter-
productive, if your child is having difficulty. For example, homework often involves repetition. The teacher may assign 15 long division problems as a way of
reinforcing that particular process, but if your child stumbles through the first
problem because he or she really doesn't understand, that's a prescription for
frustration and failure.

"An hour of homework" has no meaning in that circumstance. If that happens
a few times, then you probably should let the teacher know that the homework
seems too difficult. The flip side of that is also true: if your child regularly completes his or her homework in short order, to the point of developing contempt
for the assignments, then you might want to talk with the teacher. My own in-
stinct as a parent was to step in with homework whenever I saw signs of frustration, no matter how much time was left of that hypothetical hour.

Excellent principals make sure that teachers work as a team, so that students
in high and middle schools are not saddled with an impossible load of homework—one hour of English homework, two hours of chemistry, an hour of history homework, and so on. That can happen when zealous teachers are out of
contact with their peers.[123]

Looking It Over

Parents would be advised to take a look at their child's homework *after it's been
returned*, because they can tell a lot by what teachers write in the margins of your
child's schoolwork. A few red marks here and there or just a letter grade—even
if it's an A or a B—is not a good sign. Excellent teachers spend a tremendous
amount of time grading and trying to be as meticulous about what they give back
to students as what they're hoping to get from them.

Grading is a teacher's opportunity to have a conversation with the student
about something concrete. Excellent teachers assume that the student has la-
bored over the work. Even if they haven't done a particularly good job, they have
stressed about it and spent a lot of time trying to put it together. Excellent teach-

ers seize that opportunity to enter into a very focused, one-on-one conversation, in comments in the margins, about the work.

But before I set the bar too high, let's not forget that in many American public schools a secondary schoolteacher may be responsible for over 150 students. When I was teaching English in high school in the mid-'60s, I had at least 125 students, and because I had them writing three times a week, I had to grade 375 papers each week. I remember older teachers telling me that I was out of my mind, and I suppose I was. I'd like to think that I wrote thoughtful comments on each and every paper, but I am sure that I did not.

I swapped stories about first-year teaching with LuYen Chou, a former English teacher now developing curriculum for use with computers. Chou is in his thirties, but apparently conditions haven't changed much. "I really wanted my kids to learn how to write, and so my first year I gave every single student a writing assignment twice a week." He laughed, "And those kids really learned how to write, but it killed me. I was up until 3 A.M. every morning, trying to grade these things and get them back to them with sophisticated comments and so on."

What happened, I asked? Chou laughed again. "Some older teachers came to me and told me I was a fool. They said, 'this is the way you assess: just give them multiple-choice quizzes and have them write an essay once a semester. You don't have to do all of this work.'"

So when you're looking over homework, don't be critical if there aren't a lot of comments on *short* papers but expect thoughtful comments on *longer* papers and projects. And it's not a good idea to criticize the teacher in front of children. This will not fix the problem, and could convince the child that it's okay to be rude or defiant to teachers. Plus, since teachers often change grade levels, you may have to work with this person again.

You examine homework carefully because it's a window into your teacher's professionalism. You ought to be hoping to find a sense of passion and energy, as well as a sense of purpose. What you *don't* want to find is evidence that he or she has flipped on the auto pilot switch and is just going through the motions. Because if teaching and grading homework have become rote behavior for the teacher, it won't be long before going to that class becomes a similar experience for your child.

HOW INVOLVED SHOULD YOU BE?

It must be obvious by now that I think parents should be ready and willing to be involved, particularly with young children. If all we do is check up ("Have you finished your homework, dear?" or "May I see your homework, please") we send the wrong message to our children. It's important to be involved. Sometimes involvement means talking about the assignments beforehand, sometimes it means helping, and occasionally it means commiserating with your child about the apparent pointlessness of a particular assignment.

I think, for example that if your young child has grasped the principles and mastered the process of long division after completing seven or eight of those fifteen problems, then it's perfectly all right for her to use the calculator to finish the remaining ones. It makes sense to use a calculator to check answers, as long as you both agree that she'll go back and figure out why and how she got a particular problem wrong. No fair (and poor pedagogy) taking an eraser and just substituting the correct answer.

Ideally, there's a "learning goal" behind every homework assignment, and reaching the goal, not merely completing the homework, is the point here. If your child is struggling academically, pinpoint the problems. Does the teacher keep your child informed about what is correct and incorrect and how to improve? If you notice a problem, don't wait for the teacher to call you—make an appointment fast. There may be extra-help programs after school, or homework hotlines or e-mail chat rooms. If you don't ask, you won't find out.

Of course, there is involvement, and there is *involvement*. I once met a parent who monitored her child's homework so carefully that he was not allowed to make a single mistake. Everything had to be perfect, which meant many hours of frustration for the elementary school child. He was required to rewrite and recalculate until there were no mistakes. I argued with her that he should be allowed to make mistakes, so that the teacher would know what he was not grasping and be able to teach him accordingly. Besides that, she was turning homework into torture, having cast herself in the role of Torquemada.

OUT-OF-SCHOOL LEARNING

I do think, however, that parents can and should be actively involved in their children's learning, particularly in the summer. Which leads to my question: Ever heard of the "learning curve"? It's one of my favorite pieces of educational jargon: *useful* and *accurate* because it conjures up a picture of how most of us learn: fast at first, then more slowly. A typical learning curve[124] climbs steeply and then tapers off until it is level. At that point either no learning is going on—or you've learned it all.

Nobody talks about a "forgetting curve," but it exists. Want proof? Ask some students a week or two after school lets out for the summer to name the wives of Henry VIII, key battles in the Franco-Prussian War, or some basic principles of physics. Even if your children were honor students in excellent schools, you will see the forgetting curve in action.

The learning curve is natural and normal. We humans are curious by nature, and we learn what we need or want to know. The forgetting curve can be flattened, however, and learning can be locked in for life—or at least for the summer.

Parents can do their part, but not by emulating school. The trick is to be as unlike school as possible, actually, because schools *teach*, and you want learning, discovery, challenges, and adventure—anything *but* overt teaching.

Here are four learning experiences for children, ages 5–14, that will stick. Your children will learn important lessons about money, cooperation, argumentation, and decision-making, all of which should count for more than simply knowing about Catherine of Aragon, Anne Bolelyn, Jane Seymour, Anne of Cleves, Katherine Howard, and Kathryn Parr.[125]

Activity #1. You'll need an inexpensive, easy-to-operate cassette tape recorder for this one. Set it up, turn it on, and you're on your way. Perhaps you might begin with a mock "news" program in which you report on what you had for breakfast. Then "interview" your children about their breakfast, their birthdays, whatever. Look for an opportunity to hand the microphone to the most eager child, and then fade into the background. If the children are old enough to operate the machine themselves, show them which buttons to push and then head for the kitchen. They'll have great fun making up stuff and replaying it. When that fascination begins to fade, bring out a few pots and spoons. Add a radio tuned to a music station, and the children can turn themselves into a hot new band . . . for hours. I recall how my small children spent many happy hours making music and news. No fights, no television, and some welcome time alone for their parents. I believe they also learned lessons about creativity and cooperation.

Activity #2. Summertime is businesstime for many suburban children, whether it's a lemonade stand, a book sale, yard work, or a car wash. Selling lemonade is a hardy perennial, so let's use that example. Call me Scrooge if you wish, but I always made my children repay about half of the initial investment in lemons, frozen lemonade, paper cups, and sugar. Here why: having a real debt transforms their lemonade stand into an "adult" business. The children understand (without lectures from you) that they're not just playing; they have to produce or lose their shirts. Under my repayment plan, I got half of the gross until half of their debt was repaid—I forgave the other half.

In my old neighborhood on a hot weekend, a lemonade stand was big business, and so I was forced to work out a way to deal with my (relatively) wealthy children. Because it's never too early to learn that you don't *have* to spend every cent you earn and because I wasn't willing to order them to save, I created an incentive: I offered to match, dollar for dollar, whatever they would deposit into a savings account/money market. I followed that practice for about twelve years with three children, and it cost me about $5,000. To me, that was a bargain, because they learned valuable lessons about making, saving, and using money.

Activity #3. This is much less structured than the first two; in fact, it's more of a game, inspired by political campaigning and the debates among candidates. Whenever our younger children proposed something like a movie, a special dinner, staying up late, or a sleepover, we asked to hear a one-minute speech in favor of the proposal. I usually served as moderator, turning from one "candidate" to another, then calling for a "vote." At first, we had no time limit, but we learned that limiting their speaking time made the whole game more "real." After all, that's how candidates do it on TV! We learned that the issue had to be real and the tone light. But do not play this game too often, because once your children suspect that you're trying to teach them logical thinking, techniques of persuasion, anything at all, the jig is up.

Activity #4. Reading aloud, and reading silently. Do these two as often as possible. When you read to your children, and when your children see you reading, you are teaching lessons about the value of reading they won't forget. What do you read? Not just Harry Potter books, but also letters, recipes, and ingredients on packages and cans. You are modeling behavior you want your children to emulate. They're learning that reading is the cornerstone of all that follows. Once they *want* to be readers, they will be.

All of these activities are learning experiences that teach children to value themselves and their connections with others. Just as the brain is a muscle that needs to be exercised, learning is a habit that's hard to break, and curiosity is a virtue to be encouraged.

Activities like these[126] bring an added benefit: they keep kids away from the most forgettable activity of all: watching television.

So what "rules" emerge? Nothing hard-and-fast beyond the general belief that we parents are our children's primary teachers—whether we want to be or not (and "don't torture your children"). And because young children often enjoy having homework, the more we can do to help them maintain that attitude, the better off everyone is. Rules and procedures make sense because they provide children with structure and order, but homework is not (repeat NOT) the center of anyone's existence—and so flexibility is the first rule of all.

Learning and schooling are not synonymous, and so parents should not shy away from creating structured learning experiences for their children, always taking care that they do not turn themselves into schoolmasters or their homes into some cruel parody of school.

QUESTIONS TO ASK

- Are there only a few teachers that every parent seems to want, or are there good teachers in all classrooms?
- Are there hands-on lessons?
- Is homework meaningful?
- If you ask a teacher what his or her "learning goals" are for the week ahead, does he or she merely describe the week's homework assignments? If so, press for an explanation of the former, because homework is supposed to be related to the teacher's goals.
- Is there a "homework hotline" or some other ways that students who need help can get it?
- How much time passes between an assignment's being turned in and its return?
- Are papers marked up with thoughtful comments?
- Do teachers make an effort to reach parents if homework is not being turned in, or if it's being done poorly?
- Is your child doing his homework during classtime? This is generally not a good sign, because classtime is supposed to be for exploring new ideas and for new learning.

- Does your child have very little homework? Most schools have homework policies that set minimums and maximums. Find out about the rules and figure out if your child's teacher is asking enough of his or her students. Low expectations are a major problem in American schools, so be on the lookout.
- Is there an active PTA that works to support the teachers by, for example, accompanying field trips?
- Do parents and school work to create a sense of community by, for example, publishing a directory or holding community events like a flea market or yard sale and class picnics?
- Are there clear ways that new parents can become involved? A PTA that holds meetings in an officer's home is a problem PTA.

8

OUR KIDS ARE NOT
THE PROBLEM

While the theme of this book is "bad, good enough, and excellent," those terms do not apply to children. "God didn't make no junk," a young child once said, explaining why she mattered. All of our children matter, and all deserve opportunities to achieve and grow. Unfortunately, there is what you might call an "anti-youth virus" in our country. Just how much harm it's doing may be debatable, but its existence is not.

"It's not racism. They just don't like kids." The words came from 13-year-old Paul, a streetwise Latino boy from Manhattan, but the insight was echoed by other young adolescents, black, white, and Latino. "Sometimes grown-ups will cross the street when they see us coming," another youth observed.

"Youth" is the operative word, because Paul and the 13 others we shadowed for nine months for a television documentary series ranged in age from 11 to 14. That is, they're not hulking 18-year-olds. In fact, at only 5'6", Paul towered most of his peers, and yet adults kept their distance.

Teacher Alec Mahre supports Paul's observation. "I've heard policemen refer to the kids as 'animals' just because they were laughing and talking loudly on the street," notes Mahre, a science teacher at a Manhattan middle school. Mahre understands what these kids are really like. "They want to be grown up, and they think they're grown up, but they're still at an age where they need others to solve their problems or they need attention about something."[127]

I've met dozens of adults who admit to crossing the street if they see a group of urban teenagers coming their way. "I know I shouldn't react that way because they're just kids," a distinguished African-American woman once said to me at dinner, "but I can't help being scared."

Adult perceptions of kids are strikingly negative. An astonishing 74 percent of parents say that teenagers are "rude, irresponsible, and wild," and 58 percent describe children as "lazy and spoiled." As to the future, 57 percent of parents say that today's teenagers will make little difference in America's progress—and might even make America worse.[128] In 1997 Public Agenda surveyed adult attitudes and reported "Most Americans look at today's teenagers with misgivings and trepidation, viewing them as undisciplined, disrespectful, and unfriendly." The report said that adults feel this way about all teens, regardless of race, gender, or economic status.[129] Why do so many adults feel this way? I think it's the traditional generation gap, exacerbated by media stereotypes and by sensational coverage of the occasional outrage.

In *Ordinary Resurrections*, his sensitive portrayal of young kids in the South Bronx, Jonathan Kozol writes, "The emphasis on 'differentness' in inner city kids has been a part of sociology as long as inner cities have existed, I suppose. When I was a young teacher, 'the culture of poverty' was an accepted phrase. Similar phrases have been canonized in decades since."[130] He goes on to condemn the "wholesale labeling of inner city children," particularly by those who suggest in their writings that children in the inner city are not really children but "premature adults," perhaps precocious criminals or "predators."[131]

Actually, the young kids have fears of their own, and what they are afraid of might surprise you. "I'm afraid of the world coming to the end," Miguel Molina told us. Renata Mills says she's afraid of aliens, while Stephanie Dowie admitted, "I worry about sometimes if I wake up in the morning, my mom won't be there." Davon Carter, a 12-year-old boy who watches a lot of TV, told us he worries a lot about "Kidnappers and rapists. Sometimes that kind of scares me."

THE ANTI-YOUTH MOOD

What these kids are seeing and feeling, it seems to me, is the widespread anti-youth virus that's polluting our society. Researcher Meg Bostrom reports that today only 15 percent of American adults believe that young people had a strong sense of right and wrong, a sharp contrast to the 52 percent of adults who felt that way in 1952.[132] Consider the media—particularly television, magazines, and talk radio. The past several years have seen a spate of sensational coverage of youth crime, coverage that suggests that the nation is in the grip of a teenage crime wave of unprecedented proportions, even though the opposite is true.

A "child free" movement is growing, encouraged by books like Elinor Burkett's "The Baby Boom: How Family-Friendly America Cheats the Childless." Gated communities ban children, and there are hotels that warn patrons that children under 18 are not allowed on the premises unless they are paying guests. The organization No Kidding now has 47 chapters, up from two chapters just five years ago. Child-free Web sites are sprouting, visited by childless baby boomers, who now number 13,000,000.[133]

Between 1997 and 1999 virtually every publication on the magazine food chain put adolescents on its cover: *Time, Newsweek, U.S. News & World Report, People*, the *National Enquirer*, and on down the ladder. While isolated crimes like the murders at Columbine High School are reprehensible, the overall effect of such prolonged coverage has been to suggest that young people in America are often anti-social, depraved, and dangerous.[134]

Today, it seems to me, adult reactions to adolescents are negative and counterproductive. Or, as Karen Hein, president of the W. T. Grant Foundation, has said, "Adult attitudes can be toxic for teens."

What adult attitudes? One young high school student shocked an audience of state superintendents of education with her blunt analysis. "Adults don't respect teenagers or youth," she said. "Students are not seen as people. They're babysitting charges. You don't get respected. You don't get looked at, just glared at. . . . It's terrible the way they pounce on you."[135]

Just as harmful may be the attitudes of policymakers who view youth as a "cost-effective social investment." Jonathan Kozol writes of adults whose policy discussions "seem to view them less as children who have fingers, elbows, stomachaches, emotions, than as 'economic units'—pint-sized deficits or assets in blue jeans and jerseys, some of whom may prove to be a burden to society, others of whom may have some limited utility."[136] Can adults who speak of children and adolescents in these terms, and see them through an economic lens, connect with them on a human level?

They could . . . *if* they would spend a few days in their world. In 1995 we entered that world to talk with children about violence, a few days after a mother in Brooklyn lost her third son to gunfire. In the resulting PBS documentary, *Caught in the Crossfire*, young children spoke matter of factly about their daily lives. When I asked how many had seen guns, nearly every hand went up, nearly every child had a story to tell.

LaToya Burden, age seven, saw her uncle Gary die. He was held up just outside his home late one night. He refused to turn over any money and was killed.

Derrick Buggs was five when he saw his father get shot as he was on the way to the corner store.

Karim Smith was ten when a deranged man "with a big gun" held it to his head and pulled the trigger twice. It misfired.

Shawntrice Saunders, 15, is too scared to go outside to get the mail, so she stays indoors except when she's in school.

Yolanda Gates is a ten-year-old who was shot in the face while she and her sister were skipping rope in front of their apartment building. The bullet passed through both cheeks, miraculously missing her teeth and tongue.

But children are resilient, able to dream of a better future, and their hopes and dreams are not much different from those of privileged children in wealthy suburbs or urban private schools.

Ten-year-old Sytra Barrett wants to be a lawyer, a dress designer, or a track runner. When she was eight, she saw her uncle Danny shot.

Nine-year-old Shakia Sellers hopes to be either an artist or a lawyer.

Twelve-year-old Marcus McDonald wants to be a professional basketball player for a few years so he can make money to give to his grandmother ("because she's poor"). Then he'd like to be a policeman. Marcus's brother, a drug addict, robbed their mother only a few days after being released from prison.[137]

OUR OFFICIAL OVERREACTION:
ZERO TOLERANCE

Today's so-called "zero tolerance" policies stand as an example of anti-youth hysteria, a strong overreaction to a string of horrible, but isolated events like the school shootings. Karen Pittman, senior vice president of the International Youth Foundation, has observed that until recently the one certainty for American youth was schooling—the right to an adequate education. "But increasingly the rights of individual young people are being cut off," she wrote in *Youth Today*, the monthly paper published by the American Youth Work Center. "Education is headed down the slippery slope toward becoming not a right but a privilege. This willingness to suspend individual educational rights . . . reflects the development of a new certainty for U.S. youth: jail."[138]

Even adults who care about young people may be adding to the problem by emphasizing the uniqueness of adolescence. When they do that, those sympathetic observers inadvertently contribute to the view that the adolescents themselves are the *cause* of their problems. Once you believe that adolescent problems are the adolescents' fault, then the range of possible solutions is limited to finding ways to either change the kids . . . or isolate them from the rest of us.

An even greater danger is our demand for instant solutions, our search for the mythical "silver bullet" that will make all problems disappear. So we find state legislatures debating the death penalty for children, for example, as if that would solve complex social problems, and "getting tough on crime" by juveniles. Massachusetts law allows 14-year-olds to be sent to adult prisons; in Oregon, it's 12. Wisconsin, 10. Between 1985 and 1997 the number of young people under 18 incarcerated in adult prisons more than doubled, from 3,400 to 7,400. One in ten juveniles being held is locked up in adult jails or prisons. In 1994, according to the American Civil Liberties Union, 45 children met their deaths in adult prisons. All of this is happening even though juvenile crime has been *decreasing* for the past *six* years.

Just as it is illogical and wrong to assume that adolescents are the problem, so too is it wrong-headed to think that the solution is to punish, restrict, curtail, or refuse to support them.

THE KIDS ARE OK

Our reporting for PBS provides a powerful antidote to the anti-youth virus. For most of 1998, we shadowed 14 young adolescents, ages 11 to 14, as they made their way around New York City. These young adolescents are typical kids, representative of the 99 percent who never make the nightly news. Their lives contradict the myths about adolescents that dominate adult thinking and adult rule making. They were grappling with issues of identity, belonging, freedom, and control, just as adolescents always have. They may be defiant, and they may look and sound older, but they're still in need of adult guidance, just as we were when we were teenagers.

What's changed for adolescents today? For one thing, fewer supports and services are available. We found that most young adolescents are left on their own every day after school until their parent or parents got home from work. The plethora of supervised activities that I remember from my youth simply weren't available for these kids. Much of what was available cost money, putting it out of reach of many working families.

These kids swim in a sea of media, and many of the messages urge them to act older . . . and to buy, buy, buy![139] Sexual messages dominate the media,[140] and several young girls, ages 12 to 14, told us stories about predator males, usually 19 to 25, who tried to entice them into sexual relationships. "When one of them asks me for my phone number," one 13-year-old girl told us, "I smile and ask him for his number and tell him that I will call him. Later on I just throw the paper away."

Their teacher, Theresa Jinks, is appalled by this predatory behavior. "We need to watch out on the street for people who don't seem to care about their growth. We need to let these children take their time to grow because they need to catch up emotionally and socially with their bodies. If we, as adults, are infringing on that time by making passes at them because their bodies look appealing, then we have, as a society, lost our way."

Current data about our youth also contradict myths and stereotypes. The declines in youth crime, teen pregnancy, and high school dropouts have been accompanied by increases in educational accomplishments. SAT and ACT scores are up, as is enrollment in advanced placement courses. Between 1984 and 1997, the number of AP exams taken by high schools students nearly tripled. Minority students make up 30 percent of test-takers, up from 22 percent a decade ago.[141]

More girls are taking higher-level math and science courses including chemistry and physics,[142] and enrollment in algebra II and trigonometry increased by more than 50 percent between 1982 and 1994. According the National Assessment of Educational Progress (NAEP), science achievement is improving, with black and Hispanic students making the largest gains.[143] Reading scores have not improved very much, and math scores are mixed, with kids doing well on more complex mathematical thinking, less well on basic skills.[144]

In short, there's ample reason for us to be applauding our kids, giving them at least two cheers—and probably three—considering that we've put so many hurdles in their path to becoming successful adults.

DISSECTING THE MYTHS

Laura Sessions Stepp, a reporter for the *Washington Post*, has argued persuasively[145] that society accepts, without much examination or reflection, ten popular myths about adolescence:

1. *Adolescents yearn to be independent of adults, particularly their parents, and we must let go of them so they can establish autonomy.* Here are the facts: Only a minority of teenagers engages in wholesale rebellion against their parents. What most young people seek is not separation from their parents but opportunities to renegotiate their relationship as time passes. Several surveys have shown that most young people want closer contact with adults, including their parents. Most teenagers describe their parents as supportive and caring, and they add that they know other adults they can talk to.

Adolescents need connections to adults in order to refrain from dangerous habits, do well in school, and find their place in the world. These connections are primarily defined by love, respect, and high expectations.

2. *Adolescents are dangerous.* Again, here are the facts: Adults are responsible for three-fourths of any increases in violent crime. Four out of five juveniles murdered are likely to have been killed by adults, including family members. The rise in juvenile arrests for violent crimes exactly parallels the increase in gun-related crime. As noted earlier, juvenile crime has been declining for six years. Arrests of juveniles for violent crimes dropped 19 percent between 1994 and 1998, more than three times the rate that adult crime has declined.

3. *Adolescents don't need regular health care because, in general, they're pretty healthy.* The facts: Somatic health complaints are on the rise, as are incidents of stress-related diseases such as asthma. In short, some young people today are adopting health patterns that will have serious repercussions in later life: smoking, overeating, and not getting enough exercise are good examples.

Moreover, adolescents experience major distress in about the same proportion (one in five) as adults do.

On the other hand, many adolescents seem to be making better decisions about their own lives: drug use has dropped dramatically from the peaks of the late 1970s. Of the 4,300 heroin deaths in 1998 and the 38,000 hospital emergency cases in the first half of 1999, fewer than 1 percent were teens.[146] Drinking among teens has decreased, and teen deaths from drunk driving accidents have declined 59 percent since 1982.

4. *Adolescents are lazy and irresponsible.* The facts: Young people have an enormous desire to be useful and needed. They often seek tasks that challenge them and can make a difference. We need to create and expand opportunities that tap into their energy and idealism. To their credit, more adolescents are staying in school *and* getting involved in service projects in their communities. High school students are taking more challenging courses, girls are closing the gender gap in math and science, and SAT scores are up from two decades ago. More and more students are going to college.

5. *Adolescence starts with the teenage years.* The facts: It begins with puberty, which can begin as early as age eight or nine; moreover, the hormonal changes associated with puberty can start a couple of years before physical changes. Adolescence doesn't have an exact ending either, and the transition to adulthood (when growth stops) can extend into the twenties.

6. *Adolescents are merely "raging hormones," walking around thinking about sex every waking hour of the day.* The facts: While the secretion of sex hormones affects every tissue of the body, including the brain, the effect is not as potent as most people believe and does not make adolescents inherently difficult. Adult expectations of, and behavior toward, young people affects kids as much as, if not more than, biology. To their credit, however, fewer teens are getting pregnant these days (although American teen pregnancy rates are still higher than those in other industrialized countries). For most adolescents, the big issues are identity and intimacy—figuring out who you are and who you want to be with. We diminish the importance of this time in their lives when we focus too narrowly on sex.

7. *Adolescents are vain and egotistical; all they care about is how they look.* The facts: Adolescence is a time of physical, emotional, and cognitive growth unmatched in the life cycle, with the possible exception of infancy. What appears to be vanity is often an attempt to understand one's rapid development. In adolescence, for the first time, young people are intellectually able to contrast themselves with others, which can result in a deep sense of insecurity and loneliness.

8. *Brains shut down during adolescence, and adolescents are incapable of learning anything serious.* The facts: Adolescents develop the ability to think abstractly, reflectively, and critically. Young adolescents from 10 to 15 enjoy a curiosity about the world unmatched in the life cycle. Older youths develop the capacity for moral thought. Brain research shows a resurgence of brain activity during adolescence, the last major spurt of brain growth. Because the brain operates according to a "use it or lose it" rule, we ought to be providing positive

stimuli and challenging learning opportunities for adolescents, not conceding the field to popular culture and peer influence.

The adolescents we spent a year with were asking themselves serious questions, even as they were being rambunctious. As Ramon Gonzales, their math teacher, noted, "They're starting to ask deep questions about racial identity at this stage. 'Why am I called black, if I'm light-skinned?' 'Why am I called black if my parents speak Spanish?' 'Why am I called white if I speak Spanish?' You know these are not the usual questions that adults ask. Adults just say, 'Oh you're light, you're white. Oh you're dark, you're black.'"

These young people, if their schools take them seriously and challenge them, respond in kind. As John Goodlad, the dean of American education researchers, said on NPR, "They tend to be involved in long-term pursuits, where they're sharing, where they're reading, where they're bringing in ideas, and where they're bringing things from home. They are in effect 'into learning,' rather than merely gathering it together so they can put it back on a test. You don't see these youngsters just bending over their desks all day long doing workbooks and the like. You see them engaged in serious conversation about what they're trying to do."[147]

9. *Adolescents take risks because they think they are invulnerable.* The facts: The proportion of kids who believe "It can't happen to me" is no higher than the proportion in the adult population. They know they're not invulnerable: Many have been either victims of crime or know victims; they know people with AIDS and people who sell guns or drugs. Adolescents take risks because exploration and risk-taking—inherent to the species—are means of testing and learning about themselves. They are able to distinguish between healthy risks (team sports, for example) and unhealthy ones.

10. *Adolescents are negatively influenced by their peers.* The facts: In matters of dress, music, and language, adolescents look to their peers, but on the big issues—what is important in life, how to relieve stress, how to have healthy relationships, what kind of job to look for—adolescents are far more influenced by parents and other adults. Moreover, peers can be beneficial: they listen, care, and encourage playfulness and exploration. They also can contribute to a young person's self-esteem and desire for achievement.

As Karen Pittman of the International Youth Foundation notes, "Young people should be encouraged and expected to be learners, implementers, advocates, philanthropists, organizers, funders, critics, planners, and leaders."[148]

In some places, these things are happening. Boston has "City Year," Philadelphia has "Urban Retrievers," Oakland has "HOME," New York City has

"Beacons," San Francisco has "the East Bay Conservation Corps," and Minneapolis has "Public Achievement." The list of worthy programs for and by kids could take up many pages of this book. My own nonprofit organization, Learning Matters, has a national program called Listen Up! that trains disadvantaged young people to be media producers. It's active in 50 communities. The International Youth Foundation and the Rural School and Community Trust call attention to good works, as do the American Youth Policy Forum and the monthly newspaper *Youth Today*.[149]

Our 1999 PBS series, *Growing Up in the City*, also contradicts the clichés about our youth. One lesson to be drawn from those three PBS documentaries is that excellent schools and caring, competent teachers make a difference. The New York City public middle schools that Miguel, Villorii, Raymond, and the other adolescents attended worked hard to support, nurture, and educate—no small challenge in a society that doesn't seem to offer much support for either families or children. Teachers who care, working in a system that supports their mission, increase the odds that adolescents will develop into healthy and productive adults—despite our anti-youth culture.

Of course, there's work to be done even in excellent schools. We need more counseling and mentoring programs that connect students with caring adults in and out of school. We need teaching methods that emphasize how academic work connects to the real world, and we need more teachers who understand that children and youth learn in different ways, that brains grow in spurts, and that attention spans are variable. We need aggressive efforts to challenge all students to complete ambitious academic programs, and we need support systems to help them get as far as they can possibly go.

Children and adolescents need and want adult guidance, support, and companionship. As the number of children increases from 70 million in 1999 to a projected 77.6 million in 2020, we cannot continue to dis-invest in young people, turn our backs on them, and then dismiss them as "dangerous" or worse. That's not only a self-fulfilling prophecy; it's also a sure-fire recipe for social disaster.

QUESTIONS TO ASK

- What is the extent of after school programs for youth? Are these programs open to all? Oversubscribed? Free?

- Are there active chapters of Boys and Girls Clubs, the 4-H, the Scouts, the Police Athletic League, and other youth groups?
- Do schools have a "zero tolerance" policy? If so, was there much debate before it was adopted? Who was involved in the debate? Were parents and community groups heard from?
- What is rate of school suspension? Have there been expulsions? Are members of any particular racial or ethnic groups being suspended at higher rates?
- What do the schools do to promote links between students and parts of the community?
- Are there community service projects that link students with adults, such as helping out in senior centers?
- Are middle schools arranged into small learning communities with a strong emphasis on social-emotional development and intellectual growth?
- Does the curriculum emphasize the beginning of planning for the future (or does it hide behind stereotypes like "raging hormones" as an excuse for not taking these kids seriously)?
- Are high schools arranged so that all students cover all of the academics needed to qualify to attend a four-year college, even if the school is set up in career academies that also focus on the world of work?
- Is there adequate counseling (and other support services) for all students, perhaps including a mentor, parents, and teachers?
- Does the school provide time so teachers can talk with one another about pedagogy and the progress of students?
- What is the spirit of the school? Is it like a family, or a parole board? Does everyone in the school know what they want for students, and is everyone committed to helping them get there?
- Is there time for build this essential spirit—in meetings, celebrations of success, retreats, and everyday conversations?
- Is it a student-centered school? Are students part of creating the spirit? Does the school offer many ways for students to be listened to and be included in the decision making?
- Is this a school where you would like to spend some of your own time?

9

VALUES AND EXCELLENCE

Students of American education history know that public schools have been serving many masters since their inception. We've asked schools to provide an academic foundation, prepare workers, build good citizens, develop upright moral character, and cultivate every child's individual talents. Whether these goals would be achievable in a perfect world is debatable; it's certain that we've never come close in the real world.

With so many goals and limited debate about the purposes of schooling, educators have been left twisting in the wind, subject to "movements," fads, whims, and panaceas. Teachers get pilloried, but the responsibility for the situation lies with school boards, parents, and the general public for failing to get beyond the superficial. Schools cannot help but teach values, and the sooner we acknowledge that fact and debate its significance, the closer we will be to clarity. A close look at how schools teach values reveals just how far we are from achieving excellence.

Some of the controversy over teaching values seems to result from semantic confusion. I have the sense that the word "values" connotes either controversial beliefs (abortion or premarital sex) or simply open disagreement, which makes many adults uncomfortable.[150] Attach the adjective "traditional" to values, however, and the public's temperature goes down in a flash. Thus, a widely respected poll reveals that 97 percent of the public wants the schools to teach "honesty," 92 percent endorse teaching "patriotism," and 84 percent are behind teaching the "golden rule."[151]

How do schools teach values? Are there practices that one can identify as "excellent" when it comes to what schools do to shape the character of our young? The discussion is inevitable and unavoidable, because schools and the adults who run them (whether bad, good enough, or excellent) model and teach with every action, every policy. For years, public schools claimed to be value-free, even as they were heavy-handed in preaching such values as cooperation, sharing, politeness, and the "golden rule."[152] This logically impossible posture has twisted many schools into an untenable, unworkable position, making them what one observer calls "morally dangerous places for children."

"Morally dangerous places for children." The striking phrase seemed to hang in the air, resonating with complexity. Is that what our public schools have become, Boston University professor of education Kevin Ryan was asking me? I had been traveling around the country visiting schools, searching for values, and I had ended up on Professor Ryan's doorstep. Not by mistake, of course, for he's been thinking about the issues of character and values for many years, and he's an old friend as well.

"What does that mean, 'morally dangerous'?" I asked. His answer is that schools have bent over backward in their efforts not to offend anyone about anything. To make themselves inoffensive and studiously neutral, they have all but "cleansed" the curriculum of anything even vaguely resembling religious or ethical content.

The result is anti-historical, boring, misleading, and (in Ryan's view at least) morally dangerous for children.

A CAUTIONARY TALE

Let me go back to my own journey. It began several years ago in a small town in Pennsylvania, where the school district was torn apart in a battle over values. It's a familiar tale, one you may have read about or seen on the evening news.[153] It's always presented as a battle between the religious right, on one side, and the "values clarification" lefties on the other—with schools, students, and teachers suffering in the middle.

In fact, it's not hard to find right-wing zealots who know what's best for all of us, when it comes to values. They have taken over the spotlight and the leadership roles. "It's fine for children to discuss *Romeo and Juliet*, because that's history," a school board member told me, "but I hope the teacher will tell the students that, today, abstinence is better." Or there was the parent who said to me, "These children were given to me by God, and I will raise them."

The "lefties" are very much in evidence, too, arguing that children need to develop their own values because so many parents won't do the job.

The zealots on the right succeeded in drafting a "Parents' Bill of Rights," which (had it passed) would have given parents in that small town the right to withdraw their children from any class or class discussion they found potentially offensive. The proposal was eventually tabled (and the school board member who pushed for it was subsequently defeated in his reelection bid), but it's had a chilling effect nonetheless.

Here's what four high school students in one class told me:

"In school we're not allowed to say certain things. The school board is kind of trying to keep us in a cage or something like that. They're trying to block us off from the real world."

"We were reading *To Kill a Mockingbird* and we were talking about the prejudice against black people, and the teacher said, 'Well, I really don't think we should go into this much.' So it's kind of like she touched on it, about how people are prejudiced, but she didn't want to go into the feelings about it and everything. It was like she was afraid that if it went home that we talked about prejudice in front of the class that somehow it was going to hurt her or something."

"We weren't allowed to talk about race or racial things. I mean, how are you supposed to teach, like, black heritage if you can't talk about blacks? I mean, I just don't think that's right."

"For my book report, I picked a book about a little girl who had AIDS. And my English teacher stopped me in the middle of my report and told me that I couldn't talk about that because it wasn't appropriate for English class. But that was the assignment—to pick a non-fiction book, read it, and give a report to that class and tell them what it was about. What kind of education is that?"

VALUES AND THE CURRICULUM

"What kind of education is that?" Everyone who cares about learning ought to answer her question. It's not even "good enough," because children who are taught to be afraid of ideas grow up into ignorant, easily led adults.

We ought to acknowledge that older students recognize the "retreat from controversy" approach to education for what it is, and hold it in contempt.

In that town, some teachers are running scared. I asked a veteran (tenured) high school teacher what he would do if a student wanted to talk to him about feeling one way and his parents feeling another. He didn't hesitate. "My only re-action is, 'You're living in your parents' house, so act accordingly.'"

I pushed him. What if the student holds a value that you personally admire—tolerance for people of another religion—and he comes to you and says, "Sir, my parents are really anti-Semitic, or anti-Amish. I don't think that's right but I don't know what to do."

Again the teacher did not hesitate to support the parents, so I kept on push-ing. Suppose the kid is in tears and asks you directly, "How can I love my mother and my father when they have so much hate for the Amish or the Jews?" What would you say?

The teacher squirmed, "I can't comment, I don't know." After a minute he said, "I'd say, 'They're your parents. When you're with your parents you better do as your parents say. When you leave home then you make your own deci-sions.'"

Did he always try to avoid tough issues, I asked? He nodded, "I won't say I always succeed, but I try to."

Aren't you teaching a value lesson right there, I asked him? He agreed that he was, but he defended his position. "In this day and age I have to be very, very careful, because I could be sued. A parent could take me to task on this. I try not to interfere with what the parent is trying to pass on to their children, and I don't find that cowardly at all."[154]

To me, that's "morally dangerous" education at its worst. Fear of ideas, fear of conflict, and blind obedience—that's one heck of a lesson to teach students—but I don't blame the teacher. He's behaving sensibly, sad to say, given the in-flamed passions.

In that community, the rotting away probably started at the top; it began ear-lier, and it took years. That is, the schools didn't become a battleground overnight. It took years of what I'll call a high-level policy of cowardice, before they became a battleground.

In a thoughtful essay in the *Wilson Quarterly*, Charles Glenn places the blame for widespread confusion among teachers over values squarely upon those who trained them, the teacher educators. The professors taught neophyte teachers to be "even-handed" and "value free." Above all, they were told, don't "impose your values" on your students. "But good teaching," Glenn writes, "is all about urging those we teach to accept what we believe to be true and worthy of their acceptance. Bad teaching imposes values, too, and schools that are incoherent are not neutral or 'value free.' Cynicism, indifference to truth, disinclination to carry out tasks thoroughly, and disrespect for others—all of these can be learned in school."

Glenn writes further, "Only schools with a distinctive character to which staff and parents alike are committed can shape the character of pupils in positive ways. This is one reason why Catholic schools now enroll many non-Catholics, and some Evangelical schools serve pupils from non-Evangelical families. Parents in these cases perceive that a school centered on a religious ethos, even if it is not their own ethos, is more likely to reflect their own convictions about the good life they want for their children than a school without such a common ground."[155]

TEACHING VALUES: OTHER VIEWS

E. D. Hirsch Jr. would probably say "amen" to Glenn's analysis. I spoke with Professor Hirsch, the creator of the Core Knowledge school reform program and the author of *The Schools Our Children Need*, in the book-lined study in his Charlottesville, Virginia, home.[156] I wanted to know whether most public schools were intellectually safe places where students felt free to be curious.

"It's not as common as it should be," he said. "If I were running a school, that's the atmosphere I would encourage." Excellent schools, in Hirsch's view, value curiosity and rational persuasion. "Suppose a student has some oddball idea like 'the Holocaust never happened.' That should be discussible, but you would like to think that reason would prevail. It's like the old Jeffersonian principle: we tolerate any error as long as reason is left free to combat it."

Hirsch says that there's one best way to create that atmosphere in a school. "Model it. Create a community where intellectual inquiry is valued and where saying 'I don't know' is okay."

Hirsch, who is known for his work in elementary schools, believes that all levels of schooling should emphasize intellectual curiosity and openness. "Of all places, schools shouldn't be afraid of ideas. There has to be safety, safety to say 'I don't know' and safety also to say 'I don't agree.'"

Professor Hirsch is generally portrayed as an educational conservative, and his views upset many liberals. However, his position on this issue mirrors that of Ted Sizer, the liberal educator who founded the Coalition of Essential Schools, another prominent school reform. Now officially retired from Brown University and the Coalition of Essential Schools, Sizer remains as busy as ever writing and helping direct a new charter school, with his wife, Nancy. When I interviewed him[157] (in *his* book-lined study in rural Massachusetts) he was eager to talk about the importance of modeling of academic values.

"The ultimate test of a school is the willingness of any student to display his or her ignorance. The most risky thing anyone can do in a school, whatever your age, is to say 'I don't know. I don't get it.' But in an excellent school, the display of ignorance is applauded." He smiled at his apparent contradiction, and my puzzled look. "Unless kids can say, 'I don't get it' secure in the knowledge that the teacher is going to try to fill that void, the school is not intellectually safe."

I recalled advising my son to ask his teacher whenever he didn't understand something, to which he said, vehemently, "Dad, you don't understand. My teacher is the last person I want to know that I don't get it."

Sizer acknowledged that most schools function that way. And he added that in "good enough" schools students add to the problem. "In excellent schools kids don't laugh at wrong answers. When that happens, the kid who made the mistake immediately shuts down. Embracing mistakes and celebrating searching for the truth, that's a very difficult culture to create. When it works, when the reaction of kids is 'let me help you' instead of laughter, that warms the heart."

Sizer and his wife, Nancy, are the authors of a valuable book about kids called *The Students Are Watching*.[158] Its message is clear: kids learn what is and what is not from what they see around them, even the little things. Sizer added, "I have little patience with curricula in 'Character Education' in a school which is blatantly disrespectful of teachers, kids and serious ideas. The youngsters learn much more from what we do than from what we say."[159]

Excellent schools value intellectual struggle, Sizer concluded, and, like Hirsch, he believes that teachers and other adults must model that behavior. "Kids copy what they see, not what they're told to do." And just as surely as that teacher in Pennsylvania was teaching a lesson in values by running scared, so too are Hirsch and Sizer. Which lesson would you prefer your children learn, to run from controversy or to challenge ideas?

LEARNING TO RUN FROM CONTROVERSY

Where courage and common sense rule, "right" and "left" agree. But in another district, this one in Indiana, a middle school principal literally begged me not to pursue the story of efforts to ban "Reading for Real," a literature-based reading program. "These people are on a crusade," he said, "and they're crazy. I'm afraid they'll get me, and I'll lose my job." They were crusading against a number of Caldecott and Newbery Award–winning books that teachers have the option of assigning. They were objecting to the books' values, asserting that "schools shouldn't teach values." And that became policy! Here, too, there's cowardice, but not on the part of that principal. It's policy, you see.

"Don't offend," the policy of cowardice, has most often meant removing "religious" content from the curriculum on the spurious grounds of keeping church and state separate. How thorough is the cleansing? How about school calendars which label the school break for Christmas and New Year's "Winter Vacation," because "Christmas" has religious connotations? Or the students who, asked to explain the origin of Thanksgiving, parrot back what they've been taught: "The first Thanksgiving was the Pilgrims' way of thanking the Indians for giving them corn."

They know this for a *fact* because their teachers had not told them that the Pilgrims were thanking their God—and trying to convert the "heathen" Indians in the process. Apparently no one in a position of leadership was willing to say, "Religion is very much a part of our history, and we must teach our history." Too often leadership backs down and seeks to carve out a middle ground—no matter what the competing positions—as if truth were always in the middle.

In other cities and towns, leaders give in to demands from those on the religious right who demand organized school prayer. In so doing, they allow the tyranny of the majority to teach a lesson in values that we may come to regret deeply.

Go back to that town in Indiana, where right-wing zealots were objecting to children reading real literature. Did the leaders defend the books as nationally recognized works of literature? Did they insist that the protesters read the books themselves before objecting? Did they explain the wide variety of titles and ways in which schools and teachers can pick and choose? No, no, and no. Sadly but predictably, the leadership caved in. "We will read all the books, and we will strike from the list any book that contains even one offensive word," the superintendent announced to the protesters.

It's a safe bet that, having tasted blood, the zealots will soon be hungry again—and that schools, teachers, and children will be the poorer for it.

Schools shouldn't be perpetual battlegrounds over values. In fact, they should be the meeting ground, the common ground. As Diane Ravitch notes in her history of school reform, *Left Back*, schools "cannot be successful unless they teach children the importance of honesty, personal responsibility, intellectual curiosity, industry, kindness, empathy, and courage."[160] It *almost* goes without saying that the best way to teach these values is to embody them, to be genuine role models.

Excellent schools help parents raise children with strong, positive values. This can and does happen where educators and school boards are doing their jobs. In Morristown, New Jersey, the high school trains selected seniors to help incoming freshmen adjust. Much of what they do involves values. One period a week for the entire year, small classes of ninth-graders have the opportunity to discuss whatever tough issues are on their minds. Abortion, premarital sex, peer pressure to drink—those topics came up in the classes I visited. Playing the devil's advocate, I asked one of the teachers, "Why are you doing this in school? Doesn't this belong at home?"

Her answer: "Most parents are happy we do this. When we demonstrated what we do at parents' night, parents were pleased. In the society we live in today parents want as much help as possible."

Is that teacher right? Do parents want "as much help as possible"? The parents I spoke with seemed to welcome the program. As one said, "We don't want to be undermined and we don't want to be excluded." That high school wasn't just "winging it" when it created a program to train seniors in leadership. It marshaled community support, and it works to maintain and increase that support. Values are serious business, and the seniors who "teach" the freshmen are themselves in class studying and discussing leadership four periods a week.

Notice I haven't asked, "Should schools teach values?" That's not the right question. Instead, let's recognize that values rub off. They're copied and picked up and tested. They're "caught, not taught."

But schools have to strive to be "ethical communities," in the words of a New Hampshire high school principal: "We have to know what we believe in, and we have to live by our beliefs. Values are in the details, in the way we run our schools and our lives. Of course church and state are separate, and they should be. But that shouldn't stop us from being forthright about our ethical beliefs."

Most people in most communities want the schools to be on their side in the effort to raise children of strong character. The all-too-common educational posture—retreat from controversy—offends nearly everyone. What's more, it is driving people of all faiths, of little faith, and of no faith away from public schools.

If asked, students say they welcome value-oriented schooling. In fact, 46 percent of students feel that "the decline in social and moral values" is the biggest problem facing their generation.[161] Certainly the students I've met want school to be a place where they can honestly explore complex issues like identity, intimacy, and conflicting belief systems. We need to expect schools to be "safe harbors" for young people.

VALUES AND ACADEMICS

Can public schools be safe harbors? Can they be the meeting ground, not the battleground, in the search for values? I believe the answer is self-evident: they have to be—or they won't survive.

Which brings me back to excellence: Excellent schools understand their "core business," their mission. In excellent schools the people in charge are able to explain what they are doing, and why. I fear, however, that most public schools leaders will fail this simple test, largely because the system they work in does not encourage them to develop a true, value-driven mission. That is more likely to be found in private education, where values and a sense of purpose are expected.

Ask a public school leader what his or her mission is, and you are likely to get a blank stare or some rhetorical gobbledygook about "leaving no child behind." We need more leaders like Deborah Meier, the founder of Central Park East Elementary and Secondary Schools, two public institutions built around a system of values.

Meier understands that the primary purpose of an excellent school is academic in the larger sense of that word. "A school's focus should be the intellectual life of its students," Meier says.[162] "Kids should be able to exhibit serious, thoughtful habits of mind about whatever subject matter that school chooses. Whether they're studying about ancient China, equations in algebra, or carpentry, they should take those habits of mind very seriously. They should stop and ask themselves, 'What does a good carpenter do? What does a good citizen do?' And students may discover that a good carpenter asks many of the same questions that a good citizen does. Questions like, 'How do I know that's true?' 'What kind of evidence would I need?' 'Does that remind me of something else I studied once before?' 'What's the connection between them?'"

Meier believes that we ought to be asking those same kinds of questions about the school *as a whole*. That is, some schools cite college attendance as evidence of success, but that small slice of evidence reveals very little about the values the school has imparted, she says.

"We should ask 'What kinds of things do graduates study when they go to college? Do they vote? What do they read? What kind of relationship do they have with other people, and to their community?' Only by asking questions like those can we find out if we've created the kind of school that has had deep effects on the kids who've gone through it."[163]

Meier calls herself a progressive educator, but what is important here is not whether a school is progressive or traditional but whether it's discharging its primary duties: to educate children and to help them learn to think and act democratically.

Historian Larry Cuban has described the values, attitudes, and behaviors that both traditionalists and progressives *share*. He refers to them as "democratic virtues":

- Participation in and willingness to serve local and national communities
- Open-mindedness to different opinions and a willingness to listen to such opinions
- Respect for values that differ from one's own
- Treating individuals decently and fairly, regardless of background
- A commitment to talk through problems, reason, deliberate, and struggle toward openly arrived-at compromises.[164]

When it comes to teaching values, my own model of excellence is straightforward: the excellent school does not run from the subject of values but is clear and open about its purpose. Healthy school systems encourage value-driven education and provide parental choice, so that parents can ask questions, reflect, and (perhaps) conclude, "I agree with those values, and I want my children there."

QUESTIONS TO ASK ABOUT THE SCHOOL'S VALUES

- What does the school, as an institution, stand for or say that it believes? Asked another way, what is the school's philosophy or purpose?
- How was this statement of purpose arrived at? Who played a role in formulating it? How old is it, and how often is it discussed, reviewed, and amended?
- How are students made aware of the school's philosophy?

- How are the values made real? What behaviors are expected, and are connections made between the school's professed values and those behaviors?
- Are students expected to take the lead in passing on the values of the school to incoming students? That is, does the culture of the school allow students to say "We don't do that here" about such things as cheating or drinking? (While this is a difficult question to answer, just asking it and watching how students attempt to answer will be revealing.)
- Does the history curriculum include the role of religion (including history of the Middle Ages, etc.)?
- Do students seem to be respectful of one another? Of visitors?
- Is there graffiti in prominent places? Does the graffiti single out individual kids in derogatory ways? Is the graffiti anti-Semitic, anti-gay, anti-black, etc.?
- Are vandalism and theft problems at the school?

10

CHARTER SCHOOLS—
BUYER BEWARE

Parents searching for excellence are often drawn to charter schools, a reform that is being touted by liberals and conservatives alike. Charter schools are so named because each of these public schools receives a "charter" (usually for 3-4 years) that exempts it from many or most of its district's regulations in return for a promise of specific results. Thus, the motto or mantra of the charter movement, "Show results, or go out of business!"

I think charter schools are a good idea, mostly because I have seen wonderful results in superb charter schools. But because I have also witnessed criminal conduct, I temper my enthusiasm with the warning, "buyer beware." In my view, the word "restaurant" has about as much specific meaning as "charter school." You know a restaurant serves food, but you have to look deeper to find out what kind, its prices and so forth. And to learn about its quality, you need to consult a trusted guidebook or friends who've eaten there. Use at least that much caution and care before choosing a charter school!

That's the revolutionary idea behind 2,000 charter schools enrolling more than 500,000 students in 35 states at the turn of the century.[165] Both the fiscal management and the academic performance of every charter school are supposed to be examined under a powerful—and public—microscope. If a charter school fails to educate or if it plays fast and loose with public money, it is supposed to lose its charter and go out of business.

Charter schools are supposed to provide competition for the rest of the system, which will be challenged to improve (or be scared into it). The logic is appealingly simple: if parents are abandoning traditional public schools to put their children in charter schools, the groundswell of dissatisfaction will force regular schools to get better, particularly when the money follows the student to the charter school.[166]

Admission to charter schools is supposed to be by lottery if there are not enough slots for all applicants. In theory, this will keep charter schools from discriminating against disabled and disadvantaged children. It will also keep charter schools from becoming glorified private schools.

Determining what's bad, "good enough" and excellent where charter schools are concerned is difficult because the experiment is too new. But several of the "rules" that apply to schools generally also apply to charter schools. It follows that an *excellent* charter school will be clear about its purpose, avowedly intellectual by design, and transparent. By the last, I mean that its accountability measures are public. Excellent charter schools are not selective in admissions and serve a heterogeneous population. Finally, excellent charter schools make their results[167] public annually.

"Good enough" charter schools fall short on these measures. Perhaps they reveal academic results only under pressure, or only when it's time to renew the charter. Perhaps they admit selectively, or discourage disabled students.

I reserve the appellation "bad" for those charter schools which exist to propagandize or teach racial or ethnic separatism or superiority, and for those charter schools whose primary function seems to be to employ friends and family.

Much of what is being written about charter schools by their supporters sounds too good to be true. Where I come from, when something sounds too good to be true, it usually isn't! Parents interested in charter schools ought to be doubly skeptical, because the movement seems to be attracting more than its share of charlatans and thieves, as well as principled reformers like Ted Sizer.

Charter school laws vary widely from state to state as well, largely because of the politics behind them. In Arizona, for example, the charter law passed only because conservatives could not pass legislation authorizing vouchers (essentially tuition for private schools). In other states, pressure from teacher unions resulted in charter laws that drastically restrict the freedom of charter schools, making them essentially carbon copies of traditional public schools. And so in the final analysis, parents have to read the fine print very carefully.

Here's a sample of the range in just one city, Oakland, California. Oakland has a charter school for American Indians, a charter school operated by the East Bay Conservation Corps and a Waldorf charter school built around the educational philosophy of Rudolph Steiner. On the drawing board are plans for a for-profit Edison charter school and a charter school operated by teachers. In August, 2000, Oakland's school board rejected a proposal supported by Mayor Jerry Brown for a military charter school where students would have lived in dormitories and worn uniforms, but Brown has pledged to get a charter from another governing body, permissible under California law.

The name "charter school" in and of itself means almost nothing. That school could be outstanding (and many are), but it could also be a sham. In what follows I will take you on a tour of examples of the best and the worst of the breed.

The charter school movement seems to be a magnet for both fierce opposition and nearly reverential awe. Its detractors, most often from teacher unions or school boards, claim that charter schools take resources from the full system; some opponents see charters as union-busting, considering that charter schools are not necessarily required to hire state-approved certified teachers.

On the other hand, I've met charter school parents who seem to have lost their ability to think critically or be skeptical, so desperate were they to find some brighter alternative to the public system.

A BRIEF HISTORY

Minnesota passed the first charter law in 1991 after a three-year struggle that began at a small conference in the northern part of the state in October 1988. At that meeting, which I moderated, teacher union leader Albert Shanker, state senator Ember Reichgott, New York City Associate Superintendent Sy Fliegel, and a handful of activists including Joe Nathan, Elaine Salinas, Barbara Zahn and Ted Kolderie tried to come up with a plan to create opportunities for teachers and others to establish their own public schools.[168] After a bitter battle, the Minnesota legislature approved a watered-down bill that allowed only eight charter schools to be created.

From that seed, however, much has grown. Other states followed Minnesota's example, notably Michigan, California and Arizona. President Clinton became a supporter, and in two of his "State of the Union" addresses he praised charter schools and promised federal support to enable the number of schools to double. Florida and Texas have joined the charter school ranks with vigor, and today those two states, with Michigan, California and Arizona, account for 62 percent of the nation's charter schools, leaving Minnesota behind.

Some states passed legislation that allowed *for-profit* ventures to run charter schools, a departure from the dream and the cause of some of the movement's current troubles.

The first charter school fiasco occurred in Los Angeles in 1994 when the Edutrain Charter School was found to be spending public money on cars and gifts, not school materials. Would Edutrain turn out to be an isolated case, or would the lure of money and relative independence attract undesirables? Does the charter school movement's promise of genuine accountability hold up under close examination? Unfortunately, there's enough evidence available to raise serious doubts, and parents would be wise to probe deeply before enrolling their children in a charter school (or any other school, frankly).

Begin by looking at the school's charter, a public document outlining in great detail its plan for managing public funds and for educating its students. That's the protection, the "guarantee" of accountability. In *theory*, the application process should weed out charlatans, incompetents, and the unprepared. *In theory*, weak applicants will be rejected, or at least told to revise their plans to make them acceptable. In practice, however, a rejected applicant may ask another governing body for approval. Charter laws in California and Arizona allow any school district to approve applications, regardless of where the charter school is to be located. In some states, colleges and universities can grant charters, as can the state itself. *In theory*, schools that fail to adhere to the terms of their charters will have them revoked, but often there is minimal oversight until the charter is due to expire (usually after three or five years). That is, there's a serious gap between theory and practice, with real consequences for the education of children.

A FIASCO IN ARIZONA

I've spent a lot of time in about a dozen charter schools and found an unexpected range of quality, from outstanding to criminally negligent. In 1997 I traveled to Arizona, the home of 21 percent of all charter schools and the "Wild West" of the charter movement.

Arizona's charter schools run the gamut: early care schools, elementary schools, a school where students run a farm, schools requiring uniforms, schools that preach "community spirit," and on and on. Some charter schools are profit-making enterprises, while others are traditional non-profit organizations.

Dr. Lawndia White Venerable worked in education after graduating from UCLA in 1983. A former Miss Black Arizona, she earned her doctorate from Arizona State University in 1993 and was working in the Phoenix public schools when Arizona began its great experiment in charter schools in 1994.

Dr. Venerable saw charter schools as a way to prepare poor and minority children for the real world of business and adult life. "I thought, wouldn't it be wonderful if children could go to school and be celebrated for all aspects of their culture? Wouldn't it be wonderful if all the African-American children could learn more than just about Martin Luther King and civil rights? If the Native-Americans could learn more than the fact that they were "savage Indians?" I wanted all students to celebrate the richness of their cultures, and I wanted to prepare them for the year 2000."

"Citizen 2000" became the name of her dream school, in the proposal she submitted to the State Board of Education. The Board was impressed and voted unanimously, on February 27, 1995, to allow her to open a *for-profit* charter school, K-12th grade, with herself as principal.

She told me, "I began an office, I bought office equipment, I publicized brochures, I had open houses, and I had ice cream socials. I did all the things that you would do to develop a business prior to opening."[169] She rented space in downtown Phoenix.

Dr. Venerable also began hiring, and nearly every one of her key employees was a family member. She hired her sister to be assistant principal, her mother to teach etiquette, her brother to be head of security, her brother-in-law to be Dean of Students, her sister-in-law to teach science and physical education, and her fiancé to be her assistant. This was perfectly legal, although nothing in her application indicated her intention to do this.

She also set the salaries, as the law allowed. She paid herself $89,000, which was $20,000 more than the average Phoenix high school principal earned at the time. Her sister, the assistant principal, was paid $79,000. She listed those salaries in her application, and no one objected.

Dr. Venerable defends her hiring decisions. "Family members don't ask for overtime. When you're there at ten o'clock at night unpacking boxes and setting up desks and screwing together tables and putting in deadbolts, they don't say, 'I should have been off the clock at four o'clock and so now you owe me time and a half or double-time.'

"On the weekends when you're down there picking up trash and installing playground equipment to get the school up and open, your family members don't say, "Are we getting paid for this?" Family members pitch in whenever you need them."

Dr. Venerable also hired teachers, many of them young and idealistic. Kristin Shears remembers the opening of school. " The women on the staff received a "Save the Children" scarf and the men received a "Save the Children" tie and on certain days we would dress up and wear our little uniform too."

Everything seemed to be going well. Dawn Loch was another of the school's young teachers. "You saw healthy, happy kids. Lots of interaction in small groups, and younger grades working with older grades because we had such small classes. It left a lot of flexibility open for what we could do in the rooms."

At first parents were delighted. Victor Diaz enrolled his daughters in first grade. "When I heard my daughters coming in and doing sign language, talking to each other in sign language and the father doesn't even know what they're talking about. I mean, you can just imagine the excitement I got from seeing that."

Cheryl Finley's daughters also attended Citizen 2000. "The teachers were dedicated to the students, they were dedicated to the school, they were dedicated to the vision."

But cracks in the vision began to appear almost immediately. Teachers were the first to notice, including Eric Helming. "You can buy into a dream but if it doesn't have an attendance policy or a discipline policy to back it up, that dream doesn't mean anything if there aren't any rules, any policies."

Adds Kristin Shears, "And those concrete things were never hammered out, and that's really when things started to unravel."

When Citizen 2000 opened in August 1995, it claimed an enrollment of 500 students. Since state funds were based on enrollment, Citizen 2000 was automatically entitled to $2 million for the 1996-1997 school year, which Arizona paid in three equal installments.

Under the law, Dr. Venerable was free to write the checks. And she did, for her mother's mortgage, for renovations to her home, for her divorce attorney's fees, for jewelry, for flowers, for her income taxes, and for swimming pool supplies. Dr. Venerable says she was just paying herself back. She said that she had loaned the school a lot of her own money getting started. "I put everything in my life into this school, every asset I had."

Irregularities were uncovered almost immediately. In January 1996, Arizona's Auditor General reported that Citizen 2000 wasn't keeping adequate attendance records for students or employees. Moreover, the Auditor General charged, the school couldn't produce purchase orders, invoices, cash receipts or properly reconciled bank statements.

Arizona reporters knew a good story when they saw one. Tales of nepotism, the seemingly inflated pay structure, and Dr. Venerable's fancy Jaguar filled the pages of the local papers and the airwaves. Reporters discovered that Dr. Venerable had apparently used Citizen 2000 funds to pay the $99,000 mortgage on her mother's house. Citizen 2000 was beginning to resemble Dr. Venerable's personal "cash cow."

It turned out that Dr. Venerable had not separated her own finances from those of the school, as the law requires. "Was that a critical mistake?" she now says. "Oh yes, it was. Certainly."

However, the state of Arizona knew what was going on at Citizen 2000, but the Arizona state board of education, which was legally responsible for this charter school, did nothing. Then, six months after the school opened, Arizona's auditor general issued a public report, declaring that Citizen 2000 was out of compliance with the law. Four months later, the auditor general asked the state board to take action against Citizen 2000. It held meetings but took no action.

However, Dr. Venerable was taking action. Without official permission, she announced that she was closing the high school. However, despite eliminating four grades—basically one third of the school—she reported to the state that she expected the same number of students, 495.

The state asked no questions but simply wrote a check based on her enrollment projection. Citizen 2000 opened for its second year it reported having 247 students-half the original estimate.

Enrollment was even lower than she reported, however, according to visitors. They counted 214 students. I asked her how much the State overpaid her? "About $200,000, maybe $250,000." (The actual amount was $250,439.)

For weeks the State Board of Education debated whether to withdraw Citizen 2000's charter but did nothing. Then, with more parents withdrawing their children, Dr. Venerable acted again. She declared bankruptcy and closed the school. Ten minutes before the end of the school day on November 18, she sent a letter to every classroom: no school tomorrow, or ever again. "I am now in bankruptcy, pregnant, and unemployed. I have seen my financial stability and personal dream crumble," Dr. Venerable wrote.

Teacher Kelly Goudreau remembers the afternoon. "I taught kindergarten and I had ten minutes to explain. I said, "Boys and girls, I'm very sorry, I'm very sad, but I have to tell you that we're not having class any more. I'm not going to be your teacher any more."

"They had no idea. They did not understand. Some of them were confused and crying. I had ten minutes to get their cubbies emptied into a bag, give them a hug and have them leave my room."

Goudreau did not cry, at least not then. "I was devastated but I held back the tears until my last little one left. Then I just was crying and crying. I could cry now."

With proverbial barn door wide open and the horse gone, the State Board finally took action. Five hours *after* Dr. Venerable declared bankruptcy, the Board revoked her charter. The next day the State padlocked the school and repossessed the buses and other equipment.

Dr. Venerable says she made errors in judgment but did nothing illegal. Family members were the most qualified people available, the only ones willing to work long hours and weekends without overtime. Her ex-husband paid for the 1993 Jaguar. She had loaned the school more than $90,000 just to get the operation up and running, she says, but failed to have an attorney draw up papers acknowledging these loans. That was a mistake, she now admits, as was that infamous mortgage check.

State Superintendent of Public Instruction Lisa Graham Keegan, who voted to approve the charter, placed the blame squarely on Dr. Venerable's shoulders. "The woman who started that school did a lousy job of managing those funds, either through intent or through negligence and incapability, and we're in the midst of trying to recover those funds," Keegan told me.

The State agreed with Keegan and, in March 1997, indicted Dr. Venerable on 31 counts of theft, fraud and misuse of $179,000 in public money. Her sister was indicted on 17 similar charges. "The public has placed a great deal of trust in charter schools," Attorney General Grant Woods said in announcing the indictment. "When someone violates that trust, our children suffer. The hard work of many charter schools is diminished by this sort of activity." Woods also said that Venerable still owed the school $10,000 and that she never has paid any interest to the school. "A charter school is not a bank," he said.

Glossing over the fact that Dr. Venerable, and not the State, closed the school, Superintendent Keegan maintained that the incident proved that Arizona's charter system provides accountability. "It is a celebration, I guess, in a sense of an accountability system that the charter school can be closed down."

State Representative Jeff Groscost (R-Mesa) used the indictment as an opportunity to attack public schools. It is much more difficult to hold regular public schools accountable, Groscost said, citing several cases of public-school administrators diverting funds for private use. "If a charter school doesn't work, if it doesn't teach the kids, the parents will leave, and the school will be forced to close," he said. "If charter school officials commit fraud, we can shut them down. I'd like to see where the same accountability is for regular public schools."[170]

Keegan defiantly agreed that an occasional debacle was worth the risk. "Is it okay to open up schools and have some of them fail? Yes, it is. You bet it is." And then Keegan used the Citizen 2000 debacle as a way of attacking the public system generally. "We are failing about half of our kids in the traditional public system. It isn't as if the traditional system is working spectacularly well. There is plenty of risk in public education right now."

Ted Kolderie sees it differently. "We tend to blame failures on the operator, but in any kind of arrangement, you can have bad buyers, dumb buyers, careless buyers," says Kolderie, who helped write the nation's first charter school legislation in his home state of Minnesota. "It's important to have the rules of accountability apply to the people who granted the charter in the first place," Kolderie added, suggesting that Arizona's public officials must share the blame. "They need to make good decisions about who gets sponsored, and they need to be good about overseeing the school and making sure that, if anything goes wrong, somebody comes in and does something."

Concerned that an occasional scandal would be used to try to scuttle the charter movement, Joe Nathan makes an analogy to freedom of speech. "It is important to separate the charter *idea* from everything that happens. The idea is freedom within some limits, combined with opportunity and responsibility. Not every person uses the freedom to speak *wisely*, but we still believe that the idea of freedom makes more sense than the alternative."[171]

A month after the school closed, Citizen 2000 teacher Eric Helming looked back ruefully. "It was wonderful on paper. The things that were written in pamphlets or in brochures or in the staff handbook—that was fantastic.

"You could open up the staff handbook and find references to ballroom dancing and etiquette and equestrian-type things. But when it came right down to it, provisions were never made to do any of these special things."

At that point Helming laughed. "I can't dance. Teachers have enough things to do already without having to try to learn how to ballroom dance so they could turn around and teach it."

A SUCCESS IN LOS ANGELES

Citizen 2000 shouldn't be used to condemn the entire charter school movement, because for every fiasco, excellent charter schools like Fenton Avenue in Los Angeles are educating children and bringing new energy into public education.

I spent several days at Fenton Avenue Charter School in the spring of 1997, and it's a prime example of charter schools at their best. Fenton Avenue was a regular public school—and not even a "good enough" one—when California passed its charter legislation in 1993. Some parents and teachers saw that as an opportunity; they applied for a charter, and on July 26, 1993, Fenton Avenue became California's thirtieth public charter school. Fenton Avenue suddenly had its fate in its own hands.

Joe Lucente and Irene Sumida, two experienced educators, were hired to serve as co-directors. To others, taking the Fenton Avenue job didn't seem like a good career move. "The Superintendent spent an hour and a half telling me what a hellhole I was being assigned to," Lucente said. "It was considered one of the two worst schools in the San Fernando Valley." Sumida agreed. "When I arrived, our test scores were single-digit numbers."

They faced other serious problems besides poor academic performance: a run-down facility, and poor attendance. Standing in the way of solving those problems were two huge obstacles - the bureaucracy of the second largest school district in the United States and a powerful teachers union that was opposed to charter schools.

What were the first few days and weeks like, I asked them? "We were apprehensive at first," Sumida admitted. "It was so new and no one else was doing it. We were going to be totally independent.

At that point Joe Lucente jumped up from his chair. "And everyone was saying, "You can't do that. You're going to fall on your face." We heard that from the union, we heard that from the school board president. She said, "When you find out how little money you're going to have, you're not going to want fiscal autonomy." I just smiled because I already had done my homework. I knew she didn't know what she was talking about."

What Joe Lucente knew was that the school would receive $4,600 per student. With 1134 students, that came to just over $5.2 million . . . and not one dollar of that money had to be spent in a central district office. All of the money could be spent at Fenton Avenue, which desperately needed to have some money spent on it.

Lucente told me the story of the school's playground, now smooth asphalt with freshly painted lines marking basketball and soccer playing fields. "The playground was in atrocious condition. It was really unsafe. I queried the district as to how we could get it fixed, repaired, or resurfaced, and they told me that we were on the list but it would probably be 30 years before they would get to it, because there was no funding available, period."

But Fenton Avenue is a *charter school*, and so it did not have to wait 30 years, or even one year. They made the decision themselves, and went out and got it fixed. That, of course, is how a charter school is supposed to operate. I asked Lucente and Sumida how often they called up the Los Angeles Unified School District headquarters to ask permission to do something, and both laughed. "Never," Sumida said. "That's the secret of our success," Lucente added. "We don't have to ask permission for anything."

Sumida and Lucente cannot tell the teachers what curriculum to adopt, because that's spelled out in the charter. As Lucente told me, "We have a charter which we must adhere to. That is our bible, our operating guide." Added Sumida, "The charter outlines exactly what's going to be taught."

The ability to act rapidly impressed Fenton's teachers, including Susan Cornell. "It's the difference between having to go through channels where you have to contact this office and that office, and then they send the guy in the field out to check and the other guy finally comes to fix it. Here we're "hands on" and we can take care of it. We've eliminated the middle man."

However, the middleman does not always go away quietly, particularly when it's the Superintendent of Schools. Joe Lucente discovered this when Fenton Avenue decided it wanted to run the school cafeteria itself. Not long after Lucente received a letter from the LA Superintendent, telling him, "You are not authorized to operate your own food services program."

Lucente reacted immediately and aggressively. "I had to write a letter back on Fenton Avenue Charter School letterhead, saying 'Thank you, I appreciate your comments. However, I don't work for you, and the people I work for have directed me to operate this food services program and we will do so effective July first.'"

Fenton Avenue cancelled the district's food service contract and took over the kitchen. In low-income areas the school lunch may be the most substantial meal of the day, or perhaps the only one.[172] Fenton Avenue's cafeteria now feeds every child regardless of family income. When I was there it was offering three choices for breakfast, and five for lunch. It was as good or better than any food I've tasted in a public school in 25 years of reporting.

Fenton Avenue Charter School is different in many other ways. It has lots of computers, smaller classes, new classrooms, freshly painted interiors, and a studio for television production.

Students at Fenton Avenue wear uniforms, a decision made by parents with the strong support of Sumida and Lucente. Several students told me that uniforms were "good and bad." Good, Carla Lopez said, "because it's keeping us safe from violence outside the school, and bad because we have to wear the same thing over and over."

Uniforms were as a tangible reminder that the school's first purpose is academic. As a charter school, Fenton Avenue has the freedom to make curriculum decisions, within limits, but Fenton Avenue can act when it sees a need. Notes Sumida, "We are a really strong curriculum based school, and when we realized how poorly our kids were reading, we took action."

The school examined alternatives, chose a new phonics reading curriculum, and began using it. The entire process took only four weeks. In contrast, California recognized a statewide reading problem at about the same time Fenton Avenue did, but it took several years before it began implementing solutions.

Reading tests scores began going up almost immediately, from the single digit scores of 1991. They increased by 16.1 percent in Fenton Avenue's second year, and another 7.9 percent in 95-96. In school year 1999-2000, test scores increased another 20.8 percent. Despite the increases, Fenton Avenue students rank only in the 30th percentile nationally; while that is low, it represents continuous improvement, including a jump of five percentile points over where students were one year ago. Spanish reading test scores have gone up dramatically, from the 20th percentile to the 61st percentile in first grade reading.

Fenton Avenue's family center offers day and night classes for the parents, giving them a second chance at completing their schooling. The family center provides another benefit: Children who see their parents going to school are more likely to do the same thing.

ATTENDANCE IMPROVES

Attendance is another measure of accountability at Fenton Avenue, and Sumida says it has improved greatly, to an astonishing 98 percent. In its charter, Fenton Avenue had promised to improve attendance gradually, up to 95 percent. "We did that in our first year," Lucente laughs.

Teacher attendance is a good measure of excellence, and here Fenton Avenue shines. Teachers arrive early and stay late. During my visits I heard an announcement I have never heard in a school before. It was nearly 6 PM when the PA system came on, to announce, "Teachers, you must leave the building by 6:00."

I told that story to Lucente and Sumida, and they both laughed. "We have to chase them out," Lucente said. And then Sumida told me something that shocked me even more. "Normally they stay until eight. We usually have security here until 8:00, but tonight we have security just until six."

I had arrived at the school that morning just before 7 AM, and the school parking lot was nearly full then, meaning that many of Fenton Avenue's teachers are willingly putting in 10-hour days.

"The key is instruction," Sumida says. "The key is your teaching staff and we have a high quality teaching staff. And they've made the difference.

Fenton Avenue's teachers seem young and energetic, even veterans like Susan Cornell. "Having a charter school lets us do as teachers and as a school what we've been saying for the 22 years I've been in teaching. Which is, 'let us do it, give us the money, let us buy our own supplies, let us make our own choices, because we know what's best for our kids.'"

Arriving early and staying late . . . that's different from normal practice . . . and a challenge to union rules. Teacher union contracts spell out working hours, wages, and seniority privileges, rules that apply to all teachers in a district. But by law charter schools are exempt from following those rules. Teachers seem to like their new freedom. As Jeanette Focosi says, "We are self governing. We do not make staff selection or grade assignments by seniority."

But that anecdote is revealing in ways that Charter supporters like Joe Lucente do not intend, because *no* school will survive and prosper if it runs on what amounts to super-human effort. That's flying too close to the sun, or burning the candle at both ends, and that always ends in disappointment or worse. If Fenton Avenue, or any other Charter school, needs extraordinary effort and commitment from its teachers on a regular basis, it will ultimately become a shadow of what it was at the beginning.[173]

Lucente says that the reaction of the local teachers union was negative at first, advising teachers not to abandon seniority and warning them that they would lose all their hard-earned benefits. "They treated them more like they were renegades than they were members of their own union."

Union representative Sam Kresner disagreed. " I don't think that we were being obstructionist in what we were trying to do. I think we were trying to inform people of all the dangers, and wanted to make sure they made an educated decision." The union has persisted in its efforts to include charter teachers in one massive bargaining unit with all of LA's teachers. If that happened, charter supporters say, it would kill the charter movement in California. "We will not back down or cravenly accept the sellout of our right to determine our educational destiny," said Oakland Mayor Jerry Brown. "As we all learned from the sorry experience of state-sanctioned bureaucracies in the Soviet Union, decentralization is crucial to both freedom and excellence."[174]

The position taken by Focosi, the classroom teacher, must strike fear into the hearts of unionists everywhere. "Right now we don't need a union, but I think we need to always be thinking about in the future. It serves a purpose. It's a watchdog."

Teacher union opposition to charter schools has not gone away, but change is happening. In some cities unions are adapting . . . even to the point of helping run charter schools in San Diego, Phoenix, Colorado Springs, Kailua, Hawaii and Norwich, Connecticut. The AFT local in Miami-Dade, under the leadership of AFT Vice President Pat Tornillo, has applied to run 10 charter schools there, in partnership with for-profit Edison. NEA President Bob Chase has officially endorsed flexible working arrangements. "We need to get out of the way. We can't allow union sacred cows to block the path of members who want to pursue their own vision of school quality and reform."

Focosi says she is not anti-union, although she does embrace her activist role. "We're revolutionaries here. We're taking chances, and we manage our own funds. That gives us power. That gives us courage to take some risks."

Taking risks and eliminating middlemen has paid off at Fenton Avenue, and not just in better attendance and higher test scores. The school has also saved money. The first year surplus was spent on technology and campus improvements. After the second year, the surplus was distributed among the teachers. Each teacher received a bonus of at least $1,000. In the ensuing years, Fenton Avenue, which now has an annual budget of $14 million, has added 13 classrooms and made $3 million in capital improvements. Joe Lucente says he's negotiating with the district to build a new building that will contain a science lab, an art room and a performing arts space.

Consider for a moment how Fenton Avenue Charter School has used its freedom: For the most part, it's gone "back to basics': to phonics, to uniforms, to emphasizing family, to making the school safe. But Fenton Avenue has also embraced technology and is providing free breakfast and lunch for all students.

Freedom means just that: the power to make decisions, the power to do what seems best. That virtually guarantees that every charter school will be one of a kind.

Fenton Avenue's original charter was for five years. In May, 1997 it was named a California Distinguished School, and on June 15, 1998, the Los Angeles Unified School District unanimously approved a five year renewal of the school's charter. Academic gains have continued. Despite Fenton Avenue's impressive record[175] and the equally impressive performance of Yvonne Chan's inner city charter school(where achievement scores are up and the school has saved more than $1 million by doing its own purchasing), the Los Angeles Unified School District has not shown great enthusiasm for charter schools. LA Unified, which has 663 schools, has approved only 37 charter schools, including Fenton Avenue. California seems to be embracing charter schools, particularly under Governor Gray Davis. In 2000 the state raised its upper limit on the number of charter schools to 250.

SOME CHARTER LESSONS

Dramatic as they are, neither Citizen 2000's failure nor Fenton Avenue's success proves that charter schools are any more accountable than regular public schools. In fact, the story proves very little about charter schools generally, but it raises a warning flag about the language and provisions of charter documents. Those seeking charters are expected to make specific promises regarding educational improvements, but in some places very little attention is paid to whether those promises are being kept—until the charter is up for renewal, usually after five years (sometimes after only three).

The premise and the promise of Charter schools is "succeed or go out of business." To believe that the promise is being kept would require you to also believe in a success rate of 96 percent, for only 80 Charter schools—out of more than 2,000—have gone out of business. Some failed for educational or fiscal reasons, and some had their charters revoked for failure to abide by the rules, either academic or fiscal. Nothing works that well, it seems fair to say, and not even Charter Schools' most fervent advocates claim virtual perfection. There must be another explanation.

There is: the people running charter schools have a free hand for a remarkably long time. They are not being held accountable with any regularity, except perhaps at renewal time. A more sensible approach would require interim measures of change, such as those now being required in Minnesota and Illinois. That way, progress, or lack thereof, could be noted. Interventions could be specified in cases of failure to make progress. Such a system would restrict a charter school's "independence" somewhat, but why should a charter school be free to stay on a path of failure without some accountability?

Ted Sizer, who is co-director of the Francis W. Parker Charter Essential School in Devens, Massachusetts endorses what he calls "complex accountability." This includes the Stanford-9 test, "parental choice, regular and tough inspection, careful internal reviews and audits (including data from standardized tests), and annual reviews by outside experts of portfolios of student work." How students do once they go to college, if they choose to go, is also a measure of accountability, Sizer says.

He writes further, "This kind of "complex accountability" protects a charter school's freedom, and the shape of its design. It is practical: it can be done. However—and this is critical—it does require staff who have enough confidence in what they are doing to open their work on a regular basis to serious outside scrutiny."[176]

On the other hand, how often are regular public schools held accountable for the achievement of their students? Joe Nathan, one the founders of the charter movement, believes that opposition to charter schools comes in part from educators who aren't used to being held accountable, and who don't want to be. "The charter idea says that *all* schools should be expected to improve student achievement or be closed. This scares a lot of educators in schools which do not enroll the most troubled, challenging kids, because these schools have been largely exempt from close scrutiny, except in how many kids go on to colleges."[177]

Fenton Avenue's charter promised an increase in school attendance, a benchmark the school achieved a year ahead of schedule, but no outside authorities were monitoring progress, only those inside. It's conceivable that attendance could have plummeted and that no one with authority over charters would have known until Fenton Avenue asked for a renewal of the charter. The lack of outside monitoring during the course of a charter is a significant flaw in the reform in some states. Edward Fiske and Nancy Ladd have documented New Zealand's experiment with charter schools and school choice, and their book,[178] which is subtitled "A Cautionary Tale," provides ample guidance for those involved in this particular reform. Provisions for interim monitoring are essential if charter schools are to be successful in the United States, they maintain.

Fiske and Ladd also throw cold water on the idea that a public system would be greatly improved if all of its schools became charter schools. "A small percentage, perhaps 10 percent, would provide great incentives for the rest of the system to improve," Fiske told me in a radio interview, "But changing over the entire system ends up benefiting those who already have advantages."[179]

In their book, Fiske and Ladd describe how, in effect, "the rich got richer" when every school became a school of choice. The better schools in better neighborhoods immediately attracted most of the educationally savvy parents. And people abandoned the poorer schools, they report.

Nathan finds the comparison invalid. "I was in New Zealand and see many differences between what is going on there and the charter idea. The New Zealand plan does not allow new schools to be created, and charter laws here do. The New Zealand law allows for admissions tests, and most charter laws here do not. I really think it is unfair of Fiske and Ladd to call New Zealand a charter system."[180]

New Zealand's approach gave individual schools the power over admission decisions, as if they were private schools. That is something that no state allows here, and Fiske and Ladd agree that the difference is significant. "Admission by lottery is essential, " Ladd noted, if the experiment is to have any chance of making the system competitive.[181] Charter schools that control their admissions may be tempted to exclude children who are more expensive to educate, such as disabled students. And federal officials have already found that one charter school in Boston, Renaissance, discriminated against a special-needs kindergarten student by shortening his day, suspending him, and placing him with a teacher not trained in special education. As a result of this treatment, his mother withdrew him from the school, run by the for-profit Edison organization.

A University of Michigan study[182] came to a similar conclusion. David Plank, co-author of the study, wrote, "Our basic finding is that rules matter. Different rules[183] create different incentives and different outcomes." Plank contrasts Michigan, which uses a lottery for admission decisions, with California, where charters are allowed to select students and require parents to contribute. Most Michigan charters are in urban districts and enroll more poor and minority students than neighboring districts, but most California charters are in suburbs or small towns and enroll fewer poor and minority students than neighboring districts.[184]

Joe Nathan believes that most charter schools are succeeding despite hurdles placed in their way by hostile lawmakers, bureaucrats and unions. "Teachers and parents are desperate to create the kinds of schools that they think make sense. They're willing to be held accountable. They're willing to do whatever it takes."

The majority of charter schools seem to have struggled financially, because they operate with certain disadvantages. They never are given sufficient capital to pay start-up costs and almost never have funds to pay for decent facilities. Most charter schools reportedly work with low-income children or children from troubled families, which surprises those who assumed that charter schools would be primarily for the middle class. As Joe Lucente notes, "These are children who have long been ignored, who have not had opportunity. We want to turn it around and change that label from 'disadvantaged' to 'advantaged.'"

ARE CHARTER SCHOOLS EFFECTIVE?

What do we know about the academic effectiveness of charter schools, or is it too early to know? Evidence is spotty and inconclusive. Under Governor Jim Hunt's leadership, North Carolina has taken public school reform seriously; the state has 71 charter schools and provisions for monitoring their progress. Forty-four of the 71 charter schools operating there failed to meet their declared goals last year, and of the state's 45 "low performing" schools, 18 are charter schools. The problem with findings like these, however, is that they are based on standardized test scores from the first year of operation; one can make a convincing argument that those scores reflect what went on in the schools the kids went to *before* enrolling in charter schools.

A study of charter schools in Texas indicates that poor children in charter schools are doing no better than their counterparts in traditional public schools. However, researchers at the Center for Education Reform, a conservative education group that strongly supports charter schools, assert that students in Florida's charter schools have shown a 36 percent increase in achievement. (But it's those test scores again!) Amy Stuart Wells of UCLA found varied results in her study of charter schools.

Are charter schools helping the disadvantaged? The answer may depend on where you look, or whom you ask. David Arsen, co-author of the University of Michigan study, put it this way: "We didn't find the academic creaming that so many people worried about early on. What we found instead is creaming on the basis of cost. Charter schools generally are taking the students who are cheapest to educate, and leaving behind those who are more expensive."

The state of Michigan gives each charter school the standard $6,000 per pupil, and younger students are cheaper to educate. Those two facts explain why Michigan has more charter elementary schools, Arsen speculates. He notes that three quarters of charter schools do not provide special education services.[185]

Does the presence of a charter school (i.e., competition) lead to improvements in traditional public schools? Eric Rofes, a researcher at the University of California at Berkeley, studied 25 school districts with charter schools. He found that a quarter of them made big changes in their programs, including opening theme-oriented middle schools, establishing all day kindergarten, and providing transportation to community activities. Each of these changes, Rofes noted, mirrored steps taken by local charter schools. On the other hand, when five percent of the school children in Washington, D.C., left traditional schools to attend charter schools, the school district did little to try to win them back, choosing instead to fight the chartering process.

Whatever the academic impact, liberals and conservatives alike are supporting the charter school movement. Blanket endorsements are always risky. With the charter school movement, however, it's beyond foolishness.

What's in a name, Shakespeare asked? With charter schools, *nothing* is guaranteed, certainly not excellence. Charter schools are a good idea, but the proof has to be in the pudding. Today, America's charter schools have only *one* thing in common: the name. Whatever else you do, read the fine print. Even that may not be enough: remember what Citizen 2000 teacher Eric Helming said about his school? "It was wonderful on paper."

QUESTIONS TO ASK

- What's the admissions policy? If it is selective, how are decisions made?
- How many students have left the school after enrolling? What reasons have they given for leaving?
- What are the qualifications of the teachers? How are teachers selected?
- What is the turnover rate among teachers?
- How is the school held accountable? How often are results made public?
- What promises are made in the charter document?
- Is the charter document posted for all to see?
- How secure is the school's funding?
- What role, if any, do parents play in the hiring of teachers?
- What is required of parents?
- If the school has a surplus at the end of the year, what happens to the money? Who decides?

11

WHAT'S SPECIAL ABOUT SPECIAL EDUCATION?

The answer to the above question is either "not very much" or "not enough," depending on one's politics. Only a cockeyed optimist would assert that all is well with special education today, more than 25 years after we made a national commitment to educating children with disabilities.

Much is wrong: phony "inclusion," a bloated bureaucracy, questionable classifications, an appalling dropout rate, and a near-total lack of accountability. I say that after more than 25 years of reporting on the issue. The terminology has changed with dizzying rapidity: disabled children, exceptional children, children with handicapping conditions, special needs children, and so on, and the world of public education has been turned upside down.

During these years, I have interviewed thousands of individuals in most of the states including some of the first children to come under the 1975 legislation guaranteeing disabled children access to education; I spoke with them then, and then again in the late 1990s. I've also spent time with the Washington insiders who drafted Public Law 94-142, the former president who wanted to veto the legislation, lawyers who are driving school boards crazy, and hundreds of frustrated parents and teachers.

Determining what's bad, "good enough," and excellent in special education is ultimately an exercise in subjectivity and selectivity, I'm afraid. I believe, however, that a special education program that does not expect all students to learn (and assess them regularly to find how) cannot be labeled "excellent." Excellent special education programs provide ample training for regular classroom teachers before attempting to place special education students in the "mainstream" of their classrooms. Taking a look at the dollars a district spends placing special education students in private schools and on legal fees will tell you something about the district's backbone. I don't know how much is *too* much, but I suspect that excellent school districts manage to provide for learning disabled students without sending them away, so if lots of LD kids are in private schools with the public paying the bills, something's amiss.

"Good enough" special education programs assess disabled students regularly and provide help for regular classroom teachers. What they rarely (if ever) do is actually move kids *out* of special education and back into the mainstream for good!

Bad special education programs are dumping grounds, evidence of which can be found in the population. If disproportionate numbers of boys or ethnic or racial minorities are in the population, that should raise a serious warning flag. But look deeper even if the ratios compute and check to see if minorities are apt to be classified "behavior disordered" or "educable mentally retarded," while whites carry the "learning disabled" label.

A PERSONAL HISTORY

Special education has been a special beat for me, because I began my career as a reporter for National Public Radio just as the law was passed. I remember well the revolutionary zeal, the high hopes, and the disgraceful conditions that passed for "education" for handicapped children in the old days.

Make no mistake about it! There were *no* good old days in special education, and "excellence" was not even a dream. I remember a day in New Mexico in one of that state's institutions for the handicapped: rows and rows of children and adults strapped to their chairs in a dimly lit room, a cacophony of moans and screams. Four or five attendants stood watch over what seemed to be about a hundred "students."

Burned into my memory is the image of one young man, a quadriplegic with cerebral palsy. Abandoned by his parents and labeled "retarded," he languished for years until one day a sympathetic nurse saw in his eyes the glimmer of a fierce intelligence. "He could move his head, and he could make his eyes shine or get bigger, and I realized he was trying to talk to me," she told me.

Determined to give him a chance to communicate, that wonderful woman[186] made what must have been one of the first letter/word boards (this was in 1975). It was nothing more than a tray with letters, numbers, and common words on it. Then she fastened a small light to a hat and taught the young man to direct the light to words and letters.

I "interviewed" him that day, for my National Public Radio program, "Options in Education." He told me about his mother, asked questions about my family, and asked me if I believed in God. I cried then, tears of joy for his indomitable spirit, but also tears for the loss of thousands and thousands of lives wasted, back in those "good old days."

Today, however, when disabled students are put in the national spotlight, the glare is likely to be unflattering. Critics are calling for a complete overhaul of the law, but before we turn our backs on what has taken 25 years to create, let's take a careful look.

The Education for All Handicapped Children Act of 1975 promised disabled students access to a "free and appropriate public education," access they have achieved—5 million disabled students now attend public schools. Whether access equals education, however, is another story.

It's worth recalling that prior to the passage of the law now known as the Individuals with Disabilities Education Act, or IDEA, disabled children were often deemed "uneducable" and sent to institutions like that one in New Mexico, or kept at home. Washington, D.C., went an almost unimaginable step further and warehoused handicapped children in buildings that had been deemed unsafe—officially condemned—for use as regular schools! That is, the buildings weren't good enough for most children, but they *were* "good enough" for the disabled.

The law was controversial in 1975, and President Gerald R. Ford and his advisers wanted to veto it. Mr. Ford told me that he had prepared a veto message, based on his conviction that the law would cost too much and give "Washington bureaucrats" too much power. Mr. Ford's advisers were predicting that Congress would not provide the 40 percent of funding that the law stipulated, and they were correct. Congress has never come close, and today the federal contribution of about $5.2 billion is a staggering $12 billion short! Those bills must be paid, of course, and they are—with local and state funds.

Knowing that Congress would override his veto, Mr. Ford eventually signed the bill, but without fanfare. No official photograph of the signing ceremony exists, a sure sign of presidential displeasure.

Back then, interest groups played a major role in the actual writing of the legislation. Fred Weintraub, then as now a leader of the Council for Exceptional Children, recalled how he and Lisa Walker, a key Senate aide who had been working on this issue for some time, sat for hours in a Washington restaurant one afternoon in 1971 or 1972, talking about an "ideal" law. "At one point, I took out my pen," Weintraub told me, "but neither of us had any blank paper. So we grabbed a handful of paper napkins and basically wrote what we hoped the law would include, on those napkins. Lisa took the napkins back to the senator's office, and they became the basis for the law."[187]

The law requires that disabled students be taught in "the least restrictive environment," usually a regular classroom. Most of the 5 million children with disabilities now in public schools are described as being "included," meaning they spend their days in regular classrooms. But "inclusion," once called "mainstreaming," often results in dumping. Too often the classroom teacher has no special training and little additional support. Too often the disabled student is ignored in the corner—until he or she discovers that the best way to get an adult's attention is to misbehave.

Disciplining special education students turns out to be a complicated issue. It has become very difficult to suspend or expel a disabled child unless his parents agree or a court orders it.

And laws[188] conflict. Chester Finn, former assistant secretary of education under Ronald Reagan told me, "One law requires kids carrying guns be kicked out of school for a year, but another law says that disabled kids can be suspended for only 45 days." I recall a young boy in a wheelchair saying with a mixture of disdain and pride, "We can get away with murder. I could be smuggling drugs into the school." Former Fairfax school superintendent Robert Spillaine agrees. "Any student who is classified as disabled is now literally able to get away with anything."

The results are predictable, and nobody learns much of anything. We spend an additional $30 billion a year nationally on disabled students, 22 cents of every education dollar in New York City, and—in some extreme cases—more than $100,000 per child. Since the law's passage in 1975, nearly half of all new school spending has gone to special education programs, programs that serve 11 percent of school children.[189]

States have been trying to find ways to place caps on the number of students who qualify as disabled, in order to cut their costs. But solving one problem merely creates another. If a state caps its funding at 10 percent, districts whose population of disabled students exceeds 10 percent have to pay the excess. But that same rule encourages districts currently under 10 percent to find more disabilities to get up to 10 percent, to get the maximum amount of state money.

What does the money buy? Personnel, equipment, and transportation—but beyond it's hard to know. My impression is that most educators rarely even ask the question, but even if they do, the system is disjointed, and there's no one place to look to find an accounting of spending.

Most disabled students live in a kind of educational limbo because very few people in the system have been keeping track of how much (or whether) they're learning. In education jargon, it means they are "out of accountability." Most states in the United States have not included disabled students in regular assessments of academic success or standardized tests. It's as if they don't count. In 1999 only Kentucky and Maryland required regular testing of all their disabled students.

When he was superintendent of schools in Philadelphia, David Hornbeck shocked even his own staff when he insisted that disabled students be included in the city-wide test; they warned him that such a step would lower the overall scores (which he knew already, of course), but he insisted. His argument was that all children counted and, as he said, "All means all; what part of 'all' don't you understand?" Scores were lower, Hornbeck told me, but his action put teachers on notice: disabled children mattered, and their teachers would be accountable.

From day one, federal law has required that each disabled student have what is known as an IEP, for Individualized Education Program. But the IEP has come to mean hours and hours of paperwork instead of an accurate plan for the achievement of the student. The IEP-writing process has become so riddled with procedures that the sometimes 40- to 50-page documents can take months to prepare, time that could be spent educating the student.

These plans almost never identify outcomes ("Gloria will learn to read") but instead focus on processes ("Gloria will receive eight hours of small-group instruction in reading per week").[190] Done well, the development of an IEP forces educators to think about each child, and that provides protection—a paper trail—for parents.

However, I've interviewed many special-education teachers who've told me that they spend much of their time creating paper trails and anticipating lawsuits[191] from disgruntled parents. Many school districts have seen their legal costs balloon. For example, legal costs for Connecticut's public schools tripled between 1991 and 1994. Greenwich, Connecticut, which boasts one of the state's best public school systems, is paying tuition for several dozen students whose parents threatened to take legal action over the system's alleged failures with their "learning disabled" children. "It's cheaper and easier to pay than to fight," one Greenwich official told me.

For many students special education is the equivalent of the Eagles song "Hotel California"—a place you can check out of but never leave. That is, students who get the "special education" label almost never lose it. Once in, always in. Moreover, only 44 percent of special education students earn high school diplomas. "It's like a repair shop that never repairs anything," is the way Henry Levin, the school reformer who founded the Accelerated Schools program, puts it. And U.S. Department of Education data confirm Levin's accusation: only 4 percent of students diagnosed with learning disabilities in 1994 returned to regular classrooms.

LEARNING DISABILITIES: A GROWTH INDUSTRY

That failure rate is even more appalling when one considers that today about 52 percent of those in special education—more than 2 million children—are categorized as "learning disabled." Perhaps because the criteria are largely subjective, LD, as the learning-disabled category is known, has been and continues to be a growth industry in special education. In the late 1970s learning disabled students accounted for about one-fifth of the disabled student population, and today it's one-half. That growth accounts for almost all of the annual increase in disabled students, and in spending.[192]

By now everyone in education has heard stories of parents actually seeking out the label because they felt that it was the best way for their children to receive individual attention and special services. Chief among the advantages afforded LD students is extra time on exams, including standardized tests like the SAT.[193] Because learning disabled students were not kept in attics before the federal law was passed, critics charge that the label is also applied to children who misbehave and disrupt the class or who have a short attention span, because that will get them out of the classroom. Richard Rothstein argues that the federal law creates perverse incentives to label kids LD. Schools get extra money for disabled students, and borderline disabilities like LD don't cost very much extra (unlike, say, a multiple-handicapped child requiring a personal attendant). The child might just be a slow learner, but that won't bring in extra services, so suddenly he or she is LD.[194]

Writing in *Education Week*, Diane Ravitch and Tom Loveless make a similar point. "Alice Parker, California's director of special education, estimates that as many as 250,000 of the state's special education students are designated as learning disabled because of reading difficulties stemming from poor instruction."[195]

How dubious a diagnosis is learning disabled? Consider that Massachusetts finds that about 15 percent of its students are LD, while only 2 percent of Georgia's students are so afflicted. Is there something in the water, perhaps? Could a Massachusetts family "cure" its child's learning disability by moving south? Of course it's neither the water nor geography, but sloppy classification or vague criteria.

The special education system's strong point turns out to be process, a backhanded compliment if ever there was one. Process requires people, and special education has plenty of them. In 20 years, the disabled-student population has increased by 40 percent, but the number of adults employed in special education has grown by 80 percent. But more staff may not mean more help for students. In fact, more and more of those employed in special education work in nonclassroom settings.

Do regular and special education work together to benefit children? Do they mesh? In 1996 Brian McNulty, Colorado's director of special education, described the situation as "our own worst nightmare. We've created two separate systems of education—one for typical children and one for children with disabilities. And by and large those two systems do not interact very well."

The nightmare is worse than you'd imagine. Dr. Sally Shaywitz of Yale University tracked the progress of reading-disabled students in Connecticut. Of those identified with a disability in third grade and given special education services through ninth grade, by 1996 only 26 percent had made significant progress. The other 74 percent were still receiving special education, but had shown *no* signs of improvement.

Is a 74 percent failure rate acceptable in any other line of work? Recall Henry Levin's simile of car repair and imagine an auto repair shop with a successful repair rate of 26 percent! If 74 percent of the cars it worked on didn't run, it would be out of business in a few weeks or months. Unless, of course, nobody checked to see whether the cars actually ran, which is what often happens in special education—very little testing. When students are not assessed regularly, they and their teachers get the message that what they are doing doesn't really matter.

ADD: A DUBIOUS DIAGNOSIS

If LD seems dubious, consider the case of Attention Deficit Disorder, another fast-growing handicapping condition. We've been experiencing an epidemic of ADD, almost exclusively among white middle-class boys, since the mid-'90s. I spent months investigating ADD in 1995, trying to find out why this particular condition was suddenly becoming commonplace, and why Ritalin was becoming the treatment of choice. Gene Haislip of the Federal Drug Enforcement Administration Office was responsible for determining annual production quotas for methylphenidate and Ritalin. Haislip said that, while there was a window of legitimate use for the drug, the data suggested that "this has become a popular fad . . . especially when you realize that the United States is using five times as much as the entire rest of the planet."

As journalists are trained to do, we asked, "Who benefits?" We were shocked to discover when we followed the money trail, that the primary producer of Ritalin[196] was covertly funding parents' group known as ChADD, Children with Attention Deficit Disorder.[197] While not illegal for a pharmaceutical company to fund nonprofit organizations, the transactions (more than $800,000 over three years) were made public, if at all, in very small print. ChADD maintained that there was no quid pro quo, but its widely distributed materials recommended Ritalin by name to parents concerned about their children's behavior.

Attention Deficit Disorder is truly a dubious diagnosis. Although the American Psychiatric Association recognizes ADD as a mental disorder, the exact cause is unknown, there are no medical tests for it, no clear medical or physical evidence exists of its condition, and the identifying characteristics are blatantly subjective. They include fidgeting with hands and feet, squirming in your seat, getting out of your chair when you're supposed to sit still, and running about and climbing excessively. That's a perfect description of millions of impatient children in crowded classrooms.

Clinching the case for me, however, was the firsthand testimony of many boys and their parents, all of whom noted that the condition seemed to disappear during summers, and even on weekends. Whenever school was not a part of their lives!

ChADD, however, was telling concerned parents that ADD was a neurobiological disorder that stemmed from a chemical imbalance in the brain. Ritalin, a psycho-stimulant, presumably corrects that imbalance by activating neurotransmitters—the chemicals that carry messages in the brain.

We learned that teachers often recommend Ritalin for certain children. David Scherbel, whose son had been recommended for the drug, implicated school districts in the growth of ADD. "They're trying to cut their budgets and trying to keep big populations in the classes, and they can't have kids who are not under control. Teachers are more than happy to have kids on Ritalin, if it in fact will control their activities in the classrooms."

Some parents may accept a diagnosis of ADD because it offers a more palatable explanation for their child's behavior. Helen Blackburn, an educational psychologist for the Greenwich, Connecticut, public schools, put it this way. "Parents want a school-based reason why a child isn't doing well. And to say that a child is not bright, that he may be a 'slow learner,' or that family issues are causing the problems in school, parents don't want to accept that. They want a diagnosis and a label that then makes the school responsible for solving the problem."

And we learned that there are always doctors who will prescribe Ritalin for a child. Child psychiatrist Simon Epstein, who said he prescribed Ritalin for about 150 children a year, explained the dilemma. "If I tell them that I don't think it's clinically indicated, the parents will just go elsewhere. If that's what they want, they will go on until they find somebody who will prescribe it."

We discovered that some ChADD leaders had engaged in dubious behavior of their own, even going so far as to infiltrate parental information videos distributed by the U.S. Department of Education. On these videos, several ranking officials of ChADD state organizations present themselves as "typical parents" agonizing over their children's condition and then extolling the virtues of Ritalin. An embarrassed Department of Education hastily withdrew the videos after we reported the clear conflict of interest.[198]

At one point, I asked Dr. Parker if he felt compromised by accepting money from Ritalin's manufacturer and then recommending the drug. Did he feel "bought" by Ciba-Geigy? "I don't feel bought," he said. "I feel they owe us that as a matter of fact. I feel they owe it to the parents who are spending their money on medication. They owe it to these families to give them something back."

Dr. Gene Haislip of the DEA was incredulous. "You mean he really thinks there's nothing wrong in taking this money and keeping it a secret like they have? Well, I think it's an outlandish statement to make really, and I must say it surprises me."

Ciba-Geigy's spokesman, Todd Forte, told us that the company was pleased with the results of its support of ChADD. "We're getting big information out there and I think that's the bottom line here . . . ChADD is essentially a conduit, providing this information directly to the patient population, and they do a pretty good job of it."

We also reported that ChADD was actively lobbying Congress, something nonprofit organizations are not allowed to do. ChADD's cause? To make it easier to get methylphenidate, the generic form of Ritalin! This despite the gruesome fact that, at the time, the United States was consuming 85 percent of the world's supply of the drug. ChADD's lobbying effort was defeated, and for a time the consumption of methylphenidate actually fell.

That victory was short-lived, unfortunately. In March 2000, the White House announced an effort to reverse what it described as "a sharp increase" in the number of preschool children using Ritalin and other psychiatric drugs. In September 2000 lawsuits were filed in federal courts in New Jersey and California, accusing the drug's manufacturer and the American Psychiatric Association of conspiring to create a market for Ritalin and thereby increase its use. A similar class action lawsuit has been filed in Texas. The APA called the suit "groundless."

As I write this, as many as 5 percent of school-age children in the United States have been diagnosed with ADD, and the epidemic grows.

SO, THEN, HOW SPECIAL IS IT?

What we call "special education" is not particularly special, but I hope we'll agree that it is worth saving. Saving it requires at least four giant steps. First, we must have accountability. Disabled students must be expected to learn, be tested, and be helped when they fail. The individualized education programs must specify what each student is expected to learn—not the processes, but the anticipated results.

But accountability means more than test scores; it means asking: "Are children passing? Are they graduating, getting jobs, and finding social acceptance? Are they satisfied?" All of these are measurable, and we ought to be measuring those outcomes.

Second, dismantle special-education bureaucracies. Special educators must work with children and with regular classroom teachers, or hit the road. That money should be spent to help children and to provide training for their regular classroom teachers.

Third, deregulate in ways that will end the legal morass and system-wide distrust.

Prevention is the most important step of all, beginning with learning disabilities. Learning disabled students have no recognizable mental or physical disorders but have difficulty learning initial reading or math. With proper intervention, all but the severely disabled can learn to compensate for difficulties and can keep from falling behind in class. Early intervention, before the third grade, is the key: doing whatever it takes to ensure that each child learns to read and compute.

I think we'd be better off if we recognized that children learn differently and stopped defining "differences" as "disabilities." Our schools are too narrowly focused, and children who don't easily acquire knowledge the way most of us have—didactic teaching and reading words on a printed page—are automatically handicapped. Loosen up the system to recognize learning differences, and the disabled population would shrink.[199]

Only when (and if) our best efforts as teachers fall short should we begin affixing the label "special education" on children.

Excellence is possible, according to advocates. That is, the system is succeeding with some children. As Fred Weintraub of the Council for Exceptional Children says, "We're taking children with severe and profound disabilities, kids who were previously thrown on the junk pile of American society, and we're turning out productive citizens."

In other words, the models are there for us to copy. In 1975, our nation made a promise to children with disabilities. It's a promise worth keeping.

QUESTIONS TO ASK ABOUT SPECIAL EDUCATION

- What is the percentage of students in special education, and how does that compare to the state as a whole?
- Do the identified children differ demographically (by race and class) from the rest of the school?
- How does the school deal with disruptive behavior by disabled students? Are there, in effect, two separate codes of conduct, one for the disabled and one for other students?
- What percentage is identified as learning disabled?
- What percentage is identified as ADD?

- How many students are being sent to private institutions, with tuition paid by the district?
- How much is the district spending on legal costs?
- What training has been provided to regular classroom teachers to help them prepare for mainstreaming?
- Are aides provided? Have they had adequate training?
- What support is given to special education students? Some schools are quite hostile to providing adequate services for either high achievers or those with other special needs.
- What percentage of kids is excluded from mandated tests?
- What reasons are given when kids are excluded from tests?
- What is the "exit rate" from special education? Is anyone keeping track?

12

"DON'T SMILE UNTIL CHRISTMAS" AND OTHER CLICHÉS

The world of teaching is full of clichés, from "those who can't do, teach" to its opposite, "reach for the power—teach!" Consumers have to learn to work their way through the educational jargon and get in the habit of asking, "What do you mean by that?"

I'm also fascinated by teachers' own attitudes about their line of work, attitudes that find expression in familiar one-liners. How about a teacher who says, "I really don't need to get to know the students. I'm teaching English." Can a teacher with that attitude be excellent? I don't think so. That's like a doctor saying that he doesn't need to get to know his patients because, after all, "I'm an eye surgeon," or "I'm in orthopedics." As Ted Sizer notes, "If I care about teaching serious history, then I have to understand each kid well enough to know whether some sense of the discipline, and not just the material, is finding its way into that kid's way of thinking. It's not enough to be only a good historian."

Equally problematic, however, is the "bleeding heart" teacher who exclaims, "I don't teach English. I teach children." Wrong! You're teaching both at the same time. In my experience, teachers who "teach children" often come up short when it comes to making certain that their students acquire the habits of mind and the knowledge they need.

"I taught it, but they didn't learn it" is the most harmful attitude of all, and it's probably the most widespread, even though few teachers today would say that aloud. It is, however, the operating paradigm of American schooling, and it's an attitude that allows teachers to avoid taking responsibility for the outcome of their work. Am I being too tough on teachers here, blaming them for their students' failure? I don't think so, because for years teachers have not been held accountable for their teaching; they've gotten away with saying, in effect that they had taught it, but the students hadn't learned it. About the only teacher who could *not* get away with saying that has been the swimming teacher, who would have had difficulty explaining the bodies at the bottom of the pool. Why do we accept that attitude from teachers? Unfortunately, it's rare to hear a teacher say, "If the kids haven't learned it, then I haven't taught it."

Far better is the attitude, "If a child can't learn the way I teach, then I must learn to teach the way she learns." That's the philosophy of Ronald Williams, the principal of Newberry Elementary School in Detroit, and it's the belief system that he wants all of his teachers to adhere to. Teachers at Newberry work in grade-level clusters and share performance results and teaching tips with each other, because success is a team effort.[200]

"I don't teach; I facilitate" is another silly either-or attitude that stands in the way of the serious business of education. In that view, the teacher is no longer "the sage on the stage" but is instead "the guide on the side." E. D. Hirsch says an excellent teacher is both a sage and a guide. "It's a bad sign if the teacher's doing all the talking. There has to be some interchange because having the students talk back to the teacher is a form of monitoring. It tells the teacher whether the students understand." But, Hirsch adds, "If the teacher doesn't know more than the children, why is she the teacher?"

In short, even when the teacher is being "the sage on the stage," the class should be highly interactive and engaging, so that nobody is bored, and everybody is participating. That it's hard to be both sage and guide may explain why teachers seem to present themselves as one or the other.

CHILDREN, CHILDREN, CHILDREN

"All children can learn" is near the top of the list when it comes to educational clichés, but whether or not most of us believe it to be true is debatable. When David Hornbeck took office as Philadelphia's Superintendent of Schools in 1994, he told me that he discovered that many people there had a "belief gap." "They say they believe that all children can learn, but deep inside they really don't think they can."[201] Lauren Resnick of the University of Pittsburgh says her research backs up Hornbeck's observation. "Deep down, most Americans believe that some people are smart and some aren't," Resnick told me. "And so they expect some children to learn and others not to."[202] Resnick and others have noted that Americans believe in hard work in most other aspects of life but not in school. "I just can't do math" is an expression Americans use, Resnick observes, as if the ability to solve algebraic equations were a natural gift. Children who've just come to the United States from other countries don't say that—or think that—because they know that hard work is required.

Just how common is the cliché "all children can learn"? Reporter Andy Mollison of Cox Newspapers found it had been used 397 times in newspapers and over the Associated Press wire between January 1, 1999, and September 1, 2000.[203]

When teachers say one thing and believe another, children suffer. If teachers do not expect their students to be able to master difficult concepts, learn to write clearly, or ask probing questions, it is likely that they won't. Expectations—what we believe children need and are capable of—are the foundation of any curriculum. If we have decided that some children do not need to be challenged or will not need an "academic" curriculum (because they're going to be blue-collar workers, for example), we are denying them their birthright as Americans.[204]

So when an educator says, "All children can learn," heed the advice of another cliché, "Watch what I do, not what I say." Find out what that teacher expects and demands of all students in his classroom. That will tell you whether he believes his own words.

TAKING CLICHÉS LITERALLY

I have a theory about teachers and their training that explains why the profession is riddled with clichés and unimaginative thinking. Schooling is a risk-averse business, one in which "he who hesitates wins." When you get punished for being a risk-taker, you learn to keep your head down and follow the rules, no matter how inane.

And they get pretty stupid. The principal of my high school in the mid-'60s wrote up teachers if we failed to keep kids from writing on the desktops. How much have things changed? In 1999 my daughter was written up by her principal for failing to have her daily lesson plan in the upper left corner of her desk, as regulations require! In 2000 I visited elementary schools that order teachers to change their bulletin boards monthly. Not "suggest" but require, as if teachers cannot be trusted to care on their own.

Teacher training also squashes tendencies to make waves or to be flexible. I've listened as would-be teachers were told, over and over, "Don't smile until Thanksgiving." (Sometimes they're told to wait until after Christmas!) The idea behind the cliché makes sense: if you start out with control, it's easy to loosen up, but start lax and you'll never gain control. But apparently fledgling teachers are not told to use common sense and to treat each situation (and each child) separately and individually. Just "Don't Smile!" It's as if those training the teachers didn't have faith, and so they were trying to make teaching itself teacher-proof!

While the best teachers learn from experience to throw off these misguided lessons, rookies often take them literally. An experienced school superintendent discovered this when she went to pick up her son, a kindergartner, in the first week of school. His teacher, a rookie, had been taught that *every* kindergartner had to take a nap *every* day and so, at naptime, she told the kids to lie down and sleep. The superintendent's son raised his hand and asked if he could read instead because he wasn't tired. No, she told him. It's naptime and you have to sleep. But I'm not sleepy, he said. That doesn't matter, she told him. No reading. Put your head down and try to sleep.

It's not hard to figure out what the little boy learned in school that day. Let's hope that the teacher eventually began to doubt the wisdom of following to the letter her professor's advice about keeping control of the classroom.

"RAISE YOUR HANDS (AND SHUT UP!)"

Trainees are taught to get a noisy class's attention by raising one hand and then keeping it up until everyone has quieted down. I've seen it so often that it qualifies as a physical cliché.[205] Jonathan Kozol tells how a teacher in the South Bronx takes the concept of making a gesture to get a rowdy class's attention and elevates it from the banal. Kozol had taken over the third-grade class and found the discussion getting out of hand. As the noise level rose, the teacher, April Gamble, knew exactly what to do. "She rose to her feet and put one hand, with fingers curled up slightly, just beneath her mouth, and curled her other hand in the same way but held it out about twelve inches, maybe eighteen inches, to the right. I watched with fascination as the class subsided from the chaos I'd created and the children stood and did the same thing Mrs. Gamble did."[206]

Kozol was baffled. "Then the teacher started humming softly—then she briefly trilled a melody in her soprano voice—and some of the children started trilling in their own voices too, and suddenly I understood: it was an orchestra, and they were the flute section."

The class became calm (music hath charms . . .), Mrs. Gamble and the students put their "flutes" away, and Jonathan and the kids resumed their discussion. That is excellent teaching, respectful, imaginative, engaging . . . a sharp contrast with the literal "raise your hand and be quiet."

THE BLOB, OR "WE'RE *ALL* TEACHERS IN THIS DISTRICT"

If I have a favorite educational cliché it has to be "The Blob," because I was partially responsible for its emergence as a term of disapproval for the education bureaucracy. "Bureaucracy" itself is nearly a curse word among school critics, but we upped the ante with a report on the *MacNeil/Lehrer NewsHour* in 1987. I had been hearing tales of education's "swollen bureaucracy" from Republicans in Washington, particularly from Education Secretary William Bennett, and asked my editors at the *NewsHour* to approve a story. They gave their approval, and I, together with Producer Tim Smith, set out to find the facts and turn them into television.

After finding out what we could about national patterns and determining that school districts often classified employees as "teachers" even though they were not in classrooms on a regular basis, we decided to focus on one school district, Alexandria, Virginia. We chose it because it fit the profile, it was nearby, and one of its former teachers was Mary Futrell, then president of the National Education Association, the teacher union.

We began interviewing teachers, principals, administrators, board members, and critics. Then we got lucky. In an interview, a school board member complained about all the federal and state programs the district had to administer. "Every year we get new programs," she said, "but the old ones never go away. They just keep growing, like some giant blob."

Bingo! Suddenly all those Saturday mornings at the movies were not wasted: an image of Steve McQueen battling what looked like a giant green garbage bag popped into my head. Tim was enthusiastic, and we rented the classic black-and-white movie *The Blob* on our way back to the office. The piece took shape as we talked and watched. Ever imaginative, Tim suggested that we begin our report with the movie Blob squeezing through a vent in the movie theater as patrons ran screaming into the street. Then we would cut to me on camera, saying "Relax, that's only a movie . . . but there's a blob in your town right now. It's in your school district."

Cut to Alexandria and a careful examination of that system's personnel records, which revealed that many so-called teachers never taught at all. Back to the movie for another look at the Blob. More information about how a school system becomes top heavy as it adds new state and federal programs, which means adding administrators, all of which it tries to obscure from public view. More Blob from the movie, more school "blob," and so forth.

That night I got a phone call at home from, of all people, Secretary Bennett. He congratulated me and (sort of) asked me if I minded if he used that term in his speeches. Well aware of his own controversial reputation, he assured me that he wouldn't mention my name.[207]

The term struck a nerve with the education community, which reacted defensively. Not us, they said, but they also began trimming the administrative side of their operation. By most reports, school systems are leaner than they've ever been, but they're still afraid of being compared to the Blob.

It's worth asking administrators how many employees actually spend their days in classrooms with kids, or with kids in some other capacity such as guidance counselor. Always be on guard against the Blob!

FACTORIES AND ASSEMBLY LINES

"We have to get rid of the old *factory-model approach* to schooling."[208] According to this cliché, "public schools are nothing more than factories," grim places in which students are mere objects on an assembly line, with teachers attempting to pour knowledge into their heads as they pass by. Political candidates and other school critics can't seem to keep from describing schools as factories, in a metaphor that assumes that factories are the antithesis of quality.

Hello! Has anyone out there *visited* a factory lately? Modern factories are efficient, clean, productive, and accountable for outcomes. Would anybody make that statement about most public schools? I am *not* equating children with automobiles or any other product, but our schools would do well to emulate the processes, working conditions, and teamwork of many modern factories.

Productivity, a fair measure of efficiency, among American workers, is higher than it's ever been, while studies of schools reveal that less than 60 percent of the school day is devoted to actual instruction.

Unlike most schools, industry has discovered that workers in a clean, safe, modern factory are more productive, a message that OSHA and other regulatory groups are eager to deliver. By contrast, the average public school is more than 40 years old, and the majority were built either before World War Two or immediately thereafter. The mold, mildew, and poor air in these buildings[209] may be responsible for the increases in childhood medical problems, including asthma. A 1999 study by the National Education Association estimated that it would cost $268 billion to repair our schools. The NEA put the price tag for New York State alone at $51 billion.

Unlike most schools, factories stress accuracy. For example, Motorola rejects products that deviate as little as .000001 from specifications. Schools have trouble measuring student progress accurately and have a long history of promoting students based on their age and "seat time," instead of academic accomplishments.

Unlike most classrooms, modern factories stress teamwork. At Toyota's giant automobile assembly plant in Georgetown, Kentucky, 7,800 workers are divided into teams of four or five workers. Employees are trained in team building, according to spokesman Rick Hesterberg. Training is needed, because cooperation isn't taught in most classrooms; in fact, when students "cooperate" in class, it's called cheating. Teachers rarely cooperate. They work alone, isolated from other adults, and their work—teaching—is never seen by their peers.

Unlike most schools, modern factories practice accountability. When a Toyota team member spots a problem, he or she must take action before the car moves along the line, and team members hold one another accountable. The goal is a failure rate of zero. By contrast, teachers and administrators are rarely held accountable.[210] In a practice known cynically as "passing the trash," some teachers pass failing students, secure in the knowledge that they will be some other teacher's problem next year. They rationalize with another cliché, "I taught the material, but the kids just didn't learn it."

Factories—old and new—make things, but many schools can't say that. Instead, they're more like old-fashioned egg grading or apple-sorting plants whose function it is to sort, classify, and reject, but not to take responsibility for the rejects.

Our old-fashioned "good enough" schools look and act that way by design. They were set up to sort children into "winners" and "losers" at a time when an industrial age economy needed an efficient way of differentiating between those who would dig ditches or work in the fields and those who would get to sit behind desks and give orders. The sorting continues, with standardized tests making the decisions appear to be "objective."

However, our information age economy cannot afford "winners" and "losers." It needs workers who can access and process information, work in teams, communicate easily with others, and learn new skills. Unfortunately, the on-going national effort to raise educational standards focuses largely on test scores, not these necessary skills.

Excellent schools are *knowledge* factories in which students share responsibility for their own learning. In excellent schools, students often work in teams, and members take responsibility for others' learning.[211] In these knowledge factories, students are invited to take intellectual risks, in the name of greater "productivity," that is, more learning.

So for genuine education reform, let's try to change schools so that they resemble factories in which students are workers and knowledge is the product.

There are some key differences. Real factories use the same materials and the same processes to produce identical, interchangeable parts, because one aim of the modern factory is uniformity. But that is *not* what we want for our children, who of course are not uniform to begin with and never could be. Children are individuals with different ways of learning and with different strengths and, perhaps, with "multiple intelligences."[212] And so schools should emulate the modern factory's reliance on clear, uniform standards and its low tolerance for failure—but not its concern for uniform outputs.

The second key difference has to do with what's being produced. Students, the "knowledge workers," are actively learning and constantly evaluating their work with the help and supervision of teachers, the "knowledge factory foremen."[213] The job of the supervisors is to see that each worker achieves to the best of his or her ability and to maximize the factory's output.

Schools should be held responsible for outcomes just as modern factories are. That requires clear goals and standards. When a chip-production plant fails to achieve its goals, it doesn't blame the chips. It doesn't run for more hours or more days, the way some education reformers are pushing for more schooling. Instead, the factory examines its own procedures and makes necessary corrections. If it fails to improve, more radical steps are called for, including closing down. How often is a public school shut down for failing to educate its students?

"LOCAL CONTROL" AND "NO NATIONAL CURRICULUM"

These two expressions belong together because they deserve each other. In addition to qualifying for my personal cliché hall of fame, they are American myths. Hypocritical politicians pledge to support "local control of the public schools" with fervor and also rant about the dangers of a "national curriculum imposed by bureaucrats in Washington."

Give it up! We don't have local control, because someone else pays the bills. And we already have a national curriculum, although it was not designed by anyone in the nation's capital. Its authors are the triple towers of textbooks, technology, and television. Kids study from look-alike (bland) textbooks while they're in school. The Internet is connecting most of us with one another, introducing us to new worlds and dizzying change. Most Americans attend "class" at the University of TV with Professors Regis, Oprah, Jay Leno, and David Letterman.[214]

It's widely recognized that most teachers rely on textbooks *and* that most textbooks are remarkably similar. Because of statewide adoption policies, large states like Texas and California have a disproportionate influence over content. Publishers live in fear of offending anyone, so textbooks have been homogenized. And that's what most of our kids get.[215]

Strengthening the national curriculum is the fact that most academic subjects don't change across state lines. Mathematics, algebra, and science are the same in South Dakota and South Carolina.[216]

Although 49 states are demanding accountability and developing standards, does anyone seriously believe that the standards established by the states will differ greatly from one another? IBM's Lou Gerstner once compared the process of creating educational standards to the "bubbling up" process that IBM encourages at its regional headquarters. "It's healthier that way," he said, "because everyone at IBM has a stake in the outcome." He conceded, however, that when the process was complete, the result had to be a *single* standard because computers in New York had to be able to "interface" with computers in California.

That's likely to happen in education as well. More to the point, however, is Gerstner's simile, the world of technology. Computers in the United States also have to be able to connect with computers in New Dehli, Brussels, Tokyo, and Sydney, because technology is breaking down barriers. Perhaps we're on the road to an *international* curriculum and common cultural understandings and connections. Looking at the world from that perspective makes ranting against a "national curriculum" or for "local control" puerile.

Because we already have a de facto national curriculum, let's spend more energy improving it. The first step should be serious conversations about the purposes of education.

As for "local control," we will *not* have it until parents and children have a variety of excellent schools to choose from. That's genuine "local control."

BEYOND CLICHÉS

We desperately need to get beyond all the talk about education that claims to be "standards-based, brain-based, child-centered, site-centered, teacher-tested, results-oriented, business-backed, community-based, teacher-proof, gender-neutral, Web-based, and family-friendly." My eyes glaze over when I hear any of those expressions.

I'm sick of hearing that "children are our future" and "teachers touch the future." Ditto "developmentally appropriate" and "lifelong learners." Hackneyed expressions create a fog around the enterprise and keep us from having honest discussions about the goals of schooling.

In the end, there may not be very much to debate, because most parents want schools that teach basic skills, develop their children's desire to keep learning, provide emotional support, teach broadly shared community values, and keep their children safe. They want a school that knows their child by name, and they want to know that at least some of the adults in the building care about him or her and want each student to be a winner.

Caring parents don't sort their children into winners and losers; they figure out what each child needs to succeed and then try to provide it. The modern school ought to be set up to do that. Our economy and our society can't afford schools that pick winners and losers. Better that parents and their children have opportunities to choose schools that will work for them.

EPILOGUE

"And in conclusion . . . "

I realize that I don't want this book to end.[217] I enjoy waking up at night with my brain making connections, seeing the old in new ways. I feel alive to the possibilities of change, and I am more and more convinced that we must act to improve the life chances (including the educational opportunities) of all our children.

Every day something or someone reminds me of what's at stake, of what we stand to lose. Yesterday I was sitting in the back of a fourth-grade class, watching a young teacher at work. Earlier she had pointed out a boy who was giving her trouble, saying that he was fidgety and noisy. He doesn't understand the math, she said, so he's frustrated.

During the math lesson she began to distribute square plastic chips, which educators call "manipulatives," so that students could work out a problem involving both area and perimeter. She gave each student eight 1-inch squares and told them to make a figure that would be eight inches square with a perimeter of 14 inches. Most students arranged the plastic blocks into rectangles and then waited for the teacher to tell them whether they had done it correctly (they hadn't). The troublesome boy was looking around the room, paying no attention to the task. I walked to his desk and noticed that he had created an irregular shape with a perimeter of 14 inches. He smiled and said, "I figured it out." I asked if he could create a different shape that would also have a 14-inch perimeter. He moved one block and looked up at me. "There," he said. I challenged him to find another, and he did, instantly. By now it was a game between us, so I got three more blocks and created a new problem, which he also solved. I suggested that he help a couple of his classmates who were still waiting for the teacher's attention, which he did with apparent pride.

That bright young boy has a right to be challenged, and he needs to be. If he's not, perhaps that wonderful energy will turn negative, even anti-social. I've taught at five levels: junior high, high school, college, graduate school, and federal prison.[218] I think the most intellectually curious students I ever taught were inmates. I still wonder what twisted roads led them there. Had they been overlooked by overworked teachers in crowded classrooms in "good enough" schools?

* * * *

Despite my criticism of "good enough" schools, I have developed greater sympathy for "good enough" *anything*, because I know how easy it is to grow complacent. Most of us do it all the time in our daily lives. For example, when we find an acceptable pattern of activity (a route to the store or ways of folding laundry or brushing our teeth) we tend to stop looking for alternatives. This way, our brains conclude, is "good enough."

What sparks us to look for the new? Sometimes it's competition, or boredom, or curiosity, but we cannot assume that it will happen naturally. Left alone, bureaucratic organizations like school systems easily become complacent. They need friendly critics (and probably a few unfriendly ones as well). To ensure that schools don't settle for being "good enough," they need standards, a thoughtful accountability system, and competition.

From the point of view of children and families, choice strikes me as a right. After all, our system compels children to go to school. Doesn't that create an obligation to see that all kids have genuine choices? I think it does.

A second reason for widespread variety and choice is that there never can be "one best system" that offers solutions to every child's educational problems and needs.

* * * *

I am weary of the common defense of high-stakes tests that goes something like this: "We give students many chances to take the test." That is true, of course. Some states let students take the graduation exam as early as tenth-grade and let them try again and again. Big deal! These tests do not offer a description of what the student doesn't know, and most schools don't have the staff to provide diagnosis and treatment. Having multiple opportunities is a lot like taking a sick person's temperature over and over again. Okay, so we know he's got a fever. Now what? (Multiple testing may be worse, because if the nurse tells me every hour that I'm running a temperature, it does not make my condition worse. Failing a test over and over, however, is harmful to one's health.)

As we proceed to develop sensible high academic standards for all kids, we need to develop *multiple measures*, not provide multiple opportunities to be measured in the same way. We cannot do that unless we're willing to trust teachers.

* * * *

We could learn something about how to treat teachers by studying other cultures. In Japan, for example, teachers are given time to prepare and to meet with colleagues. Even though public schools in Japan are open for 200 or more days a year (in contrast with the U.S. norm of 180), Japanese secondary school teachers spend fewer *hours* teaching. Why? Because they are expected to be completely prepared to get their material across, and they are held accountable.

Time is something teachers desperately need, time to reflect, time to share, time to learn. Middle school teachers often work in teams (the English teacher, the math teacher, etc.). Once a day the team members who teach the same 20 or so students get together for a full period. As they share progress reports, insights, and frustrations, they are acknowledging their *shared* responsibility for these kids.

The best teachers take time from their own lives and give it to their profession, to their students. New teachers and teachers in new ventures like charter schools work long hours, fueled by idealism and adrenaline, but it's reckless policy to rely on superhuman energy. We need a system that will allow good people to grow and *become* excellent, not one that wears down and burns out its workers.

It's also reckless policy to leave the education of our young to adults we are not willing to pay adequately.[219] Teachers[220] need more money too. Why is it that our society is filled with *former* teachers? Often these men and women left for financial reasons, and many still miss the classroom. So why aren't they on the front lines today urging higher salaries for teachers?

The answer to this paradox comes back to time: how the public sees teachers using it. I spent six years (between August 1994 and August 2000) documenting school reform in Philadelphia.[221] I spent hundreds of hours with teachers and with the leaders of their union, and I cannot recall a *single* conversation about either the craft of teaching or the philosophy of education. I listened to talk of strikes, protests, parental irresponsibility, poor working conditions, cutbacks and give-backs, and other expressions of mistrust. This bunker "them against us" mentality eliminated the possibility of dialogue, which in turn reduced the chances of real change to just about zero.

Teachers deserve more money. Perhaps American society would be willing to pay them more if we saw them as intellectuals engaged in *their own* learning even as they were teaching our children. For years I've heard people say that teaching would attract "better" people if it paid more, but that strikes me as an excuse for inaction. Despite talk of a serious teacher shortage, many (perhaps most) of the men and women who are now teaching will *still* be with our children twenty years from now, so let's work with them. But if teachers and their union leaders are not willing to take responsibility for student learning—not just in contractual provisions about accountability, but philosophically—and if they're not interested in their own learning, then the entire enterprise of public education is condemned to mediocrity.

****

This seems to be a book about multiples. Relying on a *single* measure to determine whether students pass, get promoted, graduate, or earn scholarships and other awards is bad policy. Schools should develop and rely upon "multiple measures" of what a student has learned and can do. Providing "multiple opportunities" to take the *same* test is not a sensible substitute, just more bad policy.

Although I began with a list, you won't find one in this book, which is constructed instead around multiple questions. That's because making judgments about the excellence of *schools* also requires multiple measures, just as it does with students. A checklist is just as superficial as a true-false test.

Achieving excellence requires *multiple* efforts (and perhaps, multiple failures). When we are content to do things one way, we end up with "good enough" schools. Excellence is built on a foundation of choice, variety, innovation, and competition. And, of course, high expectations.

Remember the old joke about the tourist who asked how to get to Carnegie Hall? "Practice, practice, practice," was the quick reply. So how do we get to excellence? The answer is "Expectations, expectations, expectations."

The road to excellence doesn't *end* with high expectations, of course. But if we do not begin with the assumption that every child has as much potential as that young fourth-grader and is entitled to be challenged; and if we do not believe that all children deserve opportunities to go as far as their talent, intelligence, and desire can take them, we're not *going* anywhere.

NOTES

PREFACE

1. John Tulenko watched literally hundreds of hours of videotape from our archives to find the right moments to illustrate the points we wished to make. He then edited the program, another monumental task.

2. If after reading this book you want more questions worth asking, see the publications of the Center for Law and Education and Community Action for Public Schools at 1875 Connecticut Avenue NW, Suite 510, Washington, DC 20009 or on the Web at http://www.cleweb.org.

CHAPTER 1: INTRODUCTION

3. But if transportation is not provided, then choice is only available to those able to pay for it out of their own pockets.

4. These plans always end up in protracted court battles. Eventually the U.S. Supreme Court will have to decide if vouchers are constitutional. The voucher programs in Florida, Milwaukee, and Cleveland do not provide enough money to pay the full costs of tuition. Cleveland's provides up to $2,250, for example, and Florida's so-called "Opportunity Scholarship" is worth up to $3,389.

5. Charles Glenn, "The Teachers' Muddle," *Wilson Quarterly*, August 1999.

6. *The Merrow Report* on National Public Radio, Fall 2000.

7. "Reality Check," a report from Public Agenda published in *Education Week*, February 16, 2000.

8. The long-established pattern of choice for those able to afford to move reinforces the status quo and actually makes the playing field more uneven, because the school districts that people move into benefit greatly. Real estate values go up, and because property taxes provide the core of school funding in most areas, that means a larger, richer base of support for the school district. Its reputation as a provider of good education is enhanced, making it likely that it will be rewarded with a larger budget. See also "Analyzing School Choice Reforms that Use America's Traditional Forms of Parental Choice," by Caroline Minter Hoxby, in *Learning from School Choice*, edited by Paul Peterson and Brian Hassel (Washington, D.C.: Brookings Institution Press, 1998).

9. *New York Times*, "Would a Few Celebrities Please Move Here?" July 13, 2000, p. B12.

10. "Testing, Testing, Testing," a program in *The Merrow Report* series on PBS.

11. Larry Cuban, "Why Is It So Hard to Get 'Good' Schools?" in *Reconstructing the Common Good*, edited by Larry Cuban and Dorothy Shipps (Stanford, Calif.: Stanford University Press, 2000).

12. And are always building, of course.

13. There are grave concerns as to the value of the diplomas awarded to some graduates because of practices like giving credit for "seat time" or bogus classes that really involve running errands for administrators, not to mention social promotion. For more on this, see "Failing Forward," a program in *The Merrow Report* series on PBS.

14. Beginning with *Death at an Early Age*, a book I vividly remember devouring in an afternoon in 1967 and feeling forever changed. Kozol awakened Americans to the abysmal condition of many urban schools (in *Savage Inequalities*) and to the resilience of children (in *Ordinary Resurrections*).

15. *Ordinary Resurrections: Children in the Years of Hope* (New York: Crown, 2000), p. 292.

CHAPTER 2: LOOK, LISTEN, AND ACT

16. For more examples, see Samuel Casey Carter, *No Excuses: Lessons from 21 High-Performing High Poverty Schools* (Washington, D.C.: Heritage Foundation, 2000). Two of the schools featured in this book are the KIPP Academies in Houston and New York City. (KIPP stands for "knowledge is power program.") The founders of the Gap, Donald and Doris Fisher, have given KIPP $15 million in seed money to create hundreds of KIPP clones across the country. Also, Jonathan Kozol, *Ordinary Resurrections: Children in the Years of Hope* (New York: Crown, 2000).

17. *The Schools We Need and Why We Don't Have Them* (New York: Doubleday, 1996). See also *Cultural Literacy* (1987). Professor Hirsch made these observations in an

interview in June 2000. And a nugget of information for endnote readers: At least two of the 21 schools described in Carter's *No Excuses* use Hirsch's Core Knowledge program!

18. This seems to be changing. Studies estimate that at least 40 percent of American high schools have reshaped their class schedules so that many classes last for 90 minutes, not 45 or 47. Like all reforms, this is not a magic bullet. Teachers must be given some training in the use of the extended classtime.

19. *A Place Called School: Prospects for the Future* (New York: McGraw Hill) was first published in 1984 and has been reprinted many times.

20. About 70 percent of U.S. high schools have roughly 750 students, according to Tom Koerner, former executive director of the National Association of Secondary School Principals.

21. In an interview for *The Merrow Report* on National Public Radio.

22. Small high schools can and do join forces to field competitive athletic teams and have full-scale dramatic productions, bands, etc.

23. District superintendent Anthony Alvarado, assistant superintendents Sy Fliegel and Carlos Medina, and innovative principals like Deborah Meier. The story is told in Fliegel's book, *Miracle in East Harlem: The Fight for Choice in Public Education* (New York: Times Books, 1992).

24. And smaller is back in favor. In the fall of 2000 the William and Melinda Gates Foundation made 11 grants totaling $56 million to organizations that help develop small schools in Minneapolis, New York City, Boston, Seattle Providence, Rhode Island, and Alaska. Some of the grants were to community groups, others to school districts, still others to university-based organizations. The largest grant, $13.5 million, was to the Providence school district, which will devise ways to create "small learning environments," improve teaching, and strengthen community involvement. New York City has embraced smaller middle schools, and Cincinnati has eliminated junior highs in favor of a K–8 and 9–12 system. Minneapolis plans to follow suit.

25. The research most often cited comes out of Tennessee's Project Star, an experiment that began in 1988 involving 6,600 kindergartners. They were randomly assigned to classes of either 15 or 25 students and then followed through third grade. By that time, 11,000 students were involved. Students in smaller classes did better academically. Another study suggests that students who've been in small classes are more likely to attend college. The information is collected in a publication of the Education Writers Association and can be reviewed at http://www.ewa.org.

CHAPTER 3: TESTING, ASSESSMENT, AND EXCELLENCE

26. Think of it this way: The test may reveal that you consistently get wrong answers on simple addition problems, but that fact is not enough to tell your teacher why you are

making that mistake. That requires diagnosis, a careful analysis of how you are approaching the problem, and what you are not understanding. I am indebted to George Madaus of Boston College for this clarification. For more information on this and other matters pertaining to testing, see the Web site of Madaus's organization, the National Board on Educational Testing and Public Policy at Boston College (http://www.nbetpp. bc.edu). The organization issues occasional "statements," which are available online.

27. Interviews at the second Education Summit meeting in Armonk, N.Y., 1996.

28. Some of the goals were foolishly optimistic, particularly "We will be first in the world in math and science by the year 2000" (Goal Five). We didn't come close; our 12th graders still rank near the bottom in both subjects. On the other hand, the executive director of the National Science Teachers Association believes that the pressure to reach the goal has led to more coherent and focused science programs and to students taking more difficult science classes (physics and chemistry). The first goal, "All Children Will Start School Ready to Learn," was also foolishly optimistic. Only 50 percent of three- and four-year-olds are were enrolled in preschool in 1998, up from 38 percent when the goals were written, but few of these programs are considered to be of high quality. We came closest on Goal Two, a 90 percent graduation rate; today about 86 percent of 18- to 24-year-olds have earned high school diplomas. On the other hand, some individual states did as well or better than nearly all industrialized countries on the TIMSS (the Third International Math and Science Study) tests. That is, our performance is really a state-by-state problem, not a national one.

29. Originally there were to be *three* standards, including an "opportunity standard." This would measure access to educational opportunity, that is, was the playing field level or did some kids have distinct advantages from the beginning. This was scornfully rejected by most governors, who did not want someone rating the opportunity they were providing students; better to rate the students instead!

30. Imagine asking ten modern poets to name the ten greatest poems of the past century. Then count which poems are mentioned most often, and, bingo, you have a list, "The Greatest Poems of the Past 100 Years." But if you had asked ten different poets, or if you had asked them to rank order them, your list would be different. No matter, you would have an official sounding list!

31. Interview, March 2000. Most of the quotes from Mr. Gerstner are taken from this interview.

32. That is, 60 percent of those who showed up. Twelve percent of those assigned to summer school never bothered to come. Perhaps they had been paying attention and remembered what happened in the summer of 1999, when 8,688 kids were mistakenly assigned to summer school because of a scoring error. The error was not caught and corrected until summer school was over. New York City pupils had been assigned to summer school on the basis of their performance on the state exam. That's a classic example of a high-stakes test.

33. Some seniors who had attended summer school but had not taken the exam were awarded diplomas anyway, based on the considered judgment of their teachers. This was a statement of faith in teachers on the part of Schools Chancellor Harold Levy, and a victory for common sense. Next year, however, seniors in summer school will also have to pass the test, Levy said, "to prove to the world that our teachers know what they're doing," he told a meeting of educators on September 15, 2000.

34. The outbreak of World War II. See Nicholas Leman's excellent history, *The Big Test: The Secret History of the American Meritocracy* (New York: Farrar, Straus, Giroux, 1999).

35. This also occurred in Massachusetts. Students were tested in May, but results were not available until November, three months into the next school year, when most students were already in the next grade and perhaps in different schools. This seems to give the lie to the claim that these tests are for remediation.

36. The Mississippi State Board of Education says that the pressure to hold adults accountable came from the legislature. "The Mississippi Legislature charged the State Board of Education with developing an accountability plan to help ensure that local school boards, superintendents, principals and teachers are held accountable for student achievement. This plan was presented to the Legislature in December of 1999 and was passed by the Mississippi Legislature during the 2000 session."

37. Personal communication, September 2000. Madaus said that in one state (not Massachusetts) rounding *up* a score meant that an additional 10,000 students passed a high-stakes test. Rounding *down* meant those 10,000 failed!

38. E-mail, May 10, 2000.

39. Scott Stephens, "Many Switch Grades over Proficiency Test," *Cleveland Plain Dealer*, August 20, 2000. See also Alfie Kohn's book, *The Case Against Standardized Testing* (Portsmouth, N.H.: Heinemann, 2000).

40. If they stay in school. Brian Jacob of the University of Chicago and other researchers have found early indications that high-stakes testing increases the chances that low-scoring students will drop out.

41. An excellent history of the SAT, the most influential of all standardized tests, is Nicholas Lehman's *The Big Test*, cited previously.

42. The standardized testing business is also very lucrative. See Walt Haney, George Madaus, and R. Lyons, *The Fractured Marketplace for Standardized Testing* (Boston: Kluwer Academic Publishers, 1993).

43. Interviewed for "Testing, Testing, Testing," a program in *The Merrow Report* series on PBS.

44. Reported by Maria Sacchetti in the *Orange County* (Calif.) *Register*, July 18, 2000.

45. Ibid.

46. He used Mike Piazza of the Mets, then in the middle of a horrible slump in an otherwise superb year (*New York Times*, September 13, 2000).

47. We occasionally make judgments about an athlete based on a single moment, however. Bill Buckner of the Boston Red Sox is the best example I can think of. This potential Hall of Famer, who had nearly 3,000 hits over his career, will be forever known as the man who let an easy ground ball go through his legs, allowing the New York Mets to win the game and then the World Series.

48. Money changes hands in some places, however. North Carolina is paying bonuses of up to $1,500 to teachers whose students do well on state exams, and kids can earn "gold cards" and "silver cards" that entitle them to discounts at various stores, again based on their test scores. Other states experimenting with variations on "merit pay" include California and Kentucky (Jacques Steinberg, "Academic Gains Pay Off for Teachers and Students," *New York Times*, October 1, 2000, p. 20).

49. The interview is part of "Testing, Testing, Testing."

50. M. Hayes Mizell, "What Key Reformers Have Learned About Reform," at the annual conference of the National Staff Development Council, December 6, 1999, in Dallas, Texas.

51. I would prefer to say "intellectual," but that's not worth fighting about here.

52. "Testing, Testing, Testing."

53. For an example of an "exhibition," see our program "Testing, Testing, Testing."

54. "Testing, Testing, Testing."

55. Cutoff scores (cut scores) need to be valid also. That is, the term "needs improvement" has to have some consistent meaning that is based in reality and is worthy of trust.

56. "Testing, Testing, Testing."

57. The *New York Times* quotes a tenth-grade English teacher telling her class just before the state test, "Your whole life in this class depends on whether you pass one question" (October 1, 2000, p. 20).

58. One school district's plan to give a standardized test to kindergartners was defeated, thankfully.

59. And the Old Guard prevailed, in large part because of a failure of leadership on the part of the school principal and the superintendent of schools, neither of whom put their authority behind the reform on a day-to-day basis. And, of course, the veterans knew how to put on the brakes, as teachers always seem to learn how to do. The full saga can be seen in "The Fifty Million Dollar Gamble," a program in *The Merrow Report* series on PBS that aired in 1994.

60. E-mail, May 13, 2000.

61. Reported by Maria Sacchetti in the *Orange County* (Calif.) *Register*, July 18, 2000. She cites one high school that will require that students reach only the 23rd percentile to qualify for a high school diploma. That means that 77 percent of those taking the test did better on it, so perhaps that's not really "high-stakes" testing after all.

62. My favorite story of high-stakes testing gone astray concerns some savvy high school students in California who, on the eve of a mandated state test that was used to rate *schools but not individual students,* informed the principal that they would deliberately mark wrong answers unless he agreed to change some school rules about student parking privileges. Rather than have his school and his own reputation tarnished, he gave in.

63. Today students in excellent schools have access to the Internet and endless avenues to explore and learn.

64. The Core Knowledge program and other leading school reforms are examined in detail in "Early Learning," a 1996 program in *The Merrow Report* series on PBS.

65. The 32nd Annual Phil Delta Kappa/Gallup Poll, Phi Delta Kappan, September 2000, p. 14.

66. See http://www.publicagenda.org for complete details. The survey results were made public in October 2000. The same survey indicated that 41 percent of parents did not know how many standardized tests their children have to take, how difficult they are, or how much chair time is spent getting ready for them.

67. This story is told in detail in "Elementary Confusion," a program in *The Merrow Report* series on PBS. It was broadcast in 1998.

68. See "The Myth of the Texas Miracle in Education," in the August 19, 2000, edition of Education Policy Analysis Archives, published by the University of Wisconsin's Center for Education Research, Analysis and Information.

69. E-mail, May 12, 2000.

70. Two groups, Achieve and the National Governors Association, are good sources of information about standards. Achieve is at 8 Story Street, First Floor, Cambridge, MA 02138. The NGA is in the Hall of States, 444 North Capitol Street, Washington, DC 20001-1512.

71. His name was William L. Sullivan, and I was privileged to be in his English class during my junior and senior years of high school. I became an English teacher because of him. In those distant days, a "sentence fragment" was defined as an incomplete sentence, usually a group of words lacking a verb. I am certain that today Mr. Sullivan would be in harmony with the accepted view that a sentence is complete if it expresses a complete thought (verb not essential). Even then he allowed us to write in fragments as long as we used an * to indicate that we were doing it deliberately.

72. One that I still remember, nearly 40 years later, was "Turn out the light. I do not want to go home in the dark," which, we were told, were the dying words of William Sidney Porter. We had to make sense of those paradoxical words. Only later did Mr. Sullivan tell us that William Sidney Porter was O. Henry's real name.

CHAPTER 4: TECHNOLOGY AND EXCELLENCE

73. But not—repeat *not*—a threat to replace well-trained adults!

74. On *The Merrow Report* on NPR, February 29, 2000. Mr. Chou is founder and president of Learn Technologies Interactive and director of the New Laboratory for Teaching and Learning at the Dalton School in New York City.

75. *Who's Who Among American High School Students*, 1999. The fact that they use the Internet does not mean that they are cheating.

76. Teachers who attempt to control the uses of technology the way they have traditionally controlled classrooms will not succeed. For example, the teacher who is accustomed to prescribing to the last detail exactly how a research paper must be done will be frustrated if he insists that students use the Internet and other resources precisely according to his plan. In the end, students will ignore him, or cheat, or become disillusioned and do poorly in the class. Technology rewards flexibility and innovation, and it punishes those who are determined to control everything.

77. It's a psychometric impossibility, in the considered opinion of most of the experts I've met.

78. Inevitably, they will find also piles and piles of useless, unrelated information because the Internet is not yet a mature research tool. This will be frustrating to students and teachers alike, but it should not be an insurmountable obstacle.

79. "Promises, Promises," a program in *The Merrow Report* series on PBS, 1997.

80. See http://nces.ed.gov/pubsearch/pubsinfo.asp?pubid=200090 for the full report.

81. "Myths and Realities about Technology in K-12 Schools," in David T. Gordon, ed., *The Digital Classroom* (Harvard Education Letter, 2000). See also Larry Cuban's *Oversold and Underused* (Harvard University Press, forthcoming).

82. In "Promises, Promises," a program in *The Merrow Report* series on PBS.

83. Personal communication, September 2000. The teacher asked to remain anonymous.

84. Personal communication, fall 2000.

85. As Dr. Packer says, "For many students in the inner city, the ability to make an effective presentation to a diverse audience may be the most important lesson they will receive."

86. The Secretary's Commission on Achieving Necessary Skills, formed under Labor Secretary William Brock.

87. Conducted by AIR, the American Institutes of Research.

88. Ted Sizer, a founding trustee of the Parker Charter Essential School in rural Massachusetts with his wife, Nancy, shared the story of what his students are doing. "We have a serious senior project requirement, and kids are using the technology to link up with all sort of places, and we're letting kids spin out of the building into work, into col-

laboration, including some of the 'dot.com' companies that are springing up." The reaction to liberating students this way has not been entirely positive, Sizer notes. "Some adults leap to attack along predictable lines: safety, inexperience, the need for supervision to keep kids from just roaming the malls. They don't see that the status quo is for most students a waste of time at best; at worst a breeder of cynicism. Something better, something focused, something respectful of their abilities and intelligence can emerge, and technology is a big part of this." Personal communication, September 2000.

89. "How Lessons Can Compute," *Baltimore Sun*, April 27, 2000.

90. National Center for Education Statistics, "Teacher Use of Computers and the Internet in Public Schools," April 2000.

91. Private schools, with greater control over curriculum, are more likely to do this.

92. Portions of the interview are in "School Sleuth: The Case of an Excellent School," a program in *The Merrow Report* series on PBS in November 2000.

93. "Myths and Realities about Technology in K-12 Schools," in David T. Gordon, ed., *The Digital Classroom* (Harvard Education Letter, 2000).

94. It's ironic that schools are rushing to become wired even as wireless technology is emerging. In other words, old buildings will not pose as much of an obstacle as they now do, because networks are going wireless and machines are becoming more energy efficient. However, one cannot fault schools for having acted. One cannot do nothing just because things are changing rapidly; that leads to what Tom Koerner, former executive director of the National Association of Secondary School Principals, calls "technology paralysis."

95. I wonder if the school boards that authorize buying all that equipment have any idea of how the technology is used, or *if* it is! Do school boards have procedures in place to find out, or does their responsibility end with signing the check?

96. "Hi, Mom" is the bane of our existence, because it immediately destroys the illusion that we are trying to create—that we're not there!

CHAPTER 5: THE "RUSHED, CRUNCHED, AND ISOLATED" WORLD OF TEACHERS

97. Most of the teachers I have known work in the evenings at home preparing lessons and marking papers; many spend parts of their summer preparing new lessons or keeping up in their field.

98. I don't know very many adults in other occupations who could step into a classroom and have it run smoothly. The last few times I have tried it proved embarrassing, and I was a public schoolteacher for four years. It's just plain hard work.

99. For more information, visit this website (http://nces.ed.gov/timss), call 202-502-7421, or send an e-mail (timss@ed.gov).

100. Assuming they have learned how to create effective tests!

101. Other students told their parents, who then complained to the principal. The teacher, however, had kept the principal informed of his plans and all subsequent developments, and, to his credit, the principal stood firmly behind his teacher.

102. Quick now, what's the capital of South Dakota? Missouri? The longest river in North America? If you are of a certain age, you answered all three questions correctly. (And you also remember how many wives Henry VIII had, don't you?)

103. An effective science lesson could also be constructed around a #2 pencil, of course.

104. He defended his actions by saying that he could not find qualified people who were willing to come to rural Georgia. While that may be true, it's also true that the existence of the loophole provides slight incentive to look hard and long to find qualified people, especially in the absence of parental pressure or rules requiring the publication of teacher qualifications.

105. On *The Merrow Report* on National Public Radio, February 8, 2000.

106. All of this can be seen in "Teacher Shortage: False Alarm?" This program in *The Merrow Report* series on PBS aired in the fall of 1999.

107. A typical article can be found in the *Washington Post*, March 10, 1999, "Help Wanted: 2 Million Teachers."

108. Some would say "bribe," not persuade, because veterans were offered a 15 percent annual bonus for transferring.

109. We received a similar reaction to our coverage of alternative certification. The morning after the PBS broadcast, we received hundreds of e-mails, and roughly half of those writing expressed a strong interest in learning more about quicker ways to become teachers.

110. Remarks to a meeting on educational leadership sponsored by the Wallace/Readers Digest Funds, New York, September 2000.

111. In Sol Stern, "The Vanishing Teacher and other UFT Fictions," *City Journal* (Spring 2000, p. 31).

CHAPTER 6: SAFETY AND EXCELLENCE

112. Good sources of data about school safety are "Indicators of School Crime and Safety," available from the National Center for Education Statistics of the U.S. Department of Education, on the Web at http://nces.ed.gov.pubs98/safety/index.html. Also, the National School Safety Center at http://www.nsscl.org/home.html and Ken Trump at National Safety and Security Services (kentrump@aol.com). Trump believes that most high-tech equipment is a waste of money if schools aren't also managed properly.

113. "Do You Know the Good News about American Education?" Written by Jack Jennings and published by two Washington organizations, the Center on Education Policy and the American Youth Policy Forum.

114. Geoffrey Canada has written with great insight about the progression of violence. The title of his book captures what has been happening in many urban areas: *Fist Stick Knife Gun: A Personal History of Violence in America* (Boston: Beacon Press, 1996).

115. *New York Times*, "A Field Trip, A Teenager's Death and Questions of Responsibility," August 20, 2000, p. 33.

116. According to Education Statistics Quarterly, there were 95,000 school guidance counselors in 1998-99.

117. For more about school shootings, see the *Chicago Tribune*, October 15–16, 2000 (http://www.suntimes.com/output/news/shoot15.html).

118. The policies came about after the rash of school shootings in 1999, as parents and others demanded reassurance that their children would be protected. In that climate, it was difficult for boards to say that they trusted teachers to handle routine disturbances like playground fights, so they, in effect, went with the prevailing political wind. Teachers and kids are now paying for that lack of political courage.

119. Private communication, August 2000. The Student Advocacy Center of Michigan is at 2301 Platt Road, Ann Arbor, MI 48104. Phone 734-973-7860. The Web address is http://comnet.org/sac/.

120. Taken from an interview for "School Sleuth: The Case of an Excellent School," which appeared on *The Merrow Report* on PBS in November 2000.

121. Ibid.

CHAPTER 7: HOMEWORK AND HOME LEARNING

122. Katie Hickox is a third-grade teacher at Arroyo Elementary School in Tustin who writes regularly for the *Orange County* (Calif.) *Register*. This column appeared on August 20, 2000. I am indebted to reporter Maria Sacchetti for calling it to my attention.

123. John Buell, a former teacher, makes the case against homework in *The End of Homework: How Homework Disrupts Families, Overburdens Children, and Limits Learning* (Boston: Beacon Press, 2000). He maintains that homework is keeping children from such essentials as sports, the arts, and friendships.

124. Not to be confused with "learning styles." Some children learn visually, while others take in new material best by reading. Others learn best in groups, or with lots of background noise, or in silence. Whatever the children's learning styles, the learning curve is pretty much the same.

125. Finally, the names of Henry the VIII's wives!

126. For a veritable cornucopia of activities, see the works of Dorothy Rich of the Home and School Institute. Her work with families has achieved remarkable success. See in particular *MegaSkills* (Boston: Houghton Mifflin, 1992). The "megaskills" are confidence, motivation, effort, responsibility, initiative, perseverance, caring, teamwork, common sense, and problem solving. I used some of her "recipes" with my children and can testify that they work and are fun!

CHAPTER 8: OUR KIDS ARE NOT THE PROBLEM

127. In "Growing Up in the City," three programs in *The Merrow Report* series on PBS, April 1999.

128. "Kids These Days '99: What Americans Really Think about the Next Generation," a report from Public Agenda. Public Agenda, which was founded in 1975, may be the single best source of reliable information about public attitudes toward complex issues. For more information, see http://www.publicagenda.org.

129. Ibid. For more information, visit http://www.publicagenda.org.

130. *Ordinary Resurrections: Children in the Years of Hope* (Crown, 2000), p. 116. This is Kozol's most hopeful book. The author of *Death at an Early Age* is, in effect, telling us that these children do *not* die, despite the injustices and indignities of their world.

131. Ibid.

132. *U.S. News & World Report*, April 17, 2000, p. 48.

133. See "Your Kids Are Their Problem, by Lisa Belkin, the *New York Times Magazine*, July 23, 2000.

134. In the spring of 2000, a year after the Columbine tragedy, a few publications did an abrupt about face. See, for example, *U.S. News & World Report*'s cover story of April 17, 2000, "The Good News about Teens."

135. The meeting was held in Alaska in the summer of 1999. The young woman is not identified by name in the draft report of the meeting, which was conducted by the International Youth Foundation.

136. Kozol, *Ordinary Resurrections*, p. 137.

137. One year later I tried to contact some of the children and their families. My phone calls were answered by a disembodied voice, "disconnected, not in service at this time." Half of my letters came back to me, stamped "moved, no forwarding address" or "undeliverable."

138. "The Cost of Being Certain," *Youth Today* 7, no. 5, September 1998.

139. A report by the Federal Communications Commission revealed how major media companies deliberately target their advertising for R-rated movies to young children. The report was made public in September 2000.

140. For more information, see David Walsh, *Selling Out America's Children: How America Puts Profits Before Values and What Parents Can Do* (Minneapolis: Fairview Press, 1994).

141. *Do You Know the Good News about American Education?* published by the Center on Education Policy, Washington, DC, 1999. AP exams are annual tests offered in many different subject areas that give students an opportunity to demonstrate college-level achievement. Many colleges and universities offer college credits to those scoring at least a three on a 0–5 scale.

142. Ibid. However, because the research findings do not indicate whether these classes are *taught* by qualified teachers, enthusiasm should be tempered. After all, it's reliably estimated that at least 25 percent of these classes are being taught by people who neither majored nor minored in the subjects.

143. Ibid.

144. We still rank well behind most other industrialized nations, lest anyone begin thinking the battle for improving schooling has been won. It has not.

145. Laura Sessions Stepp, *Our Last Best Shot: Guiding Our Children through Early Adolescence* (New York: Riverhead Books).

146. "The Drug Abuse Warning Network," reported by Mike Males in *Youth Today*, September 2000. Males's new book is *Fear Profiteers: How Politicians, PhD.s and the Press Perpetrated the Youth Violence Panic.*

147. *The Merrow Report* on National Public Radio, February 8, 2000.

148. "Just Let Them Do It!" in *Youth Today* 5, no. 5 (September–October, 1996).

149. The International Youth Foundation can be reached at 32 South Street, #500, Baltimore, MD 21202 (http://www.iyfnet.org). The Rural School and Community Trust is at 808 17th Street NW, #220, Washington, DC 20006. The American Youth Policy Forum, which produced the memorable and influential report, "The Forgotten Half," is at 1836 Jefferson Place NW, Washington, DC 20036-2505. For ten issues of *Youth Today* (a one-year subscription), send $10.47 to The American Youth Work Center, 1200 17th Street NW, 4th floor, Washington, DC 20036-3006. Go to http://www.listenup.org for information about Listen Up!

CHAPTER 9: VALUES AND EXCELLENCE

150. Uncomfortable because "children should be seen and not heard."

151. Phi Delta Kappa/Gallup poll of public attitudes toward education, 1999.

152. Elementary schools still are very much in the business of imparting values, as a visit to almost any classroom will demonstrate. The walls will display posters urging cooperation, sharing, kindness, cleanliness, and many other shared, noncontroversial values.

153. We told the story in "The Search for Values," a program in *The Merrow Report* series on PBS broadcast in 1995.

154. I devote several pages of chapter 3 to another teacher's approach to teaching values. This man, an unsung hero, refused to flunk students in his elective class in ethics, having told them that only A or B work was acceptable. All other work would get a grade of Incomplete.

155. Charles Glenn, "The Teachers' Muddle," *The Wilson Quarterly*, August 1999. The article can be found in full at http://wwics.si.edu/OUTREACH/WQ/WQSELECT/ GLENN.HTM.

156. Much of the interview is in "School Sleuth: The Case of an Excellent School," a program in *The Merrow Report* series that aired in November, 2000.

157. For more of what Sizer had to say, see "School Sleuth," our PBS program.

158. Theodore R. and Nancy Faust Sizer, *The Students Are Watching: School and the Moral Contract* (Boston: Beacon Press, 1999).

159. Personal communication, September 2000.

160. Diane Ravitch, *Left Back: A Century of Failed School Reforms* (New York: Simon and Schuster, 2000), p. 465.

161. *Who's Who Among American High School Students.*

162. Portions of this interview are included in "School Sleuth," cited previously.

163. Deborah Meier tells the compelling story of Central Park East in *The Power of Their Ideas: Lessons for America from a Small School in Harlem* (Boston: Beacon Press, 1996). As a parent, you don't have to agree with Meier. But if you do and you're a New Yorker, you have the opportunity to send your children to the schools she founded, because that New York City district has parental choice. Choice is important because in education one size does not fit all.

164. Larry Cuban and Dorothy Shipps, eds., *Reconstructing the Common Good in Education* (Stanford, Calif.: Stanford University Press, 2000). Cuban's own essay is called "Why Is It So Hard to Get Good Schools?"

CHAPTER 10: CHARTER SCHOOLS—BUYER BEWARE

165. A good source of information about charter schools is the Center for Education Reform, an avowedly pro-charter organization that publishes a directory of charter schools every year. The sixth edition appeared in 2000. This valuable research document is available from CER, 1001 Connecticut Avenue NW, Suite 204, Washington, DC 20036. CER's Web address is http://www.edreform.com. CER's politics shine through another publication, *Charter Schools Today: Changing the Face of American Education*, which appeared in 2000. Another enthusiastic book is *Charter Schools in Action: Re-*

newing Public Education, by Chester E. Finn Jr., Bruno V. Manno, and Gregg Vanourek (Princeton, N.J.: Princeton University Press, 2000).

166. Unfortunately, this is often *not* the case because the charter law includes a "hold harmless" clause, essentially saying that the school a child leaves does not lose his per-pupil allotment. That's a serious disincentive to reform.

167. These should include more than scores on standardized tests. Attendance by students and teachers, portfolios of student work, financial accounting, and multimedia presentations are useful indicators of a school's progress.

168. A detailed history can be found in Joe Nathan, *Charter Schools: Creating Hope and Opportunity for American Education* (San Francisco: Jossey-Bass, 1996). Nathan, who was at that original meeting at Itasca in October 1988, remains a driving force behind charter schools today, as does Ted Kolderie. I recall general support for the fledgling charter idea, but Nathan recalls it differently. "Shanker did *not* agree at the conference about the charter idea we proposed. He wanted the whole thing controlled by unions and school boards—which of course, really was the status quo. . . . The charter idea we proposed called for multiple sponsors and real accountability, and neither was a part of what Shanker was talking about" (personal communication, September 2000).

169. "Education's Big Gamble," a program in *The Merrow Report* series on PBS, September 1998. All quotes from actors in the Citizen 2000 story are taken from the documentary itself or from interviews done for it.

170. I am indebted to Kelly Pearce of the Arizona Republic for this information. Her story appeared in the newspaper in March 1997. She also wrote, "The indictment also alleges that Citizen 2000 told the state Board of Education that it had 350 students last year, even though it actually had only 250. That resulted in the school's receiving $250,439 in state funding that it didn't deserve, the indictment said. That money, however, has been tied up in the bankruptcy proceedings and probably will never be recovered by the state. That has led to calls on the Legislature to tighten regulations on charter schools." Ultimately, the case ended in a plea bargain. Dr. Venerable pleaded guilty to a Class 6 Open Matter misdemeanor and was sentenced to two years of probation. She also paid a $15,000 fine to the state.

171. Personal communication, September 2000.

172. Although Fenton Avenue, like many urban schools, also provides breakfast.

173. Ted Sizer of the Parker Charter Essential School agrees. "Even the 'pioneers' cannot work ten hour days seven days a week forever; this problem is too readily finessed by many Charter schools; curiously they brag about how hard the teachers work; it is supposed to be a virtue. One wonders, when do these teachers have time to read a book or simply to ponder the meaning of their professional (not to mention personal) lives?" Personal communication, September 2000.

174. Reported in the *Wall Street Journal*, May 25, 1999.

175. Achievement scores are up dramatically. The school reports that it has saved more than $1 million by doing its own purchasing, rather than going through the school system's bureaucracy. Skeptics suggest that the last accomplishment accounts for bureaucratic hostility to charters; after all, bureaucracies are being shown to be unnecessary and irrelevant. Why wouldn't they be hostile?

176. Personal communication, September 2000.

177. Personal communication, September 2000.

178. *When Schools Compete: A Cautionary Tale* (Washington, D.C.: Brookings Institution Press, 2000). Fiske, an education consultant and former education editor of the *New York Times*, and Ladd, professor of economics and public policy at Duke, spent seven months in New Zealand.

179. Broadcast as part of *The Merrow Report* series on NPR.

180. Nathan is upset by their book, which he calls "a highly political document" (personal communication, September 2000).

181. *The Merrow Report* on NPR.

182. David Arsen, David Plank, and Gary Sykes, *School Choice Policies in Michigan: The Rules Matter* (University of Michigan, 1999).

183. Joe Nathan feels that charter schools are being held to a different, tougher standard than magnet schools, which were established to attract talented youth to city schools—and to keep whites from fleeing the system. Magnet schools are allowed to use admissions tests and are given more money per pupil than charter schools, he writes, citing a national study and press reports. *Charter Schools: Creating Hope and Opportunity for American Education* (San Francisco: Jossey Bass, 1996), p. 7.

184. California's charter school association objects, citing 38 charter schools in Los Angeles Unified, 20 in San Diego, 12 in Oakland, 10 each in San Francisco and Sacramento, as well as charters in Fresno, Bakersfield, Redding, and San Carlos. In all, at least one-third of California's charters are in urban settings.

185. Ibid.

CHAPTER 11: WHAT'S SPECIAL ABOUT SPECIAL EDUCATION?

186. She also told me that the institution sent Christmas cards to all parents every year and that, without fail, about half of them came back stamped "Addressee moved, left no forwarding address." That says so much about the helplessness that many parents of the handicapped felt in those days, when no help and little hope existed.

187. Walker notes wryly that history is rarely that neat. "Between our bull session and the actual law came two years of Congressional hearings and state hearings in Minneapolis, Newark, New Jersey, and Columbia, South Carolina, and a lot of hard work by

the Education Commission of the States," she told me. Walker worked for Senator Harrison "Pete" Williams, a Democrat from New Jersey. She also notes correctly that several states, including Minnesota and Massachusetts, were well ahead of the federal government when it came to providing educational services for disabled children.

188. Students are also protected under the Americans with Disabilities Act.

189. Richard Rothstein, "Rethinking Special Needs without Losing Ground," *New York Times*, July 5, 2000.

190. This is not an argument against the IEP. As a concept and a goal, it remains laudable; in fact, in an ideal school, every child, disabled or not, would have what amounts to an individualized plan—that is, the adults in the building would know each child well enough to be able to monitor his or her progress carefully.

191. Every state seems to have a few lawyers who specialize in "persuading" school systems to pay private school tuition in lieu of a costly court battle. An administrator at a school for learning disabled children on the West Coast told me that school records indicated that one lawyer was behind virtually all of the public school transfer students at the school.

192. Lisa Walker notes that the growth in numbers of students labeled LD has almost completely mirrored the shrinking of students identified as mentally retarded and emotionally disturbed.

193. And more controversy and lawsuits. I know several thoughtful observers of the testing industry who are convinced that before too long all of the key tests will be untimed, for everyone taking them.

194. Rothstein, "Rethinking Special Needs."

195. "Campaign 2000: What the Candidates Should Be Talking About." *Education Week*, March 22, 2000.

196. Ciba-Geigy. The drug is now manufactured by Novartis Pharmaceuticals, a unit of Novartis AG.

197. Which became "Children and Adults with Attention Deficit Disorder." The organization apparently saw an opportunity to expand its reach. In fact, Harvey Parker, the smooth-talking man behind ChADD, had a ready explanation for the disproportionate number of boys labeled ADD. Girls have it, he said, but the level of awareness isn't there yet.

198. The full and seamy story is told in "ADD: A Dubious Diagnosis?" This program in *The Merrow Report* series appeared on PBS in the fall of 1995 and won awards for investigative reporting. Both ChADD and Ciba-Geigy attempted to prevent its broadcast, even going so far as to threaten lawsuits against me, PBS, our funders, and South Carolina ETV, our presenting station. The program was broadcast as scheduled, and neither ChADD nor Ciba-Geigy sued. It was awarded first prize for Investigative Reporting by the Education Writers Association.

199. For a persuasive argument that seven different intelligences exist, see Howard Gardner's *Frames of Mind: The Theory of Multiple Intelligences* (10th anniversary edition,

New York: Basic Books, 1993), *Multiple Intelligences: The Theory in Practice* (New York: Basic Books, 1993), and *The Disciplined Mind* (New York: Penguin Books, 2000).

CHAPTER 12: "DON'T SMILE UNTIL CHRISTMAS" AND OTHER CLICHÉS

200. Samuel Casey Carter, *No Excuses: Lessons from 21 High-Performing, High-Poverty Schools* (Washington, D.C.: Heritage Foundation, 2000).

201. For the story of Hornbeck's six years in Philadelphia, see "Toughest Job in America," a program in *The Merrow Report* series on PBS. It first aired in September 2000.

202. In "School Sleuth: The Case of an Excellent School," a program in *The Merrow Report* series that aired on PBS in November 2000. Professor Resnick is optimistic. "I really do believe that everybody can learn, and I believe it because I've seen it. I've seen the kids who you wouldn't think would know how to do spectacular things, and I've seen ordinary teachers who didn't think they could do it take the kids to very high levels."

203. Personal communication, September 2000. He used Lexis-Nexis, a research tool. Even more popular was the old saw, "It takes a village to raise a child," which turned up 749 times! Clichés can be, and often are, true; the issue is whether educators and others are using phrases like "all children can learn" mindlessly, in the way that fads spread. (Speaking of fads, what's happened to all those "Save the Children" neckties that every male educator seemed to be wearing in the late '90s?)

204. We've done this before in our history. See Diane Ravitch, *Left Back: A Century of Failed School Reforms* and E. D. Hirsch Jr., *The Schools We Need and Why We Don't Have Them* (New York: Doubleday, 1996).

205. It also reminds me of Mussolini and Hitler, or maybe Charlie Chaplin's parody in *The Great Dictator*.

206. Kozol, *Ordinary Resurrections*, pp. 275–76.

207. He kept his word. Then, in what must have been one of his final press briefings as secretary, he pointed me out in the audience and gave me "credit" for coming up with the term.

208. Politicians are fond of trotting this out while proclaiming their commitment to school reform. "We've done some things wrong in education, and here's one of them: herding all students in a 25-square-mile area into overcrowded, factory-style high schools." That was vice president Al Gore on the campaign trail in 2000, but his Republican opponent, Texas governor George W. Bush, also used the same image many times.

209. Perhaps schools need an OSHA. Actually, it is the responsibility of school boards to ensure that public school buildings are not only safe, but also healthy and pleasant.

210. That's changing, but probably for the worse, as the public makes judgments based on a single measure, student performance on high-stakes tests.

211. For the argument that schools should always practice teamwork and eliminate competition, see Alfie Kohn, *The Schools Our Children Deserve* (Boston: Houghton Mifflin, 1999).

212. See *Multiple Intelligences* and other books by Howard Gardner, cited earlier.

213. North Carolina's three-year-old "bonuses for high test scores" program uses a *business* metaphor to describe teachers and students. Teachers are "shareholders" and students are "sales clerks" striving to meet sales quotas, meaning high scores on the state exam.

214. UTV has a tracking system. Some study at the University of PBS with Professors Lehrer, Rogers, and Moyers, while others go to Fox Community College or MTV Institute (and work out at the WWF gym). A sizable minority takes correspondence classes at NPR University with Bob Edwards, Scott Simon, Nina Totenberg, Terri Gross, and others.

215. Exceptions prove the rule, but some of the exceptions are worth noting. Open Court publishes distinguished textbooks in math and reading. Joy Hakim's *A History of U.S.* brings American History to life and E. D. Hirsch's series, *What Every First (Second, Third, etc.) Grader Needs to Know*, also brighten the curriculum.

216. The best argument for *higher* standards in English comes from the mouths of public figures like George W. Bush, Olympic athlete Marion Jones, and many sportcasters. Bush thanked supporters "for joining Laura and I" and then rhapsodized about "the wonderful things that have happened to Dick Cheney and I"; Marion Jones complained about the attention paid "to my husband, CJ, and I"; and the only people who have not heard sportcasters mangle the language ("just between you and I" and "there's a disagreement between he and the coach") are those who don't watch sports on television.

EPILOGUE: AND IN CONCLUSION . . .

217. Yes, I remember Bill Clinton at the 1988 Democratic National Convention getting his loudest applause when he said, "And in conclusion . . . "

218. The junior high was in Greenwich, Connecticut, where I taught summer school. I was an English teacher at Paul D. Schreiber High School in Port Washington, New York, for two years. For two years I taught English at Virginia State College, a black college in Petersburg, Virginia, where in the evenings I taught at the Federal Reformatory, also in Petersburg. I was a teaching assistant while a doctoral candidate at the Harvard Graduate School of Education.

219. As the late Albert Shanker pointed out, school systems hire lots of workers (classroom teachers) on the cheap and then pay a few other people (administrators) handsomely to watch them.

220. Do I mean "all teachers" or just "good teachers"? I would suggest redesigning schools so that the teachers function as a team and are paid, in part, according to the team's performance. To start, these teachers would have to be, in part, self-selected; they would be professionals who have made the decision to work together. Evaluation of the team's performance would require multiple measures, naturally, and would include scores on standardized tests. Team members would be quick to take note of malingering and also be supportive of those needing extra help (and guidance in tough personal times).

I also believe that individual merit must be rewarded; that system would have to be developed by the team, but the decision would, I think, ultimately be the principal's.

221. The result was "Toughest Job in America," about being an urban school superintendent. It aired on PBS in September 2000 as part of *The Merrow Report*.

ABOUT THE AUTHOR

John Merrow began his career as an education reporter with National Public Radio in 1974, when he created *Options in Education*. That series earned more than two dozen broadcasting awards, including the George Polk Award in 1982. In 1984 his first television series, *Your Children, Our Children*, earned an Emmy nomination for community service. From 1985 to 1990 he was education correspondent for *The MacNeil/Lehrer NewsHour* and in 1993 he created *The Merrow Report* for PBS, followed by the NPR series of the same name in 1997. In 2000 he returned to *NewsHour* to provide occasional reports on education.

Merrow earned a bachelor's degree from Dartmouth College in 1964, a master's degree in American studies from Indiana University in 1968, and a doctorate in education and social policy from the Harvard Graduate School of Education in 1973.

Merrow has been a teacher in junior high school, high school, college, graduate school, and federal prison. He has three children and lives in New York City.

tion leaders and meticulous, current research that's anything but boring and the result is a thought-provoking call for change . . . a brutally honest portrayal of education today. . . . It's almost a comprehensive guide on how to think about schools . . . [and] will prove useful to parents, educators, and others determined to push and pull the system beyond 'good enough.'"
— *NEA Today*

"Aristotle's wise man knew how to ask good questions as well as what constitutes good—and excellent—answers. We find such practical and idealistic wisdom in John Merrow's new book, *Choosing Excellence.* He supplies much needed clarity with the topic-specific, probing questions we should all be asking if 'good enough' is not, in fact, good enough for our children."
— Sue Bastian, president of Teaching Matters, Inc.

"The great contribution of Merrow's book is his insistence that excellent schools are possible for every child, even those whom we have historically banished to bad schools. Then he empowers anyone interested in provoking excellent education in those schools and districts by giving them the right questions to ask those in charge."
— David Hornbeck, former superintendent of schools in Philadelphia and secretary of education in Maryland

"An instructive and entertaining read for parents, teachers, and policymakers alike."
— Samuel Halperin, American Youth Policy Forum

"This wide-ranging and balanced book calls a welcome truce in the education wars. Aside from its too-sweeping denunciation of high-stakes tests, it is a wise and genial book—as one would expect from its author, John Merrow."
— E.D. Hirsch Jr., founder of the core knowledge school reform and author of *The Schools We Need, and Why We Don't Have Them*

"This book points out that there's more to a school than its four walls and reputation, and more people need to be aware of all the choices that are out there."
— *Scholastic*